✓ SMART CHOICES

SMART CHOICES

Nancy J. Kolodny, M.A., M.S.W.
Robert C. Kolodny, M.D.
Thomas E. Bratter, Ed.D.

Little, Brown and Company
Boston / Toronto

First Edition

The authors are grateful to the following for permission to use
previously published material:

Two "Luann" cartoons by Greg Evans. © by and permission of News
America Syndicate.

Two "Shoe" cartoons by Jeff MacNelly. By permission of Tribune
Media Services Inc.

"Cathy" cartoon by Cathy Guisewite. ©, 1985, Universal Press Syndicate. Reprinted with permission. All rights reserved.

"For Better or For Worse" cartoon by Lynn Johnston. ©, 1985, Universal Press Syndicate. Reprinted with permission. All rights reserved.

Drawing by Webber. © 1985 The New Yorker Magazine, Inc.

"Hi and Lois" cartoon by Mort Walker and Dik Browne. Reprinted
with special permission of King Features Syndicate, Inc.

"Archie" cartoon. © 1986 Archie® Comics Publications Inc.

Library of Congress Cataloging-in-Publication Data
Kolodny, Nancy J.
  Smart choices.

  Bibliography: p.
  Includes index.
  Summary: A guidebook to help young people make sensible deci-
sions about difficult issues, such as making friends, using drugs, and
choosing a college.
  1. Youth—United States—Decision-making—Juvenile
literature. [1. Decision making. 2. Conduct of life]
I. Kolodny, Robert C. II. Bratter, Thomas Edward.
III. Title.
HQ796.K348 1986   305.2'35   86-2916
ISBN 0-316-50163-8
10 9 8 7 6 5 4 3 2
                    RRD-VA
          Published simultaneously in Canada
          by Little, Brown & Company (Canada) Limited

          Printed in the United States of America

Dedicated with love to our children,
Linda,
Lora,
Lisa,
Edward,
and Barbara

Contents

Part 3.

Crisis Time

Part 4.

Reaching for Independence

Introduction

No matter what some people think, the teenage years aren't one big summer vacation. There's more pressure on us than anyone wants to admit.

Sally J., age fifteen

From the way TV and movies deal with adolescence, it looks like all we think about is sex, drugs, rock music, and partying. Wake up, America! That's fiction.

Tim R., age eighteen

Adolescence is like a roller-coaster ride: the highs are incredible, the lows are gut-wrenching, and the times when you coast somewhere in between make up the biggest part of the ride. Being a teenager means you have a world of opportunities ahead of you, but it also means you'll have to get through some tough times when you feel uncomfortable about yourself and how your life is going.

As an adolescent you may feel like everybody in the world expects something from you — parents, friends, teachers — and you may be hard-pressed to know how to satisfy all those demands and still be true to yourself. You may not even be sure what you want out of life, much less how to accomplish all the things on your agenda. You may assume that everyone else you know is in better shape than you are.

The truth is that no one can completely escape the low points of adolescence, no matter how attractive, how brilliant, or how popular he or she is. How many of these situations, for example, have already happened to you?

— A boy or girl you really like doesn't seem to know you're alive.
— Someone you thought was a good friend lets you down.

— You didn't get chosen for a team you tried out for.

— You got an F on an exam you studied days for.

— Someone asks you about a party you weren't invited to.

— One of your teachers doesn't like you and makes that fact clear to you and everyone else.

— Your last haircut ruined your "look."

— You have a big date and your face breaks out that day.

— A friend asks you to do something you really think is wrong.

— Your love-life isn't what you'd like it to be.

— Your parents overreact to things you say or do.

These predicaments aren't unusual. Most teenagers face them with some regularity. As if they weren't enough to complicate your life, you'll probably have to think of some of the following issues: How can I be more popular? (My attempts at making small talk wind up sounding like King Kong trying to sing opera.) Should I try drugs? (After all, won't they help me relax and enjoy myself?) How do I know when I'm in love? (Everybody talks about it, but I'm not really sure I'll recognize it when it happens to me.) Am I ready for sex? (I want to find out what it's all about and I'm not a little kid anymore, but I'm not as sophisticated as I think I should be.) What can I do to help my chances of admission to a good college? (I'm really not very special, so I don't think I have much of a chance.)

Smart Choices is a sourcebook of information to help you face these and many of the other challenges of adolescence. It's meant to be used as a guide — to help you get where you want to go by giving you insights into different areas of adolescent life. We hope it will help you make choices that are right for you when you run into unfamiliar, risky, or uncomfortable situations.

There's no guarantee that your life will instantly be improved by reading this book. But it may help open your eyes to how much control you really can exert over your life. It will show you how a little bit of effort applied correctly can solve a seemingly impossible problem, and how you can learn to communicate your needs to other people and turn the low points into highs!

The information in *Smart Choices* doesn't just come from the adult "experts" you're used to hearing from. A lot of it comes from the real "experts" — teenagers like you who spoke with us and gave us suggestions based on their own experiences at handling tough or ticklish situations and coming out winners. We hope our book can help you turn yourself into a winner.

Part 1.

Family Dynamics and Other Sticky Matters

1.

Understanding How Your Family Operates

Do you and your friends ever compare notes about your families? Do you find that sometimes it's impossible to understand the logic behind how your families operate? Does it ever seem that the rules that govern what you can and can't do, or what you are or aren't expected to do, vary? Do you think that your concepts of "family" no longer quite fit your parents' definitions?

Welcome to the club. You're not imagining things. Family life *does* change when you hit your teens. You may find it less ideal, possibly boring or confining. Even in the most secure, loving, and caring of families there will be times when relationships aren't just rocky, they're positively explosive! The parents you used to idolize may now seem less than perfect. You may notice that what they do and say in the privacy of your home doesn't always jell with the image they try to project to everyone else. There may be more tension than you remember when you were younger. This can come from many sources: your parents may be worrying about their finances, about getting older, even about bringing up a teenager. Brothers and sisters may get in your way more than ever and your tolerance level may be on the decline. In fact, they may feel you're no cup of tea either. It's important to remember that they're probably dealing with their own issues as they grow and change, and you may find yourselves on a collision course as a result. All of this creates a family system that's constantly reacting — you to them, they to you — like a tug of war between two sides that are rarely balanced.

The fact is that your needs and perceptions of the world are different now that you're a teenager. You're becoming more self-sufficient and can risk stating some strong opinions that may be at odds with your family's. As you make connections with kids and adults outside your family circle, you'll have many more people to compare your relatives to. The flaws you can recognize in your family members may have been there all along, but you probably weren't ready to acknowledge them until now.

Understanding how your family operates is important because it can help you see patterns of behavior you may not have been able to find much logic in before. It lets you put the image you have of yourself and your relatives in clearer focus. This chapter will help you do that. You'll be in a better position to understand (even if you can't fully accept) your parents' values and beliefs because you'll know how to find out where they came from, why they're important in your particular family, and why they may be important to you. You'll learn about the structure of your family, how its various parts (people) fit together, and the factors that may improve it or endanger it. Think of the process as clearing an error on your computer so you can punch in new data and come up with correct answers to difficult questions.

Family Styles

Every family has a unique personality and style.

> "The Smiths are so easygoing and casual."
> "The Joneses are so intellectual."

"The Phillipses are strict."

That family style takes years and years to develop and is usually the end product of many influences:

— the things your grandparents taught your parents about family;

— the things your parents didn't like about their own family lives when they were growing up and that they're trying to avoid doing with you;

— your parents' attempts to create a family life-style that mirrors some of the dreams they had about family when they were young;

— your influence on your parents and your responses as part of the family.

Family styles are a lot like fashions: everyone has a favorite that feels most comfortable. So even though your parents may experiment with different ways to run your family, even though they may read lots of books on parenting and try to follow new trends and ideas, it's likely that they'll return to their favorite style because it works best for them.

There are many different family styles. The majority fall between the extremes of parents-as-dictators at one end of the spectrum, and parents-as-pals at the other. Here are some of the most common family styles:

The Dictatorial Style

In this type of family there are only two ways to do things: the right way and the wrong way. The parents set the rules, and the children are expected to follow them without making waves. This is not necessarily bad. Some teenagers have no problem with this because there's very little guesswork involved — it's easy to know what's expected of you and what you have to do to please your parents. Then you can get the positive payoffs that result when a family's happy and the people in it can live with each other's expectations.

But some people have enormous difficulty living in a dictatorial family. It feels like Marine boot camp. It makes it almost impossible to negotiate or ask for compromises. It makes it hard to grow up and learn from mistakes, if mistakes are seen as a threat to your parents' authority rather than a natural part of growing up.

If you live in a family that has a dictatorial style and it's causing problems for you, try to do the following:

1. *Talk to your grandparents about the way they raised your parents.* Perhaps your grandparents were very easygoing and never gave your mom and dad much direction or attention, so your parents decided to do just the opposite with their own children. Or perhaps your parents are repeating the strict family style they grew up with because it's what they know best. Understanding the roots of your family style can help you come to grips with it, even though it may not change it.

2. *Ask your parents if you could have a family conference about your family style.* It's possible that your parents don't realize the impact their dictatorial stance is having on you. They probably don't see themselves as overly strict or inflexible. If you've already spoken with your grandparents, you could tell your parents about what you learned. Be prepared to make suggestions for specific changes you'd like to be made on a trial basis. But don't ask for the sun, the moon, and the stars — keep your suggestions realistic and reasonable.

3. *Ask your parents what they think is appropriate for a person of your age to be doing.* Your parents' style probably reflects their concerns about your safety and well-being, and not a desire to squash your social life and turn you into a slave.

The Democracy-for-All Family Style

The Democracy-for-All style operates on the assumption that each member of the family has an equal say in family affairs. In theory this is terrific, but in practice it often turns out that some family members are more equal than others. For instance, if Mom and Dad want to go to Florida for Christmas, it's unlikely that they'll agree on a skiing vacation even if all three kids vote for Mt. Snow. In a family like this, parents try very hard to be fair. They try to apply the same standards to all their children, and they expect that their kids will be reasonable and logical in how they respond to the family's requests and rules.

If this is your family's style and you're happy with it, consider yourself lucky. When you're brought up having the right to state your opinions (and being expected to), possibly influencing the outcome of family decisions, you'll have a negotiating skill that will be useful in every other aspect of your life — personal, academic, athletic, professional. But if you're brought up in a Democracy-for-All family and you're unwilling to participate in the process, you don't really learn where your parents and siblings are coming from. You may make assumptions based on inaccurate or incomplete information. You lose out on the chance to shape how your family operates. You may lead your parents to think you don't notice or care about their efforts on behalf of the family.

> I was at a P.T.A. meeting the other night. We broke up into small groups and were discussing discipline at home and how it affects discipline at school. The other parents in my group were talking about making their teenagers toe the line, and when I mentioned being flexible they jumped on me like I was a maniac. I wonder if my kids know how good they have it at home. They certainly never tell me they think our family life is OK.
>
> Mrs. N., *mother of two boys,*
> *ages fourteen and seventeen*

This can lead to feelings of being rejected on both sides, yours and theirs. In a Democracy-for-All family, you may confuse the desire for discussion with an invasion of your privacy. They're not usually the same, and you should clarify this if it's an issue for you.

The Permissive Style

"I wish my parents were more like yours. You can do anything you want."

"What a joke. My parents don't care enough to tell me

what they think I should be doing. You know how hard it
is to figure stuff out by myself? It's scary."

Kay B. and Andrea Z.,
ages thirteen and fourteen

This is the dilemma of living in a family with a permissive style. On the surface, it seems like every teenager's dream — to be able to make your own decisions and have your parents agree to almost everything you ask to do. In practice, it's tougher to deal with than you might imagine. Sometimes it may feel like your parents either don't care or don't want to get involved in your life. Sometimes it may seem like your parents are too self-absorbed to notice much about you.

If this describes your family situation, it would be useful to let your parents know that you feel like you're walking a tightrope without a net underneath. Your parents are likely to be flabbergasted. Many permissive parents have made a conscious decision not to impose themselves on their kids because they believe in the freedom to make one's own decisions and mistakes and learn from them. Some parents are permissive but *think* they're offering plenty of advice and direction where it's needed. They may not realize that *you* see and feel things differently on your end of the receiving line. Talk about it and see if you can make adjustments: speak up when you need more input from your parents, and perhaps they'll agree to try to check in with you on a more regular basis.

The Overprotective Style

Overprotective families often practice SMOTHER LOVE. This can be very uncomfortable when you're a teenager, because you need to begin to break away from your family and do things on your own. This kind of family style can sometimes feel like you're swimming upstream through Jell-O.

Overprotective parents are often frightened parents. They read the papers, watch the news, and may be supersensitive to the dangers that exist and the things that could harm you. It's not that they don't want you to grow up; they want to make sure you grow up safe, healthy, and happy. Sometimes this is difficult to deal with, though, as in the case of eighteen-year-old Marcia S., who each day of her freshman year at college received letters from her mother that included newspaper clippings about every rape that took place in Los Angeles.

On the other hand, sometimes having overprotective parents works well. Usually, in such families, parents can admit to and talk about their family style.

> Oh sure, I know I'm being a little crazy by worrying so much, but I'm a parent and I'm supposed to worry!
>
> *Mrs. N., mother of a sixteen-year-old daughter*

> My daughter knows she can't change me. She works so hard at getting me to let go. We have a ritual discussion at the start of each semester of school. She tells me what I'm not supposed to do. I tell her I'll try. We both know I'll do it anyway.
>
> *Mrs. T., mother of a fifteen-year-old daughter*

People in overprotective families need a sense of humor to keep things in perspective and to prevent angry feelings from taking over.

Overprotectiveness can become a big issue, however, when parents don't see anything extreme or unusual about how they're dealing with their children and when the children have to struggle too hard to break away. If this describes your family situation, it can be useful to discuss the following issues with your parents:

1. What is it that your parents do that you see as overprotective? Explain how they make you feel, and what you think they should be doing instead and why they should be doing it.
2. What is it your parents think other teenagers are actually doing; why do they think such behavior might pose a threat to your safety and well-being? (The fundamental issue here may be one of trust.)
3. Explain the things you know your friends really do (be honest if you want your parents to be), also explaining why your parents don't need to worry about your doing the same things.

4. Suggest some specific ways in which your parents might agree to be less protective in exchange for some promises from you not to get involved in situations that scare the dickens out of them.

Remember, though, that overprotective parents aren't likely to change their ways overnight, no matter how thoroughly you discuss this issue. In order for changes to occur, you've got to give them room to gradually accept your trustworthiness and willingness to listen to their concerns. In other words, like so many things in life, bringing about change requires a two-way interaction.

The Competitive Family Style

Some families thrive on competition. They love challenges, they love winning. This can apply to sports, games, to performance in school, even to how the parents tackle their jobs. Competition is encouraged between children in the family, and even seeps into the relationship between parents and children.

For many people, living in this kind of family is exciting. It makes life interesting. Everybody has goals to shoot for, and family members get a lot of feedback from one another about how well each one is doing. Some families may even have regularly scheduled meetings to cheer each other on or reset the goals and challenges. Each person usually knows exactly what's expected of him or her.

> I knew from the time I started piano lessons that my parents expected me to do better than my friends. I always was in music competitions. But they really put the pressure on us when my brother made it to the state finals and I didn't. By my ninth grade we both made it.
>
> *Fredericka L., age fifteen*

> There was never any question about my making first string on any team I tried out for. I was taught that anything worth doing was worth doing well and doing right. When I wanted to try out for the football team, my dad spent hours practicing with me. I think it was a little hard

on him when my arm got better than his. But I got my spot on the team, and when we throw the ball around even now I think he takes it real seriously, like he's my age and we're aiming for the same position on a team.

Paul R., age seventeen

This is all fine if you're a person with a competitive personality. Problems crop up if you're part of a family from the Vince Lombardi "win at all costs" school of thought and you couldn't care less about winning. Some people are more interested in the process of getting from point A to point B than being number one when point B is reached. Some of us aren't cut out to be leaders and don't enjoy being the focus of a lot of attention. Shy or private people may find it hard to be surrounded by competitors. If this sounds all too familiar to you, it's important to get your feelings out in the open. The parents of competitive families often think that setting goals for their children and engaging them in competition with one another brings the family closer together, giving everyone shared experiences and something to discuss from firsthand experience. They may not realize it causes you pain.

There's another side to the competitive family style that has to do with competition of a different sort. Occasionally, mothers get into not-so-subtle rivalries with their daughters, and fathers with their sons. Issues like who's better looking, who has the more charming personality, who has more friends, who is better liked can spark competitions that are really exercises in one-upmanship. If you've ever seen a forty-five-year-old mother dressed in the same outfit her fifteen-year-old daughter is wearing, or have observed a father flirting with his son's girlfriend in a too-casual way, you'll know the kind of competition we're speaking about. Teenagers usually resent this aspect of the competitive family style, and with good reason. It makes the lines of distinction between parents and children all but invisible, it's potentially embarrassing to have to deal with, and it can make you feel like your parent is a caricature of yourself. It's very tricky to ease out of this kind of competition because there may be more to it than meets the eye. The first step is to try to explain what you think you've seen happening and why you'd like it to stop. But realize that your parents may deny that they're competing with you in any way at all. They may get angry or act hurt. They may be acting out a variation of the parents-as-pals family style (see the next section of this chapter). Whatever the case, it's important to lay your cards on the table. If it continues and is something you can't overlook, you may need some counseling to help cope with this. Ask your school counselor, family doctor, or clergyperson for advice. It may be that your family would benefit from family therapy.

You may not be able to change the style of your competitive family completely, but you'll never get the chance to be your real self unless you speak up. You may find your siblings aren't any more content than you are; if you band together and confront your parents you'll have a strength-in-numbers position from which to negotiate for some changes.

The Parents-as-Pals Style

The Parents-as-Pals family style is another one of those arrangements that looks better to outsiders than to those who live with it every day.

> My mom is one of my best friends. I really love her. But she wants to be my number one best friend and she can't be. She gets insulted when I say I don't want to go somewhere with her, and she pouts when I don't tell her everything about my life. I need her more as a mother and she's having trouble with that.
>
> *Perrie T., age fifteen*

> When I was twelve my dad taught me to play golf. I got good real fast and he made me part of his foursome. We both loved it then. But I'm sixteen now and I don't want to hang around with him and his forty-year-old friends when I have free time. We've gotten into some major battles over this.
>
> *Rick K., age sixteen*

The Parents-as-Pals style attempts to erase the differences between parents and children and encourages socializing and communication on a friendship basis rather than on a parent-child basis. It can develop after a divorce, when parents jockey for the upper hand in getting your allegiance and affection. It can also happen when parents are exceptionally lonely and don't easily make friends with people their own age.

Parents-as-Pals can be terrific if it's only one aspect of your family's style and personality — for example, as one part of a Democracy-for-All style. But if it's the major focus of how your family operates, it can be tough to deal with when you're a teenager and you have a tremendous need for privacy, and when your allegiances to friends are becoming stronger than your allegiances to your parents.

Try to explain to your parents why you value them and love them as parents, and why you need them as parents more than you need them as friends. They may be surprised, because they may think they've been doing you a favor by trying to be your pals. They may be relieved to not have to play that role anymore. If your parents are lonely, or on the rebound from a divorce or death of a spouse, and you think this is why the Parents-as-Pals style is in operation, help them meet new people. Sign them up as volunteers at evening P.T.A. functions at your school. Invite a friend over and invite that friend's parents too if you think they have anything in common with yours. Give them the address and phone number of your local Parents Without Partners group (see Chapter 12 for more information). When they do start acting like parents, even if it means they tell you to do something or ground you for not doing something, let them know you appreciate that aspect of your relationship with them. Changes won't happen overnight, but they may not happen at all unless you take an active role in making them happen.

Other Family Styles

In the world of fashion, there are endless variations on a theme that result in new styles each season. So too with family styles. Some families blend these styles and come up with their own unique versions. In some families, one parent uses one style while the other parent prefers a different style. This can make you feel like you're trying to do two different dance steps at once, or it can make you feel torn — especially if one parent's style is more conservative and traditional while the other's is more casual and liberal. But you don't have to be at the mercy of your family style if it doesn't make sense to you or feel right. Figuring out the parts of that style is the first step in getting a handle on it and is very important if you're really going to be able to understand how your particular family operates.

Family Patterns

Just as there are many family styles, there are many family patterns, some of which have been popular for generations, and some of which may not have existed or weren't acceptable when your grandparents were starting their families. To determine your pattern, see which of these situations best describes your family. Do you live with both parents? Are you an only child, or do you have brothers and sisters? Are your parents divorced? Is one or both of your parents dead? Perhaps you live with a single parent who never married. Maybe you're adopted or living with a foster family. Perhaps you live with a parent who is openly homosexual or lesbian. You may live in an extended family with your parents and grandparents, or in a commune with many families not related but living together.

Family patterns can change. Sometimes the changes are planned for — your parents decide to have a baby even though you've been an only child for fourteen years. Your parents ask your elderly grandparents to move in with you when it gets too costly for them to maintain an apartment, turning your two-parent family into an extended family. Changes can also be unexpected and something over which you have no control, such as the sudden death of a parent, a divorce you didn't see coming, or a parent's remarriage after years of living as a single-parent family.

Here are some practical aspects of these situations to think about.

The Sibling Patterns: Bothered by Brothers and Sisters?

Having brothers and sisters around can be both good and bad. They deflect some of your parents' attention away from you so that you're not constantly getting the eagle eye and not having to account for everything you do. They're allies and equals in a world dominated by adults. They can stand up to your parents for you. If older, they can break the trail for you to follow, and can serve as models. They can be great friends and they can make you feel terrific about yourself — especially if they admire lots of the things you do. On the other hand, it's entirely possible that you and your siblings go for each other's throats, or that there's an iron curtain of silence separating you. If that's the case, you're probably experiencing sibling rivalry.

Hassles with siblings are a normal part of growing up, but when you become teenagers, the stakes you play for are a little higher than who'll get to ride the tricycle and who'll get the first hug and kiss when Dad walks in the door. Now you jockey for position to see who gets the car, who can stay out the latest, who can get to use the phone. The more privileges you have, the higher status it seems you have in the family. You may get into fights over "fairness," which is always tough because you and your siblings aren't the same people and don't do things exactly the same ways. What your parents think is fair may not be fair for all of you.

Rivalries between older and younger siblings usually dissolve into nuisance issues: your little sister's a pest and keeps trying to get you in trouble when you tell her to get out of your room. Your little brother interrupts your phone calls to your girlfriend and mimics the things you say to her. Your parents think it's cute; you obviously don't. Rivalries between teenagers in a family are usually more intense, especially if you're all the same sex. Though we don't have magic solutions to eliminate the aggravation from your relationships with siblings, we do have some pointers for dealing with them.

Eleven Ways to Ease Sibling Sorrows

1. Ask yourself, "Is this worth pursuing?" Sometimes it's better to let things go by than to make a big deal out of them. Have you really been hurt? In the great scheme of things, does what has happened between you really matter?

2. *Ask yourself, "Would I have done the same thing if the tables were turned?"* It's possible, once the impact of the confrontation is over and tempers are cooled, that you might be able to see things from the other side's point of view. You might even have done the same thing. It's not likely, but it's possible.

3. *Make an appointment to talk with your sibling(s).* Arrange to meet in a neutral place (NOT your room), and at a time when neither of you is rushed. Do it soon, though, while the memory of an incident is still fresh and accurate.

4. *Be straight.* If something's bothering you, come out with it right away. Be honest, direct, and have your facts in hand to prove your point. Give dates, times, and places of whatever caused the hassle.

5. *Stick to the point.* Say only what pertains to the current conflict. Don't dredge up old grudges; don't make predictions about future ones.

6. *Don't threaten.* Threatening a sibling usually accomplishes two things: your parents will be called in to "protect" your sibling, and your sibling will gear up for a big fight, which will escalate the problem rather than solve it.

7. *Don't be intimidated.* Your sister may burst into tears, your brother may turn into a mass of quivering muscles ready to spring when confronted. Don't be intimidated by their countermoves (real or theatrical). Don't be made to feel like you're the guilty one. You have a right to talk about things and clear the air even if you're not 100 percent correct.

8. *Remember the Golden Rule!* Whatever you do to a sibling will probably come back to haunt you because it'll be tried on you at some future point in time. Only do whatever you're willing to have done to you.

9. *Don't milk the rivalry for all it's worth.* This is another way of saying, "Don't beat a dead horse." Every confrontation has an end point. If you know basically why you're fighting or arguing, you should have some idea of what you're trying to accomplish by arguing. That way you'll know approximately when you've reached that goal, and you won't be tempted to keep up the disagreement just for the sake of one-upmanship or to get the last word in.

10. *Don't involve your parents if at all possible not to.* Par-

ents don't react well to sibling rivalry. Working things out among yourselves is better in the long run for lots of reasons. It sets up a good pattern that will last for the rest of your lives. It's also a way of showing your maturity to your parents. This can then be used as a bargaining tool when you need to ask for more privileges at another time.

11. *If you must involve your parents, ask them to be mediators, not judges.* The goal is to find solutions from within yourselves. A mediator guides you in that direction, whereas a judge hands down a ruling, which may or may not be the best one for you. You learn more if you do the bulk of the problem solving yourself.

The Only-Child-Family Pattern

Sibling rivalry won't surface as your problem, but parent rivalry might in this family pattern. As a younger only child you tend to be in the spotlight all the time. But when you reach adolescence, your parents may sense your need to strike out on your own and they may purposely dim that spotlight. They may spend more time with each other than with you. This can be a double-edged sword for an only child: while you like the added freedom, you may have pangs of jealousy. You might still be center stage, but in a darkened theater!

Only children should try to remember that being out of the spotlight isn't the same as being forgotten, washed up, unloved, or disapproved of. Parents need to evolve and mature through various stages of their lives just as teenagers do on the road to adulthood. It's especially scary for parents of only children to watch those kids grow up and away from them. There isn't another sibling coming up to cushion the blow and ease them into the new role. If during your adolescence your parents seem to be focusing more on themselves than you've been used to, it's probably because they need to rework some priorities in their own lives and need to plan for a future that won't include being with you on a daily basis.

The flip side of the coin is the only-child family in which the parents won't let go and instead make the spotlight even brighter. The family style of overprotectiveness is common. If this describes your situation, your job as a teenager is to get your parents to see the value of letting that spotlight dim. Try to talk to other only children and see how they've handled this. Follow the suggestions we offered in the discussion of the overprotective family style. Try to get summer jobs that take you away from home for extended periods of time. See if you can spend vacations visiting out-of-town friends or relatives by yourself. Put yourself in situations that can prove to everyone that you can make it on your own, apart, and yet still be "family." It will pay off in the long run.

The Single-Parent-Family Pattern

More and more kids under the age of eighteen are living in single-parent families. While divorce accounts for the largest proportion of these families, separation, desertion, unwed mothers, and death of a spouse are also contributing factors. Though we'll focus on the unique stresses, strains, and challenges of this family pattern in Chapter 12, we'd like to mention a few things about the single-parent-family pattern that you may not be aware of, and the things that you can do to improve a less-than-perfect single-parent-family situation.

In a two-parent family, if you have trouble getting along with one parent, a good relationship with the other parent can usually rescue the situation and preserve a sense of balance as well as everyone's self-esteem. In contrast, that balance is missing in a single-parent family. Your parent may feel like family life is perpetual combat with all the artillery coming directly from your camp!

Single parents have to cope with issues of personal loneliness and the need to form new, lasting relationships almost in the same way teenagers do. But parents have the added responsibility of being Mom or Dad. There's often a conflict between pursuing a social life and staying home with the kids. If you live with a single parent, you may also notice a tendency on your parent's part to try to win your acceptance and friendship when there's trouble between you, perhaps choosing to give up rather than lobbying for that parental point of view. This is fine if you're right and your parent's really wrong, but it's not fine if you're wrong and your parent's right and you both know it.

You really have a lot of potential and power to help straighten things out in a single-parent-family situation where your parent is obviously struggling with issues like these.

1. *Ask your parent what you can do to help out.* Something as simple as agreeing to stay home one night and prepare dinner and baby-sit may give your parent the needed free time and breathing space to feel rejuvenated and able to face the next week's challenges.

2. *Try to discuss your feelings and reactions to each other and events at home at least twice a month.* Clearing the air this way can ease a lot of tension. The more often you do it, the better the results.

3. *Don't expect the impossible.* White knights don't come charging up on magnificent white steeds too often. Taking an active role in improving things at home, and maintaining the good things that already are going on, are a lot better than waiting for that stroke of luck to change things.

4. *Try to spend time with your parent doing something you both really like.* Taking a walk in the park, going jogging, even watching TV together, reaffirms that human part of your relationship. It's person-to-person rather than parent-to-child, and it's important for your parent to know that someone still thinks he or she is actually fun to be with.

5. *Find some other adult to talk to.* There's an adult out there for every kid — you just have to do some looking. Whomever you choose to confide in can be a terrific resource and a great advisor when things get tough or tense at home, or when you just need a second adult opinion about something.

6. *Don't fall into the trap of being overprotective of your parents.* Parents, too, need room to live their own lives, just like you do.

Stepparents and Remarriages: The Blended Family Pattern

About thirty-five million people live in stepfamilies, and that includes seven million children under the age of eighteen! Luckily, the image of the wicked stepparent has faded, and the current terms used to describe these family patterns are "blended" or "reconstituted" families. Sometimes, though, the blending takes longer than anticipated, and in some families what you have is oil and water — two things that never quite mix.

If you're in this family situation and find that you're having more trouble adjusting than a younger sibling does, that's not unusual. You had more time to get used to the prior family pattern than a younger brother or sister did. You have unique needs for stability when you're a teenager, and a parent's remarriage can upset that stability. You're more sensitive to a remarried parent's sexuality than a younger sibling might be. You may feel disloyal to your other biological parent if you have to live with a new stepparent, you may dislike your stepbrothers or stepsisters and feel like your personal territory has been invaded, and you may be unclear about how you're supposed to relate to your stepparent. Adolescence is a time of making new alliances, but they're normally with peers and it can be hard to spend the time and energy forming alliances with new relatives when you'd rather be spending that time on your friends.

If you're having problems being part of a blended family, the most important thing to keep in mind is that your new family is not supposed to blot out your old family. The memories and relationships you have from that first family group can never be taken away from you. Your new family is a new challenge and a situation with lots of potential for positive things to happen — if you and everyone else will let them.

You need to give a stepfamily a chance to evolve its own style, which is a blend of some things from the old and some things that are new. See if you can discuss the possibility of starting new family traditions with this stepfamily *in addition* to the ones you had with your original family. For example, if you're used to turkey on Thanksgiving, but your stepfather and his kids like goose, perhaps this year you could have ham. Silly as it sounds, these things matter. If you're used to opening gifts the morning of your birthday but your stepmother commutes to the city, see if the family can get up just a little earlier so you can continue this tradition. It's very important for you to think about the little rituals in your life that have been meaningful and comfortable, discuss them with your stepfamily, listen to their side too, and really be able to blend together into a new-but-old, same-but-different family unit. It takes work, but it can succeed.

Family style, family patterns, family personality — these are the things to explore when you're trying to understand how your family operates. Just as you think you've got it figured out, it's likely to change, and that's where the excitement and challenge comes in. Now you should be well prepared for the challenge!

2.

Games
Parents Play

"OK, Dad, this is my final offer. It's a showdown, you or me. I'll give you Marvin Gardens and Park Place for all your properties with hotels on them, and I'll throw in five hundred dollars as an incentive. If you're as smart as you pretend you are, you'll take my offer."

"Why, you little twerp, are you trying to bury me before I'm dead? I'm plenty smart and I won't be had. I'll give you nothing. Let's see what the dice have to say this time!"

Gary P., age thirteen, and his dad

I'm gonna get those bums! I'm going for blood! Watch me make this shot!

Zane D., age fifteen, a hockey player
who also happens to be a choirboy in his church

In an interview on the Today show in August, 1985, the winner of the National Scrabble Championship admitted that some of the words he used on his way to victory wouldn't be found in a dictionary, but that his opponents didn't call his bluff on them!

Games are great. They let us live out fantasies, act out our aggressions without being punished, even bluff and be purposely deceitful without being labeled "dishonest" or "cheats." In game situations we can take on people we might never challenge in everyday life and since we're expected to try to win, we can let out all the stops, as long as we play by the rules. Parents won't ground you if you top them at Trivial Pursuit, a teacher won't fail you if you take him or her on in one-on-one basketball and win, the school wrestling champ won't pound you into the mat if you beat him at chess, and your little sister can't get you in trouble just because you beat her fair and square at gin rummy.

Actually, games are a genuine learning tool. They let us develop skills that we need to use in real life situations: defining problems, thinking clearly, developing strategy, negotiating, figuring odds of success or failure, and evaluating an opponent's strengths and weaknesses.

We all play games almost every day of our lives, but they're not necessarily board games, card games, or team sports. We play *mind games* with the people we're involved with, from relatives and friends to teachers and employers. These games have rules of their own, but the rules vary from family to family, group to group, and situation to situation. Some mind games are predictable — you almost know what the outcome will be as soon as the game is started. (The psychiatrist Eric Berne called these "scripts" because they're used so often with the same kinds of words that it's as if they're written down.) Mind games can also be a kind of recreational activity that you have fun with (like good-natured teasing) or a really bitter form of contest, a clash of wills. The point of these games varies too, depending on whether you start it or someone else (like a parent) does and depending on why the game is played and the stakes you're playing for.

You're probably a master of mind games without realizing it. Typically, they're played with parents as the opponents. Although this chapter is primarily about games parents play, we'd like to mention a few of the games *teenagers* play, so that as you read on you'll have a basis for comparison. A popular one is "Divide and Conquer," in which you pit one parent against another in order to get what you want, since it's usually harder for you to succeed against a unified front (both parents) than against split forces (one parent or the other). Perhaps you've also tried "Everyone Else Gets To," a game designed to make your parents feel guilty. It works because parents rarely check to see if what "everyone else gets to"

really is true, and also because parents often want to "keep up with the Joneses" and don't want their own kids to seem like odd-men-out. In "Bait and Switch" the idea is to disguise a real request by wearing down your parents with a string of irritating or impossible requests so that later on in the game the *real* request will seem reasonable by contrast.

Games like these can be fun because the process is fun. Game playing is challenging, shows ingenuity and inventiveness, and is a way to test those useful skills we spoke of earlier. If your parents don't respond to your games you can actually be disappointed, like winning a sports contest by default because the opposing team refuses to take the field.

Parents have games of their own, which they have probably been developing and refining since Day One of their parenthood. Sometimes they play them in response to yours. Sometimes they initiate and play them as a way of answering your requests. Sometimes they play them without realizing what they're doing. Parents' games can be just as inventive and manipulative as yours, but *you* may not enjoy playing them as much, since you're not the initiator and you haven't decided on the rules. In the rest of this chapter we'll discuss the games parents play and how you can deal with them.

"In My Day"

"In My Day" is a game with a script. Parents play it when they want to stop you from doing something they don't like, or when they want to make you feel guilty about asking for something.

> Whenever I bring up the subject of money I know I'm going to get The Lecture. I could be telling my dad that I'd just won the New York State Lottery and was a millionaire and wanted to buy him and Mom a new house and pay off their debts, and I'd get the same speech: "When I was your age I worked for every penny. A dollar a week was my maximum allowance. I walked places, I saved my bus money. I couldn't do whatever I wanted whenever I wanted like you kids do." I've heard this speech so often, I can fill in the words as he's saying them. Sometimes I can laugh about it, and sometimes I can't. Sometimes I just borrow money from friends; it can be a lot easier.
>
> *Paul R., age thirteen*

If your parents like to play this game, you're probably familiar with the following opening lines, "In my day . . .":

"... things were tougher" (implying you have it easy),

"... money was scarcer" (suggesting you're spoiled because you get more),

"... morals were stricter" (so yours aren't as admirable),

"... kids were more respectful" (trying to prove that you take your parents for granted).

The implication is until you can behave according to the standards your parents followed "In my day . . ." you can't win the game.

Parents will sometimes use "In My Day" as a substitute for a lecture. Topics that are personal, controversial, and tough to discuss calmly (like sex, drugs, and alcohol) are covered this way. You might hear, "In my day . . ."

"... living together before marriage wasn't done,"

"... sex wasn't a casual thing,"

". . . we didn't think about VD because no one fooled around,"

because that lets your parents share some information about how things were for them and clues you in on where their beliefs come from without making you feel like they're preaching to you.

If you make a request and your parents launch into this game, your countermove is to turn off their script. Be direct, and try to get them to focus on the present:

"Mom (Dad), we need to discuss how things are *now*."
"I'd like to clarify my reasons for asking you."
"What are you really trying to tell me?"

There's no guarantee that your strategy will work. If they slip back into another "In My Day" move, you can try again. "Mom (Dad), could we talk about me and *my* day?" or "I'm always glad to hear about how things were for you when you were my age, but I don't really think my situation is exactly the same. Could you help me see how I can deal with *my* situation?" Your parents won't feel as though you've put them down (if you haven't confronted them in a shouting match) or that you're discounting their advice. Respond to their game by inviting more *focused* discussions, with the focus on you — not on them.

"Do as I Say, Not as I Do"

"Do as I Say, Not as I Do" is a frustrating game to have to respond to.

My parents are forever on my case to improve myself. They're immigrants and I'm first-generation American. That means a lot to them in terms of their dreams for themselves coming true in me. But they're driving me crazy. My dad in particular. He runs numbers in our neighborhood and makes a good living on the side that way. Mom is very religious and pretends she doesn't know what he's doing. Whenever something comes up that they think will hurt me — like my boyfriend's new motorcycle and the friends he's made as a result — they start in with this "Do as I say, not as I do" routine. They want me to be perfect. How can I be? They're not.

Louisa T., age sixteen

"Do as I Say, Not as I Do" has two basic premises: parents can set all the rules (because they're parents), but they don't have to *follow* the rules (because they're parents). Ironically, this is a game that usually starts out because the parent player wants the teenager player to win. It's meant to compliment you for your strong points by making it seem as if you have the chance of being better than your parents. Unfortunately, it's a game that can get out of control and turn into a no-win situation for both sides if your parents want you to be a Xerox copy of the "do as I say" image. No one can be that perfect.

If you encounter this game, you can try dealing with it by being assertive (without provoking a fight). This isn't as easy as it sounds, especially if you're a younger teen (your parents may still think of you as a child rather than an adolescent). Try saying, "I really care about you and want to live up to your expectations. But I think they're unrealistic. Could we compromise?" This strategy often works because you don't come out and say your parents are hypocrites who don't live up to their own standards (even though you may think this). Instead, you emphasize your willingness to be the kind of kid they want, within reason. It doesn't force your parents into a defensive posture where they have to prove that what they want for you is right.

Asking your parents, "What will happen if I don't do as you say, but I do as you do?" is an interesting tactic, but can lead to some heated discussions. If you have a comfortable relationship with your parents, you could try this. It works best when you're older and have had experiences, such as working at an after-school job or living away from home during the summer, that you can compare with your parents' experiences and use for the sake of discussion.

"Yes, but . . . No, but . . ."

"Yes, but . . . No, but . . ." is a favorite of parents because it gives them the chance to be creative in the "but" part of the maneuver. It lets them say all the things they think parents should say without actually destroying or denying your request. If you play it often enough with your parents you'll find that certain "scripts" emerge, just as they do in "In My Day."

"Yes, but . . . No, but . . ." is a game of limit setting and boundary building. Your parents try to set limits and build boundaries and you try to test the limits and break down the boundaries!

> It's so funny in my house whenever any of us asks if we can take the car. We always get to; we're all good drivers, we pay for the gas we use and each put in $100 towards the cost of our insurance every year. It's not like our parents have any real reason to worry about whether we can handle the responsibility of a car. But my mom always, and I mean always, says "Yes," and then adds a string of "buts": "Be home by 11," "Don't speed," "Don't drink," "Don't forget to wear your seatbelt," "Don't pick up hitchhikers." My dad's as predictable. He always says "No," and then about five minutes later he'll come back and say, "But maybe I overreacted," or "But actually I don't need to go anywhere tonight, so you can have it." It's like they want us to know our limits without having to be our jailers. It's kind of nice that they're consistent about something.
>
> *Kerry A., age seventeen*

"Yes, but . . . No, but . . ." is much easier than the other games to deal with. Often, parents are so programmed to add the "but" to any conversation that they don't realize they're doing it. There are several ways you can react. The simplest is just to listen politely, not trying to offer a comeback at all, and your parents may assume that you've agreed with what they've been saying. In any event, you've avoided *promising* you'll do something a certain way, but your attentiveness suggests that since you've listened you'll take it under consideration. You have nothing to lose by listening, so it's a good game-playing strategy. Another approach is to say, "Mom (Dad), do you hear what you just said? You tacked on so many conditions I'm not sure what you really mean!" Another possibility is to keep a notebook in which you record every instance of this game for a period of a week. If you have an easygoing, open relationship with your parents you can show them the log after it's complete and use it to explain why it makes knowing what they expect from you a little difficult. Playing "Yes, but . . . No, but . . ." that way can actually be fun. Basically, it's a game that you're more likely to win than your parents are.

"Ask Your Mother (Ask Your Father)"

This game is the parent's version of a teenager's "Bait and Switch" or "Divide and Conquer." It's a useful strategy when a parent doesn't have the time, information, or desire to respond *immediately* to a request because it buys time for your parent to learn more about what you're asking for.

> My eighth-grade French class was planning an end-of-the-semester trip to Quebec City. I really wanted to go so I came home and asked my mom. I didn't have any handouts to show her. She thought about it and said, "You'll have to ask your dad." But my dad was on a two-day business trip, so I had to wait until he called to ask him. He said, "It's OK with me if your mom agrees." I didn't realize it at the time, but my mom had spent the rest of that afternoon and early evening making inquiries about the trip, calling other parents, and rechecking the stuff I told her. I thought it was pretty clever of her to put the thing off on my dad's shoulders. She saved face, I guess, and we avoided a big fight, and when she said, "Yes" finally I knew she felt *she* had made the decision rather than me forcing the issue and fighting with her to make it.
>
> *Amy H., age fourteen*

"Ask Your Mother (Ask Your Father)" may be played because one parent doesn't want to alienate or offend you by saying what he or she really thinks about your request at that instant. It's a good game for parents to play when they feel angry or pressured because it's actually a way of saying, "Time out!"

You *can* play and win at "Ask Your Mother (Ask Your Father)." Try saying, "Mom (Dad), I asked you because I want to know what you think," or "It's important for me to get this settled soon. Couldn't you please go out on a limb and answer me now?" If your parent refuses to make a move, and if you force the issue, you may provoke an outright "NO" to your request. If that happens you may get frustrated. For this reason, it's sometimes best to bide your time and wait for your other parent's response. Usually, the longer it takes for parents to say "No," the more likely it is their answer will be "Yes."

One last point to keep in mind: in some families, one parent is the primary decision-maker and disciplinarian. If this is the case, prevailing on your other parent for permission to do something major is just setting up the "Ask Your Mother (Ask Your Father)" game. If you know in advance that this is how your family operates, save yourself some grief by going directly to your decision-making parent with your important requests. It's more efficient.

"The Guilt Glut"

"The Guilt Glut" is a game with endless variations and predictable scripts that start out, "If you would only...," "I thought you loved me," "If you loved me (respected me, took my feelings into consideration) you would...," "Look what I do for you...," or "How could you...?" It's the parent's version of a teen's "Everyone Else Gets To" and is very much like fencing, with many thrusts and parries that are meant to throw you off balance and eventually wear you down. "The Guilt Glut" is a game most parents swear they'll never play because they hated it when their own parents did it with them.

The other day I was shopping the January sales with my oldest daughter. She had picked out several things and we'd spent close to $100 — that was on clothing reduced by 50 percent and more, to give you an idea of the quantity. I told her I wanted to look in my department for a couple of things before we left and she had an absolute fit, telling me she was exhausted and had homework to do and phone calls to make. I blew up on the spot and told her I thought she was ungrateful, didn't appreciate anything I did for her, and never even said "thank you" to me. Then I realized I sounded just like my own mother used to and I remembered how I used to hate those lectures. I don't know why I overreacted that way.

Mrs. L., age forty-two

"The Guilt Glut" usually makes everyone feel awful, so it's a game in which there are no winners, only losers. There's no point in arguing with a parent who feels put out or hurt enough to say the things the game strategy dictates.

How should you respond? Emotional outbursts like, "I hate you," "You don't understand me!" or "You don't care about me," don't work because they just add fuel to the fire. Instead, use logic and refocus the game. Try saying, "Mom (Dad), this has nothing to do with whether or not I (love you, respect you, etc.). It has to do with me and ... (fill in the blank)." You could also try this, "I'm sorry that whatever I've said (done) makes you think I don't care (am ungrateful, don't love you, etc.). I do care about you and we're not making an issue of that. We're talking about ... (fill in the blank)." Oddly enough, playing "The Guilt Glut" like this with your parents can lead to some useful insights about each other and can improve the way you communicate.

"Why Can't You Be More like . . . ?"

"Why Can't You Be More like ... ?" is a refinement of "The Guilt Glut" but isn't usually as unpleasant for you to have to play. That's because it starts when a parent isn't quite ready to come out and hit you with "You blew it," or "I'm disappointed in you," and isn't feeling hurt, angry, or frustrated enough to play "The Guilt Glut." In "Why Can't You Be More like ... ?"

your parent is more controlled. Here are some examples that might sound familiar.

> "Why can't you be more like Mrs. Smith's daughter? I understand she's a straight A student, goes to church twice a week, does all the cooking for her poor old mother, and writes operas in her spare time."
>
> "Why can't you be more like your cousin Larry, who's captain of the basketball team, an honor roll student, *and* has a job at the grocery store that pays him a hundred dollars a week?"
>
> "Why can't you be more like your brother? *He* never asks for money and he always puts his dishes in the sink."

How should you play? It depends in part on the tone of your parent's opening move. Is it said aggressively, meant to get you so angry that you'll hear "Why can't you be more like . . ." as a challenge and you'll take the bait, rise to the occasion, and *achieve*? If that's the case, you could respond by saying, "Are you suggesting I get into a contest with X to see who does better in the next few months?" You could also ask, "Why is it you'd like me to be more like X? Could you be very specific so I could see if there's a way for me to make those changes?" You could ask for information: "Why have you waited until now to bring this up?" "How do you know X is so great? Who told you?"

It may be that the tone of your parent's opening move is wry, almost satirical, like a left-handed compliment meant to convey the message that you're every bit as capable as the person you're being compared to, but that the parent thinks you either haven't hit your stride or haven't put in enough effort. If that's the case ask, "Am I hearing you right? Do you think I'm really OK but just need a little push to do better? Are you trying to give me that push?"

There's always a chance that "Why Can't You Be More like . . . ?" may not be a game at all. It may be an honest question said by parents who want to know why you aren't more like the person they're talking about, want you to take a good look at yourself by using someone else as a role model, and want you all to be able to discuss it calmly. If that's the case, "The Guilt Glut" tone of voice, that sense of hurt, anger, and frustration, will be totally absent.

"Because I'm Your Parent"

"Because I'm Your Parent" (with variations of "Just because," "I said so, that's why," and "I'm older than you are and know better") is another one of those games with scripts used by many parents who don't want to come across as disciplinarians, or seem too old-fashioned, and who don't want to have to lay down the law and get into a confrontation with you. It's hard to respond to because the chances for communication are limited.

How can you handle this? When you were younger you probably responded with "That's not fair" or persisted with endless repetitions of the same request until your parents dropped the game, gave in, gave up, or you gave up, but these responses usually do not improve things at all.

If you're playing for high stakes and your parents pull this strategy, it can cause great conflict between you. There will be some times when parents pull rank on you and put you in a no-win, checkmate situation. Your best shot is to withdraw gracefully and try again at a later date.

Family Games:
"Happy Family"

Family games are different from parent games because they go on for long periods of time and dominate everything your relatives do, say, or react to. They exist as an undercurrent that, similar to the background noise of a radio when you're studying, you may sometimes be acutely aware of, sometimes be able to ignore, or even completely forget about. A family game is like a whirlpool that sucks you into it: the more you struggle against it, the more you realize its power, since you can't control it or get yourself out of it.

"Happy Family" is a game people play to pretend everything is right when, in fact, everything isn't.

> My mom and dad want everyone to think of them as pillars of the community. My dad is on the bank's board of directors, and Mom volunteers all over the place. Right now she's president of the local hospital auxiliary and is my sister's room mother at school. But what no one else sees is that Dad drinks too much, Mom is addicted to Valiums, and they fight all the time — sometimes actually pounding each other with their fists. We are NOT a normal family, but we look like one on the outside.
>
> *Marjorie Z., age seventeen*

Families who play this game usually have family secrets. In fact, some parents who play "Happy Family" believe they've succeeded in hiding their problems from their own kids. They don't want to look like failures; they don't want anyone to realize that things aren't functioning smoothly at home. The secret might be that a parent is an alcoholic or drug abuser, or that mental, physical, or sexual abuse (the most extreme of which is incest) happens between family members, or that their marriage is in trouble. Secrets can involve family history: there may be something that someone did years or even generations ago that could jeopardize the family's standing in their community or get them into legal trouble if discovered. There are as many kinds of secrets as people, and the game is more common than you might imagine.

Hiding something can create a lot of tension in your home. "Happy Family" is often played to reduce that tension. You learn the game rules very early on and will know (sometimes by instinct) what you can and can't discuss either among yourselves or in public about how the family really operates.

If you're caught in the middle of such a game, it's hard to refuse to play since it seeps into every nook and cranny of your routine. But you may find that rather than being a tension reliever, it is a very stressful game to have to play and you may try to avoid playing it at all, or you may rebel and refuse to play by the rules. Your parents may resist you if you refuse to play, and they may try to make things unpleasant for you if you buck the tide.

What should you do? It depends on the nature of the secret that's being kept. If it's something that you can live with because it doesn't really affect you directly, then leave it alone and don't try to change the game rules. Let's say Uncle Harry was once in jail for stealing money from his boss and now has moved to your community. However, your dad's an accountant and is afraid he'll lose clients if anyone finds out about his brother's past, because of guilt by association. So they've made up a story about where Uncle Harry was for all those years. You can stick to the story because it really won't hurt you to do so, and it may make the difference between things going smoothly at home and things getting all messed up. But if the game is played to hide any kind of physical or mental abuse and you are a consistent loser in the game (because you are a target of the abuse), *you must refuse to play and get yourself out of the situation.* This can be scary and difficult, and it takes a lot of courage to do, but your first responsibility must be to yourself. There are some secrets that may not be as dangerous as abuse but still can be devastating. In those cases you should go talk to someone you trust who can help you sort out your feelings and decide what to do.

Parent and family games (and even your own games) can be a normal, though sometimes frustrating, part of growing up. They give you a chance to practice all kinds of useful communication skills and negotiating strategies in your family, and then take what you learn and apply it to other situations: school, friendships, romances, jobs. Playing these games with your parents can help you learn to handle rejection, frustration, and anger, as well as how to win graciously. Game playing teaches you about limits and boundaries that apply to your own family, because when you play games you learn very quickly how far you can go before the game is won, lost, or forfeited.

Some parents regard game playing in terms of winning or losing, never a draw. If they win, it bolsters their sense of being "good" parents because they can retain their authority over you and make you toe the line. But the fact is that games don't often result in a "winner" and a "loser." Their outcome affects all of you, and it's more likely that either you and your parents both win or you both lose.

What's in it for you? The payoff is that being satisfied with yourself and your family is very dependent on how well you can make the various decisions that are involved in the game process. You'll find it much easier to succeed in later life if you sustain battle scars from skirmishes within your family before you have to go out and slay some strange dragons.

3.

The Art and Science of Communicating with Parents

Mom and Dad are living in the past. Everything they expect me to do is based on rules they had to follow when they were my age.

Karen P., age fifteen

We don't seem to be speaking the same language.

Karen P.'s mother

My parents completely ignore my point of view and pretend that no other kid they know of would ever consider discussing the things I think are important.

Alex F., age fourteen

Alex and his sister suddenly become hard of hearing the instant we open our mouths.

Alex's parents

A major challenge you'll have during the next few years is to get your parents to listen to you, understand you, and respond to you as you'd like them to. It can be an exciting task, but it's guaranteed to present some frustrating moments. Your parents may think you're ignoring their attempts at communicating with you, and you may think the only times they'll notice you is when you create some chaos in the family. You and your parents may be operating on different wavelengths, and there may be too much static between you to be able to hear each other out.

Clearing up the static and learning how to express yourself and listen comfortably and effectively is part of the art and science of communicating with parents. It involves learning some new skills and being willing to put them to the test. This chapter will give you the information to set that process in motion.

The Parent-Teen Communication Crunch

Communication is a process of sending and receiving messages — "transmitting information." That sounds simple enough. Why, then, can communication be such a problem? The answer lies in three ingredients of your communications: motivation, content, and style.

Motivation refers to the *real* reason why someone does or says something. Often, it's hard to know what that motivation is unless you and your parents are so honest with each other that you never play any of the games we discussed in Chapter 2. Since very few of us are that honest, it's possible to become suspicious of the motivations that lurk beneath the surface of a communication. That's not unusual; it's human nature.

> **Father:** *"I had a funny feeling when Danny asked me for the car last weekend. I didn't want to come out and accuse him of anything but I found it hard to believe that the only reason he wanted it was to drive to the shopping mall to select a Mother's Day gift. It was so gorgeous out that I thought for sure he was going to pick up his girlfriend and go to the beach, and I was worried that they'd be drinking beer there or maybe worse."*
>
> **Danny:** *"My dad always does this to me. He never believes me and always assumes the worst. I feel like I can't win and I wish he'd just come out once and for all and tell me what's on his mind and what he really thinks of me."*

Parents are often afraid that you're hiding something, being manipulative, or lying. You may react to many of your parents' communications, especially their questions, as invasions of privacy. What your parents may think are reasonable topics for discussion may seem like propaganda or commands to you. It's almost impossible to have clear, open lines of communication when you're suspicious of each other's motivations before you've barely begun a dialogue.

The second and third ingredients in communicating with your parents are *content* and *style*. Think of the process in terms of a picture in a frame. The actual picture represents the content: what is being said, the message. The frame represents the style: how it is being said and how it comes across to the other person. Just as a frame and picture are linked because a frame can make a picture look good or bad, so are content and style closely linked.

Style refers to the way you choose to communicate, the attitude that comes across as you speak, listen, and respond. Style is a combination of things: *body language* (Are you facing each other? Are you shaking your fist as you speak? Does one of you have an arm around the other person while you're talking? Are your arms folded tightly across your chest?), *eye contact* (Are you looking directly at each other? Are you rolling your eyes in disgust? Do you refuse to return the other person's gaze?), and *tone of voice* (loud and brassy? soft and sweet? condescending? sarcastic? angry?). Your style can make or break the outcome of a communication with parents because certain styles lead to certain predictable results. Here are some examples of how style can ruin communication or open the door to understanding:

How to Ruin It

Father: *"Young man, I think we need to talk about your grades."*
Tone of voice: *angry.*
Eye contact: *glaring, eyes slightly squinting because face is tense.*
Body posture: *erect, finger pointed at son and parent shaking it as he talks.*
Content of message communicated: *"I'm going to punish you for getting bad grades."*
Son: *"What's there to talk about? They stink."*
Tone of voice: *even angrier than father's.*
Eye contact: *none.*
Body posture: *back to his parent, walking away as he responds to father.*

Content of message communicated: *"I won't get into it with you."*

How to Open the Lines of Communication

Father: *"Young man, I think we need to talk about your grades."*

(Tone of voice, body posture, eye contact, *and* content *are same as above.*)

Son: *"Dad, I'm upset enough as it is. I really can't talk about it right now. How about later this evening when I'm not feeling so down?"*

Tone of voice: *calm and in control.*

Eye contact: *focused on father's face; responding directly to father.*

Body posture: *tense but not defiant.*

Content of message communicated: *"I know I messed up but I can't deal with it now and I don't want to get into a fight with you. So let's wait till I'm in control to talk."*

Style can make a difference. Even though you can't be responsible for a parent's opening style, how you respond can either smother communication like a wet blanket or make it possible for you to have a meeting of the minds.

The Seven Don'ts of Communicating

1. *Don't begin a communication by putting down the other person.* If you say things like "You don't know how it feels," or "You're hopelessly outdated" to your parents, it automatically puts them on the defensive and makes it unlikely that you'll have a productive exchange of information or ideas. If your parents start a conversation with a putdown or a lecture about how you've disappointed them, realize that if you respond in kind you'll only end up aggravating and hurting each other, and chances are none of you will pay much attention to whatever's said next.

2. *Don't use a "nonresponse" when your parents say something to you.* If you're asked, "How was your day?" and you reply, "OK," or if your parents want to know, "Where are you

going tonight?" and you answer, "Out with the kids," or if the question is "Did you finish your homework?" and you tell them, "Sort of," there's nowhere for the conversation to go except down the tubes. In fact, you probably wouldn't like it very much if your parents responded this way to you. Nonresponses don't permit any exchange of information, and that style infuriates and upsets everyone.

3. *Don't distort what your parents are saying.* If your parents say, "You can't go out tonight because you have two final exams tomorrow," and you respond with "You hate me, you think I'm stupid and that I'm going to fail!" then you've distorted what your parents said. Distortions are common and they're an enemy of understanding. One good way of avoiding distorting is to try to see a situation from your parents' point of view. If you succeed in doing this, it may help your parents see things from *your* viewpoint once in a while.

4. *Don't yell in order to get your point across.* People usually yell when they are frustrated or angry. While yelling may help you let off steam, it throws a monkey wrench into the communication process. In fact, it's usually just a verbal temper tantrum. If you find yourself on the verge of yelling, you can do one of these things: (a) swallow hard and force yourself to talk quietly and deliberately; (b) end the conversation and go somewhere alone; (c) admit your feelings of anger and frustration and ask to end the conversation temporarily.

5. *Don't consistently undermine your parents' attempts at talking.* Saying things like "Can't you see how much I have to do?" or "I'm busy now and I have a lot of phone calls to make and then I have two hours of homework" makes parents feel left out and hurt, and may eventually make them believe it's not worth trying to discuss things with you when they need to. That situation can lead to parents who dictate to you rather than parents who negotiate and give you options to choose from. Again, think how frustrating this is when your parents do it.

6. *Don't act as if you're hopelessly bored when your parents are talking to you.* Acting bored says that you're not interested in what your parents are saying. If nothing else, this will make it a bit more likely that they won't be interested in listening when *you've* got something important to say. A word to the

wise: try to *look* interested when your parents are talking to you (even if you're not) because it will pay dividends in many ways.

7. *Don't be sarcastic, silly, or coy (as if you were playing a cat-and-mouse game) when you and your parents talk.* All this usually accomplishes is to make your parents question your maturity level, your common sense, your seriousness. It's better to be yourself and leave the theatrics for another time.

Communicating effectively with your parents means making a major effort to remember about motivation, content, and style. It also means fine-tuning a few more skills — sending clear messages and learning how to listen.

Sending Signals Clearly

The best way to get your point across is to send a clearly stated message. If you do that, there can be little question about the content of your communication and your motivation. But sending clear signals isn't always easy. In fact, communicating clearly is definitely an acquired skill. If you think about the process of driving a car you'll see what we mean. When you first start to drive you're hesitant, you make mistakes, and it feels funny because the instincts that let you proceed with confidence aren't there yet. The more you drive, the more practice you get on different kinds of streets and roads in different areas, the less you need to think about what you're doing as you do it, and the better driver you become. That skill eventually becomes second nature to you; once learned, it's never forgotten.

As with driving, part of learning how to communicate clearly with parents — or anyone else for that matter — is knowing what *not* to do as well as what to do.

Don't say something you don't really mean. You and your parents can be equally guilty of doing this. Consider the following conversation:

Karen (age fourteen): *"Mom, would it be dangerous for me to use birth control pills?"*

> **Mom:** *"You're too young to be thinking about birth control pills."*

Karen's question was a loaded one that caught her mother off guard. Her mom wanted to say, "They're not as dangerous as getting pregnant at your age could be." However, she was afraid if she said that, Karen might think that her mom approved of teenagers having premarital sex. So Karen's mother did what so many parents do when faced with the prospect of having to be completely honest with their teens — she skirted the issue to avoid controversy and confrontation and ended the discussion. Karen, meanwhile, really had wanted to get some information about birth control. She had hoped her question would generate a discussion of facts and that her mom would help her find some books to read on the subject. But her question didn't convey the message clearly at all; instead, it triggered a parental panic attack! If Karen and her mom had been more skillful at sending clear messages, the dialogue could have gone like this:

> **Karen:** *"Mom, I've been hearing a lot of rumors about birth control lately because all my friends are talking about sex. But they're afraid to ask their parents about things. I know I can be straight with you. Can you answer some specific questions I have? My main one is whether the pill is safe and who should use it and when."*
>
> **Mom:** *"Well, dear, it depends on many things — your age, your health, the kind of pill. Why are you suddenly so interested? I hope you're not planning on having intercourse yet."*
>
> **Karen:** *"I don't know much about anything, Mom, and I was hoping you'd help me get some information."*
>
> **Mom:** *"I'm really glad you asked. I have to tell you at the start that I don't approve of premarital sex, but I think you have a right to know about birth control. Do you have time to come to the library with me?"*

Do you see the difference? This conversation could continue for weeks. The other version was at a dead end before it had the chance to warm up.

Don't send mixed messages if you want to be a clear commu-

nicator. Mixed messages are basically like the "Yes, but . . . No, but . . ." game we discussed in Chapter 2. When you or your parents send mixed messages, one part of the statement negates the other. Have you ever heard your parent say, "I don't expect you to be perfect, but how on earth could you have gotten a B on that test? The exam was so important!"? or "You're way too young to be wearing so much eyeshadow and mascara . . . (three minutes later in the conversation) . . . Can't you act more grown up? You're not a kid anymore, you know"? The signals are confused, almost like crossed wires on a telephone line when someone else's conversation bleeds over into your own and garbles the conversations for both parties.

Mixed messages can also happen when there's an obvious difference between words that are spoken and the nonverbal messages we send through body language. If a dad says to his son, "How was your blind date tonight?" and the son answers, "She was nice enough," but says it in a flat tone of voice with zero enthusiasm and a skeptical look on his face, the dad ends up not knowing what his son really thinks. If your parent says, "I'M NOT MAD AT YOU!" but booms it out through gritted teeth, speaking each syllable distinctly, slowly, and dramatically, you'll realize the words don't match the tone of voice and you may wonder when your parent will explode.

Don't assume the other person is a mind reader. It's easy to forget to be specific when you talk to each other. A parent may say, "Don't make any more phone calls this evening," but when you're back on the phone fifteen minutes later that parent gets mad. You say, "*I* didn't make the call; my friend called me!" You ask your mom if you can borrow the car this weekend but neglect to say which day, and she takes it on the day you wanted it. You get annoyed. She says, later on, "You didn't stop me or remind me, so I assumed tomorrow was when you wanted it." Forgetting to be specific is an oversight that occurs in families because people think they know each other so well that most things don't need to be spelled out. Communicating under that assumption leads to garbled, unclear signals.

Don't Wait!
Try These Eight Ways to Send Clear Signals

Fortunately, it's easier than you may think to send clear signals. If you start using these techniques your parents will definitely notice something different is going on. You may even find your parents starting to use them too, even if they never had before. Here's a list of skills to develop.

1. *Use "I" messages to state your feelings and expectations.* "I was hoping for a raise in my allowance" states a fact and a feeling and leaves no room for your parent to guess what's on your mind. It's a lot better than saying, "You're so cheap" or "You never give me enough money to cover expenses" — even though you may feel that way — since those approaches just put your parents on the defensive. Similarly, look at the difference in these two messages from a parent to a teenager.

Message 1: "You're always leaving a mess in the bathroom." (Is your parent angry? Annoyed? Is she telling you to clean up or just trying to make you feel guilty? It's not clear.)

Message 2: "I get annoyed when the bathroom's messy. I'd like it if you'd help out by keeping it neat." (There's no need to guess at the message sent here.) Using "I" messages eliminates a lot of second-guessing and aggravation.

2. *Rehearse ahead of time what you want to say and how you'll say it, if it's about something really important.* Doing this is useful if you have a crisis you need to tell your parents about, or if you have questions about emotionally charged subjects like sex or drugs. You can write an outline of what you want to discuss. You can tape-record imaginary dialogues. You can rehearse in front of a mirror. You can write it out as a debate and try to list every rebuttal you think your parents will make to your arguments. If you do any of this, you'll be less nervous when it comes time to bring up the subject.

3. *Make your needs clear.* Since many conversations touch on a number of different issues, state your case clearly and up front in the conversation, including, if necessary, a list of the things that are very important to you, somewhat impor-

tant to you, and the things you'd be willing to let slide by at this time.

4. *Don't beat around the bush.* Most of us hate it when parents lecture and get long-winded, and parents don't like it very much when their kids seem to be deceptive. Even if it takes a lot of courage to be direct, it can pay big dividends because parents won't have to waste time second-guessing you, and you can get started on creative problem-solving right away.

5. *Try to make your parents feel that you love them, especially if you're about to hit them with a whammy.* "I love you, but I want to move into my own apartment" is easier for a parent to process than "I can't stand living with you anymore and need out." You can sometimes forget that your parents need to know that you love them. Even if the words stick in your throat at first, if you have any positive feeling about your parents, give them a clue that it's there.

6. *Get feedback from your parents.* Double-check as you go along in a conversation to see if you're making yourself clear. You all benefit from this.

7. *Be aware of your parents' attention level.* If Dad is sitting in front of the TV, attentively watching a World Series game, it's not a good time to try to have a heart-to-heart talk. If Mom is in the shower getting ready for a big night out at the annual company dinner, it's not a good time to talk to her about a problem you're having in school. Try to choose sensible times for communicating, when no one's rushed or preoccupied with another activity or problem. After all, this is how you'd like to be treated, isn't it?

8. *If you think you're going to have trouble talking face-to-face, write your parents a letter.* This method is good because it gives you a chance really to think out what you want to say, and because, once written, it states your message without interruption. Use letters to tell your parents good stuff as well as problematic things. You can use letters as a bridge from a state of embarrassed or tense silence to a more comfortable conversational style by which you communicate. A word of caution, though: letter writing shouldn't be the only way you communicate if you're all living under the same roof.

Learning to Listen

The thought of having to listen to your parents can be a turn-off if you've heard the scripts we discussed in Chapter 2 so often you have them memorized. Learning to listen, though, is one of the most useful communication skills you can acquire, and if you try it using the following guidelines, we think you'll be pleased with the results.

Give your full attention to your parents. If you listen with only half an ear, you may miss a key point in what your parents are trying to tell you, and then you may react on the basis of thinking something was communicated when it really wasn't. If you pay close attention, the chances of that happening are reduced.

Try not to seem impatient or disgusted with your parents as you listen to them. No one expects you to like everything your parents will have to say to you. But if you expect them to give you an open-minded hearing when you want to talk, and if you want to be treated on the basis of your ideas and not how cleverly you present them, then you need to extend the same courtesies to your parents as you listen to them.

If you're in a hurry to get somewhere or do something, tell your parents and make an appointment with them to discuss whatever it is later, and at leisure. Parents may need more time than you want to give them to explore a topic, and if your mind is on something else the communication will be short-circuited. If you know this in advance and can make other arrangements with your parents, they'll appreciate your willingness to hear them out, and your discussion may be more fruitful. If you do make an appointment, make sure to follow through and actually meet with your parents. Otherwise, they'll end up angrier, more frustrated, or more annoyed than they would have if you had "listened and left" in the first place.

Once in a while ask your parents if they'd like to talk, even if they haven't requested a discussion. These unexpected, odd-moment exchanges can be the most successful. You may find your parents have a lot to offer, especially if they're not feeling pressured to solve a crisis or give an instant answer to a request. Sometimes parents feel you really don't care about what's going on in the world of adults, so a "What's new?" asked while standing in the grocery checkout line, or "How's work? You've seemed tired lately," while you're raking leaves together can be a good way to sharpen your listening skills and let your parents open up.

Listening is an active process that requires a lot of energy and effort because it is more than just hearing words. It's not a difficult skill to learn, it just requires that you clear your head of "clutter" and focus on your parent's message. Active listening doesn't guarantee that you'll like what you hear; it just means you've received an accurate signal and can respond appropriately.

The Silent Treatment

The silent treatment is communication by omission. Many of us are masters of this art, using it to cover up blunders, to mask anger or pain so the feelings don't have to be acknowledged and discussed immediately, or to signal a need for privacy. Sometimes it is used to *get* attention. The trouble with using the silent treatment as a communication strategy is that it usually puts parents into a panic and sets their imaginations into high gear — they automatically assume the worst.

> Last spring, Tad got really quiet all of a sudden. He used to come home every day and talk about work and about the money he was saving to be able to go to the junior prom, and he'd make my husband and me feel like a part of his life. Then it just stopped. He basically became a ghost, a presence in the house that slept and ate here, but that was it. We did something we swore we'd never do — we searched his room for drugs and read through some of his private papers. We felt awful, but we couldn't think of what else to do. He was like a zombie. You know, as soon as school was out he started acting normal again. We've yet to find out what was going on. Teenagers!
>
> *Mrs. P., age forty-six, mother of three teenagers*

In all fairness to Mrs. P. and parents in general, there is reason for this panic, since prolonged silence can be a sign of depression or other kinds of mental conflict, a sign of addiction, or even a signal of impending suicide. So give your parents a break. Don't rely on the silent treatment too often. Just state your need for privacy, say why, and then hope your parents will accept it.

What if your parents give you the silent treatment? It depends on when and why they do it. If they almost never talk with you and rarely say what they're thinking, you have no yardstick against which you can measure your behavior. You may feel like they don't care one way or the other or maybe you'll assume they approve of everything you're doing. But most parents use the silent treatment sparingly because it's so hard to do. Being silent means not criticizing, not offering advice or opinions that weren't asked for. A parent who uses the silent treatment occasionally may be trying to give you a chance to become just a little more independent, even if it increases the chances that you'll make a few more mistakes than you would if that parent was giving you instructions along the way. It's also possible that something's bothering your parents

if they're excessively quiet. If you think that's the case, why not ask about it?

Compromise

Compromise is an invaluable skill to learn if you and your parents are going to communicate without major hassles. For example, your parents want you to stay home this weekend because your grandparents just called to say they're coming up from Florida to pay you a surprise visit. However, you were invited by your best friend to go to her brother's homecoming weekend at his college two hours from your town and you had already finalized your plans to go with her. To keep peace in the family, you compromise — you agree to spend Sunday with your relatives if your parents let you spend Saturday at the homecoming game. Compromise means that both you and your parents must give up a bit of what each wants in return for something. *It does not, however, mean giving up.* It's like walking a tightrope — you each need to find the position that enables you to be in balance.

Ten Ways to Erase the Static When Communicating with Parents

1. Don't put down your parents.
2. Don't assume you know what they're going to say before they say it.
3. Don't assume they'll never be able to understand you.
4. Do cool off before you talk, because anger is not conducive to clear communication.
5. Try to understand your parents' viewpoint, but don't allow yourself to be pressured into agreeing to something you don't really want or like if there's room for compromise.
6. Try not to demand things or make threats; these tactics have a tendency to backfire.

7. Know when to drop the discussion — that is, don't beat a dead horse.
8. Don't turn the communication process into a contest for power.
9. Be an active, accurate listener.
10. Don't think of your parents as The Enemy.

Part 2.

Dealing
with Everyday Realities —
Facts and Feelings

4.

Touchy Subjects

The little things in life matter a lot. Whether or not your hair combs out just right after your morning shower, whether your clothes capture the look you want, whether you have access to the car, what your parents have to say about you can make or break a day even before it's started. They're like tiny pebbles that get into your shoes when you're out jogging — they won't cause much damage, but they can be irritating in the long run.

One of the reasons they may be sources of conflict has to do with the different values you and your parents place on each of those miscellaneous matters that come up day after day: your clothes, your makeup, your jewelry, your driving privileges, your chores, and so on. Your parents may ask, "How can you get so worked up about something so unimportant?" or "Why can't you be logical about this? Why can't you put it in proper perspective? Why can't you see things my way?" You may argue that yours *is* the proper perspective, and not only is the issue important, it's critical to how your life will play out in the near future! You may think that your parents are making a mountain out of a molehill, and you can't understand why they're on your back about it. In this chapter we'll explore some of the miscellaneous matters that are sources of irritation and see what can be done to erase the aggravation factor from them.

Hair

How you wear your hair can drive your parents up a wall, can cause them anxiety attacks, and can make them feel as if they've failed in their efforts to raise you properly. It can make them say things that you think are absolutely silly, like

> "If you wear your hair that way, no college admissions officer will take you seriously."
> "That hairdo will make everyone think you have no common sense."
> "You'll lose all your friends if you go out looking like that because no one would want to be seen with you."

It is true that some of the more outlandish hairstyles may put some people off, and that if you choose to enter the military or certain other professions like trial law, you'll have to give up your streaks of orange, blue, or green, and you'll have to switch your braided tails for tailored tresses. It isn't true, however, that how you wear your hair defines how nice you are, how smart you are, or how successful you can be (unless you're a model, when a hairstyle may be a factor in your success). A hairstyle is a hairstyle, and while it might help you feel good about yourself, help you identify with a group of people who wear similar hairdos, or help you capture the look of a favorite soap star, movie star, or rock artist, that's as far as the equation goes.

You don't have to wear rags tied on top of your head like Madonna or elaborate beaded corn rows like Stevie Wonder to get your parents involved in a confrontation about hair. "Your bangs are too long, dear; I can't see your face" is a common complaint of mothers to daughters. "Your sideburns are uneven," "The nape of your neck looks messy" are things that boys frequently hear. "You wash your hair too much," "You don't wash your hair enough," "When are you going to get a haircut?" "Didn't I just give you money for a haircut?" are all part of the same process. The attention your hair gets from your parents may make it seem as if it has a separate life of its own.

When parents put so much focus on your hair it may make you feel like they can't accept you as you are and that they care more about how you look than about anything else (which may not be true). It can make them appear to be hopelessly out of touch with "style" as you define it, and may make you think they want to impose their standards on you rather than letting you develop your own (but *they* may be thinking they're giving you the benefit of their experience). These kinds of feelings and messages need to be erased and replaced with accurate ones. Here are some suggestions for how you can handle your parents' reactions to your current hairstyle and clarify your own feelings without fighting about it.

Show them a yearbook from your school. If the majority of students don't look appreciably different from you, you're on your way to winning the argument about your hair.

Look through family photo albums. Put place markers on the pages where there are photos of your parents wearing hairstyles unlike the ones they're currently wearing. Sit down together and look at the pictures and then discuss your reactions. Your parents may decide *you* look pretty good, after all, in comparison to how they used to look.

Call your grandparents and ask them how they reacted to your parents as teenagers. Take notes as you talk so you will accurately remember specific incidents and dates. Later, tell your parents about the conversation. Jog their memory a bit and ask them to try to recall how they felt when their own parents made hair a big issue. Then see if you can tell them how it makes you feel when they do this to you.

Arrange to see Woodstock *or* Hair *with your parents.* (You can rent a VCR and these movies if they're not playing on TV.) Discuss the way people looked (*Woodstock* is a documentary; *Hair* is not), what your parents remember about the sixties and early seventies, what they did to their own hair (and whether it was in response to what friends did to make a statement, and so on). Compare it to what you are trying to accomplish by wearing your hair the way you do.

Try to compromise occasionally. If it's very important to your parents that you tone down your hairstyle for a particular event (a wedding, graduation, funeral, job, college interview) and there's any way you can do it temporarily and without losing face (even if it means using hats, scarves, hairpieces, wash-in color), do it. It will show your parents you respect their feelings and will also contribute to family harmony.

Do some research about hairstyles in history. This is a good tactic if your parents are sure your hair is going to be your downfall. Eighteenth-century wigs for women (and even men) make punks, Cyndi Lauper, and the early version of Boy George look positively dull by comparison. Many successful people have worn their hair in less-than-conservative styles. Elvis Presley and the Beatles both caused a cultural uproar with their hair styles. Share your information with your parents. If you take the time to do this, they may be so impressed by your inventiveness that they'll drop the whole issue.

The point of all of these suggestions is to get a dialogue started. Talk to one another and see if there isn't something more at stake than just the hairdo that is the irritation. It's certainly worth a try.

Clothing

How you dress can create similar kinds of tensions as how you wear your hair. Both of these things often boil down to being issues of control: your parents feel their influence slipping away as you develop your own sense of style (and with it your own sense of who you are) and may struggle to keep the control just a little longer; you need the opportunity to make decisions for yourself and will probably fight for the right to do so.

Some parents actually believe that you either don't love them anymore, don't appreciate them, or don't think highly of them if you reject their suggestions about your clothing. You may not realize this, but many parents feel just as insecure as their kids do and don't know how to speak openly about their feelings. When a lot goes by unsaid, a good deal of tension can build up and arguments about clothing hide what really needs to be discussed. If you think this is the case with you and your parents, a first step is to say something like "I love you and really appreciate your help with this, but my taste is a little different from yours," or "That's a great-looking outfit you've picked out for me, but my body type doesn't quite match the style," or "I think that sort of thing would look great on you, but I'm not sure I can carry it off just yet."

Other parents say they can't understand what you're try-

ing to do to yourself when you pick out certain outfits. Here's
what the father of a high school sophomore had to say:

> My son is built like a Greek god. Do you know that all he
> wore to school this year was a pair of hospital surgical
> scrub pants and a matching top! The only variety was that
> one outfit was a sickly green and the other was a washed-
> out blue. Now, I think back on the days when I criticized
> his picture T-shirts and blue jeans and I wonder why I
> didn't like them. At least you could see the person under
> the clothes. I'd think he'd want to show off what he's got.

If you're a person who happens to like fifties- and six-
ties-style clothes similar to what your parents wore as teenagers, that's no guarantee that clothing won't be an issue.
Why? Your parents probably have lost their "eye" for the particular clothing fad. All you need to do to understand this is
look at the contents of your closet. The clothes that seemed so
"in" last year and made you feel you looked really great tend
to appear hopelessly out of style one or two seasons later.
Cases in point: wide vs. narrow ties or lapels, high-top sneak-
ers vs. traditional Keds or Nikes, long vs. short skirts, floods
vs. wide-bottom pants. Put yourself in your parents' place for
a moment and perhaps you'll understand why they can't easily
get accustomed to the looks you like.

What if you really like your parents' clothes better than
your own, are the same size as your mom or dad, and tend to
borrow clothes without asking and without returning them?
Try to realize that when you borrow clothes this way, your
parents don't necessarily feel complimented. They may, in
fact, feel that their privacy has been violated. They may think
you're trying to grow up too fast, to fit an image that's too sophisticated, and this can cause as much turmoil as when parents dislike your clothes. On the other hand, it may be an
issue of economics: their things are probably much more
costly than yours, and if you don't take care of them and return them in the same condition as when you took them,
there's bound to be trouble. To avoid major headaches, get
permission before you invade a parent's closet, and find out
the ground rules for wearing the clothes.

The clothing issue isn't as difficult to negotiate as hair

issues because it's easier to change your clothes than a haircut. Here are some guidelines to ease the aggravation potential.

1. *Make sure you own one or two things that you can put on when you go out with your parents and that you know they'll approve of.* Tailored clothes are always a good bet, and you can add some oomph by accessorizing if you want to wear them when you're with friends.

2. *Try not to feel personally attacked if your parents don't like your clothes.* Make allowances for the fact that if you don't care for everything they put on, there's no reason they should have to like all your things.

3. *Try to educate your parents.* Show them current fashion magazines (every public library has some). Invite friends who dress like you do to your home. Ask your parents to come to some school activities so they can see what the popular looks are.

4. *If your parents pay for your clothes, practice the art of compromise.* You'll probably find something that captures the basic look you're trying for without offending an adult's sensibilities. That way you won't get your parents so annoyed that they'll refuse to let you buy anything at all.

5. *Find a few friends you can trade clothes with occasionally.*

6. *Shop in thrift stores.* If you pay only a few dollars for an item it's doubtful that your parents will react as strongly as they might if you spent a great deal more.

Earrings, Other Jewelry, and Cosmetics

My dad is a therapist who works with really tough kids, dropouts, runaways, and he's seen it all. That's why I was totally freaked out by his reaction to my ear. I've had pierced ears since I was nine and I triple-pierced my right ear last week. My mom thought it was fine, but he went out of control. I mean I could have come home in leather and chains with spiked hair and he would have been calmer.

Marcie N., age fifteen

The guys at school are wearing rubber washer rings that we get from the auto mechanics classes. My mom didn't mention the ones I wore on my fingers but when I started wearing the bigger ones as ankle bracelets she had a fit. She told me I looked like a fool and was embarrassing her. At one point she threatened to ground me if I didn't throw them out. I couldn't talk to her and she made such a big deal out of it I felt like I had to fight for my rights. If she hadn't done that, I'd probably have given the whole lot to my sister.

Phil B., age thirteen

Last Sunday I was getting myself ready to go out to dinner with my mom and grandmother. I put on a real dark green eyeshadow I had just bought and flecked it with some silver glitter. It looked so tough. My mom came into the bathroom to ask when I'd be done, took one look at me, and slapped me in the face. She told me I looked cheap and made me wash everything off. I was so angry I refused to go out with them.

Joan R., age fifteen

What you do to your body and put on your body in order to look attractive can generate intense reactions from the adults in your life. It may not matter to your parents that centuries ago pirates wore earrings, or that in many cultures people wear jewelry in places we consider odd, like noses, cheeks, toes. It may not even matter that there are many cultural definitions of "beauty" — so many, in fact, that if you and your parents were to read anthropology books you'd find that some people stretch their upper lips with wooden plates, others keep adding rings to elongate their necks as they grow, some daub themselves all over with clay or mud, and others tattoo their bodies in elaborate patterns. Most parents will tell you, "I don't care what anyone else does; this is what you should do."

For girls, wearing earrings, other jewelry, and makeup can be sources of conflict with parents for a number of reasons. They tend to transform you from "child" to "more adult" very quickly. It's one thing for you to play dress-up, it's another thing entirely when the playing turns into everyday routine. They really mark a transition point in your life, the way buying a first pair of high heels probably did in your mom's. But it can be scary for parents to see this happening because it means that you're growing up, and growing up leads to growing away from them.

Why parents react strongly to heavy applications of makeup or triple-pierced ears, for example, also has to do with their images of their daughters and what they want other people to think about these girls. Let's say that your parents have always imagined you as a Miss Teenage America type. You, on the other hand, are trying for something entirely different. Your parents may mistakenly think that the way you are choosing to express your individuality means you've thrown away the values or morals that they imagine go with that Miss Teenage America look.

> My daughter came home from camp last summer a different person. She didn't look like anyone I knew. I sent her there with a fresh-scrubbed look and she returned looking like something I thought belonged on Forty-second Street. We got into huge fights over her makeup and the tacky jewelry she was wearing. I bought her real gold studs for her ears; she wore safety pins. I took her to get a Mary Kay facial; she went out and bought red mascara and blue lip gloss. I was afraid that she was going to end up on the streets. You know what? She got straight A's in school and was elected class treasurer even with the makeup and the jewelry. I know she's still a virgin, and, believe me, I was concerned about that too. It took me a long time to be able to tell her what I was afraid of, and to admit I was wrong, but I did it. I still don't like how she looks, but I see it isn't hurting her at all.
>
> Mrs. F., *mother of a fifteen-year-old*

Try to understand that many parents have trouble admitting what Mrs. F. did and instead will say things like "You look ridiculous" when what they really mean to say is "I care about you and I'm worried that other people will get the wrong impression about you," or "I'm worried that other people will think I'm a bad parent if you go around like that." Explore these issues with your parents, and put all your cards face-up on the table.

The issue of jewelry and cosmetics for boys is a little different than for girls. A lot of it is tied up with parents' images of what boys are supposed to be like, the whole macho image. Many parents just can't accept the fact that boys wear earrings (perhaps they don't know that movie star Rob Lowe is currently wearing not a stud in his right ear, but a dangly drop earring) and this doesn't necessarily mean that they are homosexual. Many parents also have problems with boys and other kinds of jewelry. You have to understand that when many of your dads were teens, men were just beginning to wear neck chains and bracelets again. There were much stricter cultural "rules" about what men could or couldn't wear.

Boys who wear cosmetics are also a relatively new phenomenon, and if you do, you can expect a lot of flak from your parents, who may not know about the guys in Duran Duran who share their makeup with their wives. Again, parents may not state their anxieties out loud to you. After all, it's taken a long time for men's colognes and skin-care preparations to be accepted by the general public, and it will probably take even longer for the idea of makeup for boys to be considered "normal." But if you are a boy who is intent on wearing earrings, jewelry, and cosmetics, you do have a responsibility to ask your parents if it worries them, and if it does, why. You may not persuade them that your style is the right style, but if you can clear the air it will make room for other more important issues to be discussed.

Tattoos

My daughter went into the city yesterday with a group of girlfriends, and every one of them came home with a tiny tattoo inscribed on the bottom of her left foot. They told me they got the idea from reading a magazine article about a tightrope walker who had one on his instep. I was beside myself. But what can I do?

Mrs. J., *mother of a seventeen-year-old*

In some schools tattoos are "in." However, on a popularity scale of 1 to 10, most parents rate them somewhere between 1 and 3! So if you surprise your family with a permanent tattoo, you'll probably have a lot of explaining to do. There are some valid reasons why your parents might get upset about one.

1. Tattoos involve injecting dye under the skin. If they are not done properly, there is risk of infection or scarring.
2. They're permanent. Plastic surgery is about the only thing that can remove them, but the results aren't always good, and the surgery is expensive.
3. Your girlfriends or boyfriends may change. If you have their initials or names tattooed on your body, you may have a lot of explaining to do to future dates or mates.
4. Your tastes may change. The adorable turtle that looked so good on your sixteen-year-old thigh may not look so cute to you when you're forty.
5. Your body will change. Tattoos can fade, and they'll stretch or sag as your skin ages.
6. Your parents may be completely unable to understand what you've done. Many parents think of tattoos as a form of self-mutilation rather than something that's artistic or decorative.

If a tattoo is really important to you and really a problem for your parents, there are some semipermanent stick-on/peel-off tattoos that can fool most people. Go that route for a while. If your parents get used to the idea and you still want a real one, they may have no problem with the idea if you go ahead and do it.

Driving

Driving is a turning point for both teenagers and parents. It means you're on the road to independence (no pun intended); it's one of the tickets out of childhood that lets you into the world of adult privileges and responsibilities. For many parents, it's the first tangible sign of having to let go of their kids.

When they hand over the car keys, your parents may say, "I hope all we've taught you in the past has sunk in," which is a way of telling you they're concerned but know you have the skills and judgment to be a safe, responsible driver, and the rest is up to you — you're in control and they can't protect you.

There are a few basic things you might try to understand about what parents think about when they see you driving off in a car.

Parents often worry that you may not get home safely. Accidents, drunk drivers, highway snipers, hitchhikers who are kidnappers or rapists tend to loom larger than life in parents' imaginations. Some of their concerns are well founded — anyone who reads a newspaper knows there are certain real risks to driving. Discuss the fears your parents may have and obey the ground rules they establish for you. Those rules (like no driving alone at night, no picking up hitchhikers) are for your safety and aren't meant to make you feel untrustworthy.

Parents often worry about their cars. A major concern is that you'll misuse or abuse the car in some way. Some of the things that aggravate parents are neglecting to replace the gas you've used up while driving, turning a clean car into a mobile version of your room at home, taking the car to areas where it gets very dirty (like off-roading, the beach) and then not washing it or waxing it, or when your driving habits are sloppy and you cause mechanical damage (because you shift improperly, gun and flood the engine frequently, let the car idle and overheat). It's a good bet that if any combination of these situations happens too often, you'll find yourself walking or taking a bus. A simple way to avoid this is to have a checklist of what car maintenance procedures your parents expect you to follow. Keep it in the car's glove compartment and refer to it each time you take the car.

Parents expect you to be a safe and responsible driver. This is nonnegotiable in most parents' minds and means you'll often be reminded of a series of dos and don'ts. Don't speed, drink and drive, overload the car with passengers. Do wear seatbelts, be a courteous driver, make sure to use your turn signals, and so on. The reason many parents make such a big deal of these things is that they know good driving is largely a matter of good habits, and poor driving often the result of bad habits. They want you to develop good habits even if it means they'll have to nag you a lot at first. Rather than turning the nagging into an issue, think of your parents as fitness coaches who are trying to get you to achieve your best performance. It may be easier to take that way.

Many of us don't own cars. Driver's education courses offered in most high schools may be the only way you'll have access to a car. Try to take a driver's ed course no matter what the chances are that you'll have a car any time soon. Not only will you learn to drive and get road time, you'll get classroom lectures about safety, and you'll be shown movies that graphically depict actual crashes and what can happen when you ignore the safety rules. Driver's ed works. Teenagers who successfully complete such classes pay lower insurance rates than those who don't because their driving records are better. That doesn't mean that if a parent teaches you to drive or you go to an independent driving school you won't be a good driver. It's just that the positive impact of driver's ed has been proven year after year, and it's something worth thinking about.

Telephones

We've heard parents say they wish their kids had to take a required "telephone user's education course" during seventh or eighth grade. Junior high seems to be the time when you begin to use the family phone as an extension of the schoolday, and in many homes the phone starts to ring the instant you walk in the door after school.

It may be that for you, using the phone is really a necessity.

> "There's no public transportation in my town and my parents both work. My best friend lives too far away for me to bike to his house easily. So we use the phone to hang out together."

> "I do a lot of homework over the phone. It's really the only way to practice my French vocabulary. If we walked

around speaking French in public our other friends would think we were nuts."

"I can say things to my friends over the phone and I know they'll be private. I don't have to worry about nosy little sisters eavesdropping, or other kids listening like they do on the school bus. When I talk on the phone and go over stuff that's happened at school, if it gets repeated and back to me, at least I know who has leaked it and who can't be trusted anymore."

The telephone can be an important tool in your social and communication network. But there are some understandable reasons why your telephone habits can annoy your parents. If there is only one phone line in the house and you're monopolizing it, your parents may miss important incoming calls. "When my best client couldn't get through to me and had to call my boss about a contract change, that's when I suspended my daughter's phone privileges for a month," one dad told us. A good solution is to tell your parents you will pay for "call waiting" — a clicker system that indicates someone is calling while you are talking. You put one person on hold and answer the click. This eliminates the possibility of missed calls due to a constant busy signal. Information about call waiting is found in the front of local phone directories.

Cost is another issue that arises if you overuse the phone. Some calls cost extra, and they're not necessarily long-distance numbers. In some areas the town next door to yours may be a toll number. When you dial a radio station to request a favorite record or to try to win a contest you may be adding to the base rate on your phone bill. Prerecorded answer calls, such as dial-a-joke, can cost fifty cents apiece, as do the calls when you dial a number to vote "yes" or "no" or to answer a question. The best way to avoid hassles about the phone bill is to find out if your parents will give you a phone budget: a certain number of dollars you can spend each month on such calls. If you don't use up that amount, see if they'll credit your account for the next month. You can offer to pay for such calls yourself if your parents won't agree to such a budget.

If your parents are willing and you can afford it, having a separate number for you can reduce much of the tension

about phone behavior. If you have your own phone, your parents won't have to be your personal secretaries when you're out of the house. In fact, your parents don't even have to hear your phone ring if that's how they want it, because it can be installed in a separate part of the house or apartment. If you get your own phone, it is important to discuss ahead of time who will be paying the monthly fee, who will pay for repairs. If you buy a phone rather than renting one from the phone company and the phone conks out, will you have to replace it or will your parents?

Finally, there is the matter of phone etiquette. Some parents get really furious when they answer the phone, it's for you, and your friends don't identify themselves, are rude, or, worse, hang up when they hear the adult's voice. The time of day or night that calls come in can be sources of tension too — some families don't like to be disturbed during dinner, others don't like to have the phone ring past nine or ten P.M. Discuss these things with parents and relay the information to your friends. If your friends don't respect the phone rules at your home and get you in trouble by ignoring them, they may not be such good friends after all.

There are some phone don'ts you should be aware of. Don't give out your family's personal access code or credit card number to any friends and don't use someone else's, no matter how tempting it may seem. You're responsible for the charges if you get caught. Don't make harassing, prank, or obscene calls. They can be traced and you can get into a lot of trouble. Don't let the phone dominate your life so that it interferes with your schoolwork and other responsibilities. If you are reasonable about the phone, you'll find that your parents will be, too.

Music

Since many parents grew up listening to a wide variety of music and still have the habit of tuning into rock stations or oldies stations for part of each day, it may seem odd to you that we'd mention music as a source of conflict. It is, though, and the issues tend to be very predictable. Parents complain about the loudness of the music, the money spent on records, tapes, or discs, and the annoyance factor of portable players like boom boxes.

These issues are easy to resolve. Either don't play the music when your parents are at home or agree to keep the volume at a level everyone can tolerate when there's a full house. Use headphones. Instead of buying all your music, trade with friends or make your own tapes from the radio. Don't bring your box when you go out with your parents. It means you'll have to make some concessions to their taste, but it'll be worth it in the long run.

MTV and rock videos are a new issue that has emerged in the music category.

> My mom used to tell me how her parents worried about her watching Elvis on TV and that they thought some of the lyrics to what she called "makeout music" might give her ideas. She always laughed about that. So I never thought she'd worry about me and the music I listen to, but she's really scared that MTV will corrupt me or something!
>
> *Caryl Anne T., age fifteen*

Parents tend to take these videos much more seriously than you do, and many can't see that they're reacting the way their parents did when Elvis, Little Richard, Janis Joplin, or the Beatles got popular. You can ease the tension by inviting your parents to watch some videos with you. Point out the special effects. Talk about the skills needed to make those video productions. Discuss the merits of the music. Try to point out the humor and satire. If you dissect the video the way you might analyze a story or poem in English class, your parents are likely to be both surprised and impressed and may stop worrying about the impact rock videos may have on you.

Neatness

Did a teacher in school ever tell you that "neatness counts"? Well, it counts at home, too. You probably hear your parents scream, "Clean up your room!" at least once a week, and problems crop up when what you define as "clean" is different from how your parents define "clean." Here's what you can do to ease the tension.

1. Ask your parents to pretend you're the cleaning service coming in to do the housework. Have them tell you what they expect done in each area you're responsible for. That way, there's no room for guesswork.

2. Discuss a "neatness quotient" with your parents. What can they tolerate and what won't they tolerate? Do they have stricter requirements for neatness in places like a bathroom or family room that everybody shares than they do for your private space, like your room? Compare and contrast their formula with what you can and can't tolerate. Compromise is often possible, and it usually involves your being neater in the shared areas and their being less strict about your room's appearance.

3. Once in a while surprise your parents by cleaning up not only your space but theirs too *without being asked*. Then, they may be more willing to be flexible when things are a mess and you don't have time to deal with it.

What if you share a room and you're neat but your sibling isn't? Keeping a chart of whose turn it is to do what chore or dividing the room into clearly separate areas may help. Make sure your parents know that you're making an effort (if you are) so you won't get blamed for something you didn't do.

Language

I told my mom she looked "bitchin" yesterday and she took away my car privileges for two weeks.

Carson L., age sixteen

I was joking around with my dad and called him an "old fart." My mother came flying in from the next room and called me a disrespectful kid and said I deserved to have my mouth washed out with soap.

Marlena F., age sixteen

You and your friends are probably a lot looser with language than your parents may like. As a result, kidding around can get misinterpreted as disrespect and can turn discussions into confrontations. Every parent has the right to require that certain types of language not be used in their home. Even if you think these rules are silly, it's easier to respect them than constantly test the limits of your parents' patience. Believe them if they tell you, "I'm your mother (father) and I don't want to be talked to the way you'd talk to your friends."

Sometimes it's necessary to apologize and admit you're wrong to have said something offensive even if deep down you believe you're not. When your parents were younger it's a good bet that there were stricter lines dividing what was OK to say in the company of adults and what wasn't. The commonly used four-letter words that pepper so many conversations weren't socially acceptable in your parents' day. So it's not unreasonable that adults may feel uncomfortable or even threatened if you speak to them in a slangy way.

It's generally not too useful to try to negotiate this point with parents. If it's an issue for you, it's one of the few times we'll recommend that you don't express yourself so freely. You won't really lose anything if you pretend to be a bit more formal than you'd like to be, and you might even gain a larger vocabulary as a result of having to find other ways to say what's on your mind. You might as well leave the loose language for other times and be more controlled when speaking to your parents.

Manners

There's a wonderful children's book, *Dinner at Alberta's*, about what Arthur the alligator's family must do to prepare him to be a civilized guest when they're invited for dinner at his friend Alberta's. It's easy to laugh about such problems when you're baby-sitting and reading the book to a four-year-old; it's not so easy to laugh about when they're your problems and your parents constantly correct your manners and give you daily doses of etiquette. In fact, it can make you very angry.

But as with driving or language issues, many parents have certain nonnegotiable expectations regarding manners. Some parents go crazy if you put your elbows on the table at dinner, others get furious if you start eating before everyone else is served. If you've heard such things all your life and refuse to play by the rules, *you're* the one who's making the mountain out of a molehill.

Try to put yourself in a parent's place. There are many times when first impressions count. What if you're on a job interview and you're invited to eat out with the personnel director? How would you feel in his or her place if you acted like Tarzan rather than Lord Greystoke? What if your date's parents asked you to their home and served food you hated? You could really insult those people if you didn't know how to let your manners work for you. Try *not* to automatically discount your parents' advice about manners. They may be talking from experience!

There are other manners to be learned besides table manners. Promptness, courtesy, looking interested when someone is talking to you (even if you're not) can really boost your standing in other people's eyes. While you may think paying attention to manners is phony and that "anyone who likes me will have to like me the way I am," you may not be an objective judge of how you're coming across to others.

It's not usually too hard to play by parents' rules about manners, and if you choose to, you may find they'll react very positively. Allowing yourself to learn manners can make you a very impressive person and cut down on hassles at home enormously.

Money Matters

Money certainly does matter, and the earlier you learn to handle your finances the better. That's hard to do unless you have some money to handle. Whether you get that money in the form of an allowance from parents or from working for other people, you may find yourself at odds with parents about where the money should end up.

To avoid arguments, try to discuss the following things with your parents and review your ideas a few times a year.

1. *Budgets.* Does the family operate on a budget? How much do they put aside each week? Do they expect you to follow a budget that mirrors theirs?

2. *Bank accounts, checking accounts.* Will your parents let you open your own accounts and let you be responsible for keeping track of your own finances? Do they expect to act as your money managers?

3. *Ownership.* Is your money all yours, or are you expected to contribute to the family expenses?

4. *Borrowing.* If you are short of funds, do your parents approve of your borrowing money from them or from other people? What is expected of you in terms of paying back the money?

5. *Credit cards.* Will you be allowed to use the family's credit cards? What penalties will they impose on you if you can't pay for your charges when they come due?

6. *Mistakes.* Will your parents give you the chance to make decisions about what you want to spend your money on, even if they're 99 percent sure you're making a mistake? You can actually learn a lot about money matters through these goofs, but you need to anticipate what kinds of reaction to expect from your parents if you blow a bundle of cash once in a while.

7. *Cost of living.* Do you and your parents have accurate facts about each other's expenses? Do your parents realize what you need to spend money on? Do they know about the cost of dating, clothes, books, etc.? Do you know about household expenses, the cost of food, utilities, medical and dental expenses, etc.?

Don't be afraid to talk about money with your parents and don't let them baby you and say it's not your concern yet. It should be your concern, and it's an important part of growing up. You wouldn't want to go swimming without the skills needed to stay afloat, and you shouldn't start spending without the information needed to stay solvent.

Jobs

To work or not to work? While working is a form of education, a part-time job can disrupt studying, social life, and extracurricular activities. On the other hand, it can teach you the value of money and the meaning of responsibility and commitment to an employer. To decide whether working is a good option for you, answer the following questions.

1. Can you handle the extra time and energy the job would take? Are your grades good? Do you budget your time well?
2. Will the job cut into your social life too much?
3. How badly do you need the money? What do you plan to use it for?
4. What type of job can you get? Will you be disappointed if all you can get hired for is a low-status job?
5. Will you take your work seriously?
6. What hours will you have to work? Do your parents approve?
7. Can you get to and from work independently or will you need to rely on parents or carpools to get you there?
8. What do you imagine this job will do for you in the long run? Is it worth it?
9. Have you talked to any kids who've had the same job you're applying for? What were the benefits and drawbacks for them?
10. What will you do if you hate the job?

Information about finding your first full-time job is discussed in Chapter 17.

The miscellaneous matters we've been talking about are the stuff everyday life is made of. Even though many of them may be touchy subjects, they make life interesting, and they usually can be negotiated with parents. With luck, you'll now be in a stronger position to win these negotiations!

5.

Your
Social Scene

Up to this point, we've been focusing on you and your family. Now it's time to turn our attention to another important dimension of teenage life, your social scene, complete with friends and enemies, acquaintances and confidants, good times and bad.

The predictable thing about your social life is that it rarely works out exactly as you planned, hoped, or thought it would. The possibilities for surprises (pleasant and less-than-pleasant) are endless. Your best friend tries to steal your boyfriend or girlfriend, you expected to go to *the* big party of the year but didn't get invited, you're pressured by the kids in your clique to do something you don't feel is right for you, your parents put the whammy on your weekend plans by imposing a too-early curfew. Kids you assumed wouldn't look twice at you ask you to join their group, romance blossoms from what you thought was a platonic friendship, you help a friend in trouble by doing all the right things and really make a difference in that person's life.

Your social scene — variable as it can be — is a mixture of the people and situations you're involved with daily. Sometimes it can seem like you're not in control of your social life: your parents' rules make it hard for you to do what you want when you want, your friends make unexpected demands on your time, people you'd like to get to know don't seem to be receptive to your efforts. When there's an obvious difference between the social life you'd like to have and the social life you do have, you can end up with a case of the blahs or worse — and suffer self-doubts and wonder about your popularity. It can be a shock, like looking in a fun-house mirror that throws back a reflection you weren't anticipating.

But the contrast between your ideal and your reality doesn't have to overwhelm you or shock you. In this chapter, we'll discuss what makes your social life social or not, and the adjustments you can make in your thinking and behavior so that you minimize the lows, maximize the highs, and get the most out of your social experiences.

Popularity — The Big Question Mark

My worst fear has always been that people will think I'm a dork.

Mark P., age fourteen

I'm well liked but I'm just a shade under what you'd call popular.

Jennie F., age sixteen

Popularity? It's a curse. Once you get it, you have to work too darn hard to keep it.

Beryl M., age fifteen

Is it possible to have a good social life if you're not popular? Is it possible to *be* anyone if you're not popular? Not in my school.

Philip S., age fifteen

Most of us operate on the assumption that if you're going to have a good social life you have to be popular. The popular kids are the ones in the "in" groups. *Popularity* is one of those terms that we use without always knowing what it means, and that's what's so funny about it — we aspire to popularity but since we may not be clear about what it consists of, we don't know how to achieve it.

Popularity means different things to different people. Your definition may be having a few good friends you can really confide in and trust. You may think that being popular means belonging to a group — being instantly recognized and identified by the way you dress and act and by the kinds of things you do in and out of school. You may define popularity purely in terms of dating — how many dates you can get, how many names you can put in your diary or address book. Some kids only feel popular when they have tangible proof that they've been recognized for their abilities, such as when they're elected to a school office. Still others assume that being popular means you have all of these things happening at once.

To be perfectly blunt, popularity confers a kind of power. It sets you off from the crowd, it gives you a reputation that other people would like to have, it means that other kids will assume you're OK without your having constantly to prove yourself. The label "popular" is shorthand for "fun to be with," "a mover and shaker," "dependable," "attractive," "friendly," "person with status."

Is it possible to *learn* to be popular? The answer is "yes, maybe . . ." It depends on how much of your own personality and how many of your values you're willing to bend or change to match the profile of the "popular person" as defined by the kids in your group, school, or community. That, of course, assumes that you've spent time observing the popular people and can describe what sets them apart and makes them special, and it also assumes you've done some thinking about whether they are so very different from you or not. Ask yourself these questions:

1. What's so appealing to me about this group?
2. Do I have anything in common with the people in it?
3. Do I really like them, or do I just like the power they have, or what they stand for?

Learning to be popular may mean you'll have to develop a few new social skills, like learning how to enter conversations without seeming too pushy, or tooting your own horn without seeming stuck up. It may mean you have to temper a nasty streak, or learn to keep your mouth shut when you really have a strong opinion that clashes with the popular kids'. You've heard of protocol at the White House and how people are supposed to conduct themselves in the presence of the President of the United States? Well, sometimes popularity depends on having a sense of social protocol and being able to carry it off appropriately when you're with the people you want to like you.

Other pointers you can follow to increase the odds that you'll be popular are:

1. *Make sure you're well groomed.* Unfair as it is, kids may shy away from you if your deodorant constantly fails, your shampoo doesn't do its job, and your fingernails resemble an eagle's talons. First impressions can lead to lasting impressions, which in turn may result in a reputation that cuts off your chances for others to get to know the real you.

2. *Be honest about yourself.* There's always a temptation to introduce yourself to new people by pretending you do things that you really don't, or that you're very interested in areas that you haven't the slightest inkling about.

> My big mistake last winter was to let everyone think I could ski. I got invited to go on a YMCA weekend trip with the bunch of eighth graders I was dying to be part of. I had the outfit and the gear, and I looked OK, but I ended up on the bunny slope and they all went to the top of the mountain. My weeked was spent with eight- and nine-year-olds. I was never so embarrassed; I don't know what made me think I could get away with it. Now I'm constantly having to prove that I'm truthful about other stuff with them.
>
> *Abby T., age fourteen*

While you don't need to be *so* honest that you hit people with your complete life history, shortcomings and all, truth in advertising is generally preferable to deceptive packaging.

3. *Stick to your guns (a.k.a. "be true to yourself").* It may seem that in order to be popular you'll need to give up a lot of your ideas and values to become part of the group and to blend in with the crowd. While a shot at popularity does partly depend on having shared interests with other kids, it doesn't mean transforming yourself into a clone or a robot.

LUANN   BY GREG EVANS

Often, the people who are the most popular are those who successfully blend the ability to be like the other kids while keeping their unique personalities or sense of style — the things that make them really special. It's not necessary to sacrifice yourself for the sake of a group.

4. *Read at least one magazine a week.* Whether it's *People, TIME, Muscle and Fitness,* or *Soap Opera Digest* doesn't matter so much as the fact that you can talk about stuff you wouldn't necessarily pick up in school. Being able to insert a juicy tidbit into an otherwise predictable or boring conversation can open people's eyes to your presence, and make them sit up and listen to what you have to say.

5. *Avoid criticizing others unnecessarily.*

6. *Don't try to be "cool" all the time.* It's OK to show you have a few flaws, to open up sometimes.

7. *Don't try to be center stage all the time.*

8. *Keep your word; follow through on things you promise to do.*

9. *Learn to listen without interrupting and without being argumentative or constantly contradictory.*

10. *Don't be the kind of person who needs to rely on one-upmanship to gain status.*

11. *Don't be the group gossip.*

There are times when you're popular because of circumstances that really have nothing to do with your personality, but rather with what you have or what you can do for other kids.

My dad remarried last year and his new wife is on one of the TV soap operas. All of a sudden, girls I barely knew started calling me. It took me a while to figure out that they wanted to meet her, but when the sixth kid asked if we could do something on a weekend when I stayed at my dad's, and offered to meet me there, it dawned on me.

Jessica H., age fifteen

It's only human to want to cash in on other people's good fortune. But popularity based on the new car you got for your sixteenth birthday, or the swimming pool your parents had installed in the backyard of your suburban home, or the extra spending money you have because of a legacy left you by a rich relative isn't the most desirable kind of popularity. It can disappear as quickly as it came, and it usually doesn't withstand the test of time. That's not to say you shouldn't enjoy basking in the attention people give you, but if you do, realize that the likelihood is that *you're* not the focus of their interest — what you have or can do for them is. Some kids call this "being used" and resist it; others like it and are able to keep it in the proper perspective.

We often make assumptions about other people's popularity and what it does for them. This is the "grass is always greener" attitude and it may make you believe other people are more popular and so must be happier than you are. "I wish I could be as popular as X" may not make allowances for the fact that the kid who is glib, can come up with the best one-liners at parties, seems upbeat, and looks popular may actually not feel popular at all. Such a person may not have any close friends, may know all the right things to say and do to fit in on the surface but may not have the skills, or be willing, to get beyond superficial relationships. Don't assume the grass is always greener; appearances can be deceiving and you may actually be more popular than the person you're looking at with envy.

Whether or not you can be, will be, or are popular depends in part on how clear you are about what popularity means to you, and what steps you're willing to take to get to that goal. Whether or not being popular — as you define it — will be worth it in the long run is something only you can decide. As you get older, though, your definition of popularity is bound to change, and the people you wanted so much to be with and be liked by at thirteen or fourteen may not be the ones you seek out at seventeen or eighteen. There's something else you might keep in mind — popularity doesn't guarantee a perfect social life even though it seems that one leads directly to the other. If you can't get into the popular group, it doesn't mean you're a social washout; it may just mean you're over-looking some people or situations that might be better suited to you.

Everything You Always Wanted to Know about Friends and Friendship

Friends are like food. You need them but sometimes they can make you sick!

Meg B., age thirteen

Friends are like family, only more so because not only are they there for you, but if you dump on them they under-stand, and if they don't they'll call you on it right away. Plus you pick them; you're not stuck with them.

Alonzo Y., age fifteen

A good friend will tell you things about yourself that no one else would dare to, and you don't get all hyper — you can take it from a friend.

Sara R., age seventeen

Friends and friendships are definitely the building blocks of your social scene. There are many different kinds of friend-ships, ranging from the casual acquaintances you say "hi" to when you pass each other in the halls at school or on the street to the best friends with whom you spend the bulk of your time and share your most intimate thoughts. Between the two ex-tremes are many other categories. There are friendships of convenience — you have a neighbor who's not "your kind of person" but you get together occasionally because you're close by, and can amuse each other when there's no one else around. There are classroom friendships that start because you've been made lab partners and have to spend lots of time together to do your projects. There are platonic friendships with members of the opposite sex that don't involve romance, and there are summer friendships that evaporate when camp or the summer job that threw you together in the first place is over. There are common-interest friendships that develop because you're in a youth group or club or on a team together and relationships form on the basis of the common interests or focus of the group. You can probably think of many more categories.

The point is that the potential for friendships is anywhere you look, and it doesn't take much to get one started. Asking for a person's phone number and following up with a call is a great way to begin. Being complimentary about something — "I like your hair" or "You played that piece better than anyone else in the band" — can break the ice. Sometimes a remark that's very direct — "Are you in the market for a new friend?" — works wonders.

Most of us only need a few close friends to feel popular, and don't require an army of admirers to have a good social life. A few kids who genuinely like each other and have common interests can have great times together, even if they don't get invited to all the parties and aren't members of the "in" crowds. What are some characteristics of close friends?

1. Friends are people you like being with, who understand that you don't have to spend all of your hours together to prove the strength of the friendship.
2. Friends are honest with you but aren't out to put you down or hurt your feelings with that honesty.
3. Friends are often able to overlook (and even confront) each other's shortcomings.
4. Friends can weather the bad times in order to have some good times.
5. Friends can usually be counted on and trusted.
6. Most of the time, friends will give you a second chance if you mess up.

Problems with Friends

As terrific as it is to have friends, it can also be very stressful. Once the "honeymoon phase" of a friendship is past — when you first establish that you like each other (by being especially sensitive to each other's needs, trying hard not to offend one another, and building up a base of trust and good times), the "down in the trenches" phase takes over. That's when you let it all hang out, and you stop walking on eggshells. You begin to take each other for granted and treat each other more like you do your family. You let your needs come to the forefront.

Almost as quickly as a friendship got under way, you may lose interest in people you've been hanging out with, or you may get into fights with kids who were your closest confidants and now seem to be your arch-enemies. Anger and fights can occur because close friends often become intensely competitive. You may actually be rivals — you like the same people and enjoy doing the same things, and you may be thrown together so much that you find yourselves competing for the same spots on a team, the same academic honors, or for status in the same group.

> My best friend and I went to a summer program at the University of Rochester. We shared a dorm room, dated two guys who were friends, took the same classes, and spent our weekends with the same crowd. By the fourth week the tension was unbearable. We got into a fight over a plastic inflatable dragon the local gas station gave us when we filled up the car's tank. We didn't speak for three weeks, and that's not easy when you're living together. When we finally made up we realized we were fighting to be Number One — I was jealous that her French grades were always a few points higher, she was jealous that my boyfriend called more often than hers. We practically ruined each other's summer. When I think of what I said about her . . . !
>
> *Diane N., age seventeen*

Problems also crop up when cliques disband and then re-form, and you may find that the balance of power in the group has changed and your place in it isn't clear anymore.

Sometimes, instead of supporting one another, you and your friends make unreasonable demands on each other. You may pressure (or be pressured by) your friend to do something by setting up an ultimatum — "If you don't, then I won't . . ." or "If you were really my friend, you'd . . ." and those demands in the name of friendship may strain the limits of the relationship. It's hard to say "no" to a friend who does this sort of thing because you may worry that the friend will equate your refusal with rejection of the friendship. It's hard to say "no" because it may make you seem wimpy or chicken. It's hard to say "no" because you know that disagreements can lead to fights, and fights can lead to breakups. But sometimes you must say "no" — even at the risk of messing up your current social life.

When should you put your foot down? If you're asked or expected to do something illegal, something dishonest, something that will cause physical or emotional damage to you or someone else, or anything that really goes against your personal sense of ethics and values. You can always blame your parents for your decision to not do something, even if you haven't mentioned it to them. You can blame it on your health — "I can't take dope because I have a heart murmur and it could trigger heart failure" — be creative in your excuses. If they sound logical, chances are you'll get away with it, save face, save the friendship, and at the same time remind your friend what your limits are.

Trust and Friendship

You may have many close friends, but not every one of them will be the kind of person you can call on when you have problems. Be careful to not make an automatic assumption that if you're good friends with someone he or she will be available to hear you out and can be trusted not to betray your confidence. Recognize that someone can be your best friend today, but if you tell him or her something intensely private and your friendship breaks up later on, that secret might be used against you. Also, some close friends just can't cope with the pressures of having to keep your secrets and may back off from an otherwise terrific relationship just to get rid of the pressure. Similarly, some kids can keep secrets but don't want to have to confide secrets and may be put off if that's what you expect of them.

It's important that you don't let the glow and comfort of a close friendship blind you. Every one of us has weak points, and there are limits to the things we can do for one another. Short of saying, "How many secrets have you been able to keep in your life?" you can use the following checklist to help you decide if a close friend is a candidate for hearing your true confessions.

1. How long have you known each other? In what situations?
2. What other friends does this person have? Are they gossips?
3. What is your friend's "reputation"?
4. What kinds of personal things does your friend tell you?
5. Have you ever caught your friend in a lie?
6. Does your friend talk about other people behind their backs?
7. Does your friend start rumors or respond to rumors?
8. Does your friend have a romantic interest that he or she might spill the beans to in a moment of intimacy?
9. Does your friend tell a lot of things to his or her parents? Do those parents repeat things to other parents?
10. Does your friend carry grudges?
11. Are you and your friend very competitive?

Ironically, then, friends can be the source of big problems in your social life. It's actually normal for you to go through several strings of friends before you find the few people compatible enough to form long-term relationships with, but it can be tough to have to weather the stormy times of arguments, silent treatments, making up, and renegotiating the terms of your friendships.

Jealousy and Friendship

Jealousy is one of the most serious threats to existing friendships and it's one of the hardest to admit to and confront.

> We'd been best friends since sixth grade. It was always "Amy and Barbara." Everyone knew that where one of us was, the other one would be there too. We started having problems at camp after eighth grade. We shared an upper and lower bunk in the same cabin. I got real interested in learning Japanese from one of the girls, whose parents came from Tokyo, and we spent hours of free time together. Amy got furious with me, and told me she thought Suki was trying to take me away from her. I couldn't believe my ears. I told Amy that no matter how close we were she didn't own me and never would, and that I could be friends with anyone I wanted. She didn't talk to me for two weeks until our counselor locked us in the cabin and said she wouldn't let us out till we got our heads on straight.
>
> *Barbara S., age fourteen*

Jealousy and possessiveness become issues when people want to branch out of cliques or best-friend situations and develop close relationships with other kids as well. This poses a threat to the existing friendship system and stirs up the kinds of scared or skeptical feelings that go along with having to deal with someone or something who's unfamiliar. Jealousy prompts remarks like these:

> "I thought you were my best friend!"
> "You'll have to choose between me and him (her)!"
> "Do you think you're too good for us now?"
> "She's (he's) trying to take you away from me."

Feelings of possessiveness and jealousy are like an advancing avalanche that will destroy everything in its path. The best way to combat them is to admit they exist and then have the guts to do something about them. Here are a few suggestions about how to accomplish this.

1. *Get the feelings out in the open.* If you're having trouble talking about it face-to-face, you can write a letter explaining how you are feeling and why. Try to discuss what you think is happening and why. Listen to your friend's point of view as well as stating your own.

2. *Specifically define your concept of friendship.* You can write out a list of the things you think you have a right to do within your friendship, such as "I can count on a friend to stick up for me," "A real friend won't mind if I have other good friends," and ask your friend to do the same, then compare lists and use any differences as a starting point for a discussion.

3. *Discuss jealousy and what it means to you.* What comes across as jealousy to one person may be another person's way of saying "I care for you." You need to make sure that it's jealousy you're really dealing with, and not just a misplaced expression of affection.

4. *Discuss what each of you hoped to gain from your friendship.* It's possible that your expectations are very different, or that they may have started out similar and then changed without your realizing it. Did you want a person to confide in? Did you want the friendship to get you into a certain clique? Did you think the relationship would enhance your status and power in school? You need to talk these things out, because it may be that your friendship is turning into something different from what you need or want.

5. *Discuss "What if I want the nature of our friendship to change?"* Friends should explore the possibility of expanding their social horizons. Talk abut the fact that it's possible to have more than one really close friend at a time, and that it's possible for a best friend to become just a good friend. You need to acknowledge that if you grow apart, the time you spent together isn't downgraded in any way, and that it doesn't mean you were dishonest with each other about your feelings in the past. Discussing these things ahead of time, even if they never actually happen, is useful because it adds to your understanding of what friendship is all about.

It's possible to put jealousy into perspective and save a friendship, but it takes a lot of effort and honesty to do that.

Cruelty —
When Friends Turn on You

People aren't all that different from animals — when they're backed into a corner they may lash out at you; if they're sick or injured they can turn on you; if they're under stress their behavior becomes less than reliable. Sometimes friends get into similar situations. When a person is facing overwhelming problems or situations, when he or she is very jealous of someone, seems to be losing social ground, and needs a way to reestablish social status, a natural impulse may be to blame someone or try to put that pain and anxiety off onto another person. Putdowns, cold shoulders, starting false rumors, scapegoating, blackballing, or any other forms of suddenly excluding someone from a group are a few of the ways kids exhibit cruelty to each other. Unfortunately, you can often be the target of a close friend because he or she knows you so well, including your vulnerable spots — so you're an easy mark.

> I've had bad skin for years. My best buddy never made fun of it. It just wasn't an issue. He'd try to get dates for me, and when he saw I was uptight he'd tell me I had a great build and any girl worth trying for had to look below my neck and give me points for my biceps and my abs. Last week I overheard him call me "zit face" to someone else; then today he called me a "pocked pig" at lunch. It was like he put a stake through my heart. But I found out his dad just lost his job and they have to move. Maybe he's trying to make it easier for us to split.
>
> *Casper P., age sixteen*

> Marilyn didn't get into Vassar and I did. After we found out, she started spreading rumors about me — that my parents had bought my way in through contacts, that I cheated on the S.A.T.'s — all lies. It hurt me so much. Things can never be the same between us.
>
> *Melinda Z., age seventeen*

It's rotten to be the target of someone's cruelty, and it hurts even more when someone you thought was your friend is the one who's dishing it out. You can do something about it.

Though there's no guarantee that you'll succeed, here's a game plan that you can use as the basis for handling the situation.

1. *Try to pinpoint exactly when your friend's behavior toward you changed.* Was there a "trigger" event? Ann's friend didn't get into college; Jon's friend was dealing with major family problems. Did you get an award, get elected to something, snare the cutest kid in the class? Look for the obvious, and then dig deeper.

2. *Keep track of the things your friend has said or done to hurt you.* Keep a list with approximate dates, times, places, and situations. You'll be able to see if there's a pattern or if things seem to heat up in random fashion. Having a record like this that you can look over and think about when you are at some emotional distance from the actual events can help you make some decisions. Maybe they're not so bad after all and maybe they were even justified. On the other hand, you may end up thinking your friend is a real rat. Be reasonable when you're judging what's been going on. Not sitting next to you on the bus because your friend had to do homework and didn't feel like chatting, or accepting an invitation to a party you weren't invited to may make you feel lousy but aren't the kinds of slights we're speaking about.

3. *Confront your friend, list in hand.* Having the list prevents the possibility that you'll back down if your friend says, "It's all in your mind," "You're making it up," or "You can't prove a thing." If you confront your friend, though, you need to be in control. Throwing the list at him or her and screaming "Here's proof of what you're doing to me" won't help much and it will just show the other person that he or she has the upper hand. Instead, try to aim for the tone of a formal debater: direct, strong, self-confident, prepared. Your message must be that you don't like what's going on and you won't be someone's doormat or scapegoat.

4. *Be willing to ask some tough questions (but realize that you may not like the answers).*

"What has happened to make you turn against me?"

"Why are you trying to hurt me?"

"What are you getting out of this?"

"Have I done something I'm not aware of?"

"Are you trying to tell me something you're afraid to come out and say directly?"

"Do you want to try and work things out?"

"Will you be willing to make up for what you've done?"

"Will you tell the truth and set the record straight about me?"

"Do you still want to be friends?"

We'd like to be able to say that friends don't usually know when they're being unfair or cruel to one another, but we can't, because they do. What's more likely to be true is that so-called friends who do these things don't automatically assume they'll be found out and then be asked to account for their actions. That's why cautious, creative confrontation is a good way to deal with friends who turn on you. You'll either learn something from the episode and have a renewed relationship (though the terms of the friendship may change), or you'll be rid of a friend who probably wasn't right for you in the first place. Such confrontation sends the message that you're not someone who can be dumped on, and may dramatically cut the chances for a repeat performance.

Parties

Giving parties and going to parties take up a lot of time and energy. They can be a major focus of your social scene, or they can take a back seat to your other responsibilities. Parties are fun — most of the time — and give you the chance to let parts of your personality that may be stifled at school or work shine through. You've probably seen the transformations we're talking about, the one-track-mind math genius who turns into the break-dancing fanatic at parties, or the class slob who turns up at the prom looking like he stepped out of the pages of *Esquire* and has the most elegant manners of any of you! Parties make it easy to do things you wouldn't try elsewhere — flirting techniques and "lines" that might seem ridiculous at school seem OK at a party, even if they don't work. Parties give you a chance to be more socially aggressive than you would otherwise — you can openly look for someone to get involved with and not seem pushy, cheap, oversexed, or crude (unless you really overdo the hunt). Parties are great places to "show your stuff" — you can come dressed to the hilt, look like you're out to impress someone, sing, dance, play the piano (or whatever shows you off to advantage), and rarely will you be put down for it or labeled a show-off.

Parties and Parents

Like it or not, parties and parents are connected. Party going and party giving may or may not be a big issue, depending on your age, the friends who'll be there, the reputation they have, the kind of party, and how well your parents actually know the kids you'll be with. You may notice that when you hit the ages of fourteen or fifteen, your parents begin to take a much greater interest in your parties, to the point where you feel they're turning into detectives who want to know every detail of your social life. This isn't unusual — even for parents who never seemed to think twice about letting you invite friends over (or go to their homes), have sleep-overs, or go to dances.

The reason parents' radar activates when they hear "party" as you get older is that they know there are some real temptations and risks for you in the form of alcohol, drugs, access to cars, and sexual pressures, all of which are increased in a party environment. And while your parents may be concerned with these things, they may not be willing to ask you direct questions about them, or they may not know the right questions to ask.

Frequently, parents overreact because of rumors that circulate about the things kids in your community are allegedly doing.

> I was invited to the junior prom even though I'm just a ninth grader. My parents talked with the parents of the other ninth-grade girls who got invited and they all agreed we could go. Then one of the moms read an article about how a lot of the older kids in our school were doing beer bombs by guzzling the stuff through funnels and passing out. It made it sound like every guy was doing it, but only a few were. But she called my mom, who got crazy and said I couldn't go. My date doesn't even drink because he's on the swim team and is always in training.

It was unfair. My dad calmed her down and we worked
things out.

Carol D., age fifteen

Most of the time, parents try to be fair, realistic, and reasonable. They don't set out to try to ruin your fun or keep you
tied to their apron strings. But many worry more than they
should, and this tendency can cause them to make the wrong
decisions occasionally. They may come across as overly cautious and overprotective. It's often up to you to keep your parents adequately informed of the current social scene. You can
relieve a lot of a parent's anxiety by being straightforward
about the good and the bad stuff, and you can let them know
where you stand without having to tell them every single experience you've ever had. It is possible to keep the lines of
communication open without laying yourself bare. But if you
are told you can't do something or go somewhere and you
really haven't given your parents any reason to say "no" to
you, you can try to negotiate.

"Could you please tell me what you're worried about?"
"A lot of the kids are saying their parents have been
stricter than usual about parties and curfews. It seems
that way here too. We can't figure out what we're doing
wrong. Can you give me a clue?"
"I'm beginning to feel like you don't trust me too much.
Can we discuss why you think I shouldn't be allowed
to. . . ?"

We want to stress the word *discuss*. If you threaten, have a
temper tantrum, or go behind their backs and do the thing
anyway and then get caught, you're just cooking your own
goose. Discussions may not guarantee that your parents will
change their minds, but at least you'll clear the air and know
where you stand. Your parents will probably admire your effort, and your maturity quotient may go up enough notches to
strengthen your position the next time a party becomes an
issue.

Here's a list of things you should tell your parents each
time a party is planned.

1. Who you're going with, who will be there.
2. Where the party is going to be held.
3. What time the party is scheduled to begin and end.
4. Whether there will be adult chaperones and who they will be.
5. How you're getting there and back.

In addition, you might want to have an emergency procedure arranged with your parents. This doesn't mean you're a baby or can't handle yourself. It's just good planning. If you're going to a party with people you don't know well and you think you might run into problems, see if your parents will agree to stay home that night in case you need them to pick you up. If you find you want to leave early, you can call and give them a prearranged message. You can use any number of ruses. "I need to call home and see if I can stay out later; I'm having so much fun." But your prearranged code to your parents was "I want to stay out later." They can then agree, but call you back at that number a few minutes later and say, "There's been a family emergency and we need you home to watch your younger sister while we take care of it." You might need your parents to pick you up if your date is too drunk to drive. You can save face and also get out of uncomfortable spots by creative preplanning.

It shouldn't be parents vs. teenagers when parties are discussed. It can be parents and teenagers planning together to assure the best times and fewest hassles for everyone.

How to Guarantee Your Own Party Will Be the Best It Can Be

You don't have to have Huey Lewis and the News in person to play the music, you don't need a circus tent pitched in your backyard to set the theme, and you don't need waiters in tuxedos serving a candlelit sit-down dinner to ensure that your party will be a success. But there are some details you should work out in advance, with both friends and parents, whether you're planning a get-together for four or a bash for the entire football team.

1. Tell everyone what kind of party it will be. There's

nothing worse than going to a party expecting one thing and finding something else. Imagine how a friend would feel if he or she was the only one who didn't realize it was a costume party and came dressed for a normal evening out! Imagine the embarrassment of friends who didn't know it was a birthday party and didn't bring you gifts. If you let everyone know the kind of party you're having, your chances of a successful event are increased dramatically.

2. *Agree that no drugs will be allowed in the house.* Moral values aside, drugs are illegal, and your family could potentially get in trouble if someone on the premises was caught with them. Tell your friends point-blank that this is how it's going to be, and that this rule is nonnegotiable. Blame it on your parents if you must, but make it clear that there will be no party if there are drugs.

3. *Make it clear that you won't be providing kegs, wine, or hard liquor.* Here again, you can lay the blame on your parents. But the fact of the matter is that even if drinking seems like the social thing to do, serving liquor to minors is illegal. Also, you and your parents can be held responsible for any alcohol-related accidents and injuries that occur as a result of your serving liquor and letting your friends leave your party drunk. Alcohol doesn't guarantee good times at a party. Your friends can do their drinking somewhere else. They know that, and if they really are your friends, they'll go by your rules and come to the party even if all you serve is punch and diet soda.

4. *Decide with your parents what will be done about crashers, especially if you're having an open house.* Remember the party scene in the movie *Sixteen Candles?* Crashers can cause damage to property, rip things off from your home, and can trigger fights, especially if they're part of competing cliques or gangs. Will you let a few crashers in, but set the limit at a certain number? Will you have someone checking the guest list at the door so no crashers get in? At what point might you call in the police? It's better to be aware of the worst possible scenario and be prepared than have a party ruined because you were caught by surprise.

5. *Discuss how late the party will last and who will bring it to an end.*

6. *Will bedrooms (or other areas) be off limits to guests?*

7. *Who will chaperone? How obvious will the chaperones be?* Some parents agree to stay in the house but out of sight, while others like to be in the same rooms as your friends. To avoid embarrassment, know which format your party will have and plan activities accordingly. Also, tell your parents what other parents do in terms of chaperoning, especially if yours are the eagle-eye variety and no one else's are. It may be that they'll check with these parents and alter their style accordingly.

8. *Think about what you want to accomplish by having this party.* Is it a payback for invitations you've had in the past? Is it a get-together for your closest friends? Is it a casual thing or do you want it to be *the* talked-about event of the year? Knowing what you want from a party can enhance the chances for success.

Your social life can be the source of high drama, incredible comedy, darkest tragedy. It's changeable and challenging, and you can get a lot of pleasure from it if you know how to control it rather than letting it control you. By having a realistic sense of what you want from your social life, what you can do to get it, and what might happen to trip you up along the way, you should be in a better position to do that.

6.

School Days, School Days

What do I think of school? Sometimes it's the pits but sometimes it's the best because I feel like I'm in charge of me. My parents can't say *they* did it when something goes right.

Emmie T., age fourteen

Emmie has really hit the nail on the head and captured what school is all about — making it or breaking it on your own. Parents aren't there to protect you or make excuses for you, and they certainly can't do the learning for you. School is unique because it's a place where your decisions and actions count for everything. If you do well *you* get the credit, if you mess up *you* take the rap.

Spending six or seven hours a day nine months out of each year getting educated is a major project. It gives you the chance to learn more than English, math, science, history and a foreign language. It's an opportunity to learn (and practice) what it takes to get along with many different kinds of people — kids and adults — and cope with various academic and social stresses. These skills will stay with you for the rest of your life.

When you're in school the focus is on you. Sometimes that focus is positive, like basking in a spotlight. Sometimes the focus is scary or painful when it reveals flaws. Many of us aren't prepared for these ups and downs and don't know how to deal with the tensions and pressures. Some students stop trying or even decide to drop out of school. Some of us mistakenly believe everyone else coasts through each semester without a hitch and we get really depressed when that fantasy doesn't turn into reality for us. We may not know how to define "success" and so don't give ourselves credit for the great things we do, or we may not know when real problems are brewing and don't get adequate help as a result.

This chapter will serve as a map to help you navigate through your school experiences, pointing out the most direct routes to successes and steering you away from potential roadblocks.

"I Feel like a Pizza That Everyone Wants a Slice of!"

School is demanding. It requires that you follow a certain schedule every day, it sets limits on your behavior by imposing rules and regulations that are nonnegotiable and if broken have predictable consequences. It gives you a lot to do: take the courses required for graduation, attend classes, participate in class discussions, do homework, take and pass exams. On the social side of things (although there are no actual requirements) you're supposed to make friends, get along with people in general, maybe take part in extracurricular activities like sports, clubs, and student government, and above all have "school spirit." Your parents may have their own ideas (which may or may not be either realistic or reasonable) about you and school and may impose their own rules about things like what electives you can take, how many hours a night you're supposed to spend studying, the kinds of grades you're expected to make if you're going to be allowed certain privileges (phone, car, TV, going out), even the group of kids they'd be willing to approve of you hanging out with. Friends can put their imprint on your school experience because they can make it hard or easy for you to be a conscientious student, and they can make you feel obligated to follow what the group does rather than deciding things for yourself. In fact, friends can be a lot like dictators who demand certain things and will punish you if you don't deliver.

As a result, it can often feel like all the people you deal with — teachers, coaches, counselors, friends, even your parents — have their own agendas for you, their own personal ideas of how you're supposed to act and what you're supposed to do in school. Fifteen-year-old Cary P. put it this way, "I feel like I'm a pizza that everyone wants a slice of!"

One problem is that while you're being bombarded by all these different demands and expectations (which sometimes overlap, sometimes conflict) your own sense of identity and purpose may get lost in the shuffle. Your personal goals can get transformed as you try to please everyone else.

> My mom and dad got a call from school from my American Lit. teacher. She asked them how they'd feel if she recommended me to be editor-in-chief of the school paper. My parents were ecstatic and said, "Yes, do it," without bothering to ask me. They assumed I'd be flattered just as they were. They assumed I'd think it was a great thing to put on my college applications and would be an "in" for getting a job this summer. I've always done well in English. It just comes naturally. I've been a reporter on the paper but never one of the kids who'd stay late to put the thing to bed. I don't really love it. But now even my friends are adding in their two cents' worth — they're pushing it from the "senior power" angle. Frankly, I'd rather spend my time at the gym — my body needs more work than my mind — but now I'm stuck with the prospect of a job I don't want and everyone's so proud of me. Except me. I don't know if I'm scared, angry, or excited. But I'll do it; how can I say *no?*
>
> *Carole B., age sixteen*

Carole's situation is a perfect example of what we've been discussing. She knows the pros and cons of accepting the job and what it feels like to bow to the pressures from teachers, friends, and parents who assume it's the best thing for her. Like many situations you face in school, this one is two-sided: if she says "yes" she gains recognition, power, the appreciation and respect of her parents and some teachers, and her "value" to her friends goes up as her power increases in school. If she says "yes" she loses too, because this isn't what she really wants to focus on in her senior year. If she says "no" she risks disappointing her teachers and parents and maybe even risks getting a reputation of being unappreciative, or someone who won't go that extra mile to make it to the top. On the other hand, if she says "no" she won't have the pressures and aggravations that go with being editor-in-chief of a school paper.

Carole accepted the job. But she said that she really didn't like the lingering feeling that she was pressured into it rather than having decided to try out for the job on her own. Sometimes at school we're forced to make tough decisions that are every bit as significant for us as decisions parents might have to make about their work. Fair or not, other people do have their own expectations and requirements that influence you and can make you feel like a pizza everyone wants a slice of. The good thing is that you have the freedom to make choices in the face of these pressures.

"Whose Expectations Do I Have to Live up to Anyway?"

How can you come to terms with trying to play so many roles at school and please so many people without feeling as though you're being squeezed into a mold that doesn't fit? It's really important to get into the habit of defining, updating, and re-defining what you're aiming for and are interested in as soon as you start junior high school and to keep up the habit till the day you graduate from high school.

When you enter the world of higher education you have lots more options than you did in elementary school and you're expected to make many of the decisions that previously were made for you. What language do you want to study? Do you want to participate in choral music or band? Are you planning to take college prep courses, industrial arts, work-study, fine arts? Having to make these decisions when you're twelve or thirteen can seem ridiculous because you don't necessarily know what you'll want even two years from now. Yet you have to, so that the schools can fit you into a slot and schedule you and educate you.

So what do you do? Ask other kids who've been through school. What teachers are good? What classes did they like best? Which courses are easy and which ones are tough? Ask your parents what they think you should take. What did they like when they were your age?

Use this information to help you make your own decisions but don't forget that *your* instincts are the most important. Unfortunately, lots of us make mistakes and are unhappy with our school schedules because we don't take enough time to figure out what we *really* want for ourselves and add that into the equation. We end up like Carole B., doing things that other people think we should do but that somehow don't feel quite right.

It's not always possible to avoid making mistakes, but there are a few techniques to use to help make sure your school years will serve your own needs and interests and not someone else's. A good way to start is to keep a *Me* list and a *Them* list at the beginning of each quarter or semester. On the *Me* list write down the things that you want to accomplish (academically, socially, personally) during that time period. On the *Them* list write down the things you believe others (family, teachers, friends) will expect from you during that time period. If the two lists coincide there's no problem and you shouldn't feel too pressured or at odds with everyone else. If they're radically different (or even moderately different) you might want to discuss the discrepancies with those people. Your parents or teachers may not know exactly where your most current interests lie and may be accidentally pushing you into academic, extracurricular, or social situations that don't suit you now, or that you're not ready for. If friends are getting on your case, this technique can help you set them straight.

What else can you do to avoid having to live your school years according to someone else's goals or plans for you? *Try to be realistic about what's possible and what isn't.* Not everyone is cut out to be a star quarterback of the football team, or the computer whiz who sells a game program to Apple Computers and makes enough money to cover college tuition before the end of his or her junior year. Not everyone can pull off 500s on their SATs, much less 800s, and very few work-study students end up earning as much as their teachers by working evenings at extensions of their school-related jobs. Just because some teenagers do (and get lots of good press) doesn't mean you have to downgrade your own accomplishments if they pale in comparison.

A good way to determine your strengths and weaknesses at school is to talk with the experts — your teachers and counselors. If you're feeling pressured by some unrealistic expectations about what you should be accomplishing, you need an educator's objective opinion to help set the record straight for you and your family. Teachers are a good resource because they're hard to fool (though you may think they're easy to con). They generally spend more hours a day with you and talk more with you than your parents do when you're a teenager. They see you at your worst and at your best and know the kids you hang around with probably much better than your parents do. They know what kind of learning style you and your friends have and can tell the difference between a student who really can't handle the work and one who isn't willing to. Teachers also know about your performance on standardized tests designed to show not just how much you know, but your learning potential. They can give you all this information if you ask for it and, with the help of a school counselor, can help you decode your permanent record file (which is *by law* open to you and your parents; you just need to make an appointment to see it). You may discover that your teachers think you have strengths in areas you've never thought about. You may find that your real talents are in subject areas your school doesn't currently give classes in, so not only aren't you getting credit for talents you have, but you have no opportunity to explore them.

Teachers and counselors can help you enormously if you want to maximize your "peaks" and minimize the "valleys" in school and avoid spending years trying to be someone you're not capable of or interested in being. They can help you answer the question, "Whose expectations do I have to live up to anyway?" with a response that really works for you.

"Is It OK to Be Average?"

Our society puts such a high premium on achievement and excellence that we tend to sometimes forget that it's also OK to be average. Many of us associate being average with being lazy, or taking the easy way out, or being mediocre. Actually, you could be a genius and any of these descriptions of behavior could apply. The idea of being average has a bad reputation.

What being average really means is that you can do most of your required schoolwork well, but that you're probably weaker in some areas, stronger in others. It means you get along with other students without major problems, you participate in extracurricular activities (but not necessarily as a bigwig), you have a group of friends you're tight with (though they may not be the school's movers and shakers), you tend to get along with your teachers even if you're not wildly enthusiastic about them or vice versa. If you're average you're part of the majority of students, though it can be a silent majority that may not get a lot of attention and may not take credit for what it actually achieves.

You have every right to be average, if being average is what makes you happy and if average represents the extent of your abilities. But what if you are part of a family that doesn't believe it's OK to be average?

> My mom and dad want me to be a superman. They have me taking piano and doing competitions twice a year. I'm in a soccer league, lacrosse league, and I'm also on the swim team at the Y. On top of that I'm in a theatrical dance class on Saturdays and I have a huge amount of homework each night. I practically kill myself to make B minuses and I think that's fine. I'm not a great student but I really love the sports. They think they're being reasonable when they tell me I should aim for A's. I can't. I really can't.
>
> *Tony B., age fourteen*

From the description of his extracurricular life, Tony is anything but average — he's overextended! But his family's style seems to be competitive and the definition of "average" really pertains only to the grades he's making. If you and your family are at odds over your "average" school performance, here are a few suggestions for constructive negotiations.

1. *Discuss your definitions of "average" and see if there's room for compromise on either side.*

2. *Figure out how efficiently you're organizing your time.* Are you giving your school work the time and attention it needs? Are you willing to make any changes?

3. *See if you need to rethink and reshuffle your priorities.* If being average in your school performance is causing problems for you at home, can you eliminate anything in your schedule without making yourself miserable so you can spend more time on your work?

4. *Do your parents understand all you have to do?* Give them a written description of your "typical" day and see how they react.

5. *Is there a possibility your parents might be right?* Jot down a list of all the things they're absolutely correct about. Discuss your understanding of their position with them.

6. *Decide on a trial period of six weeks, during three of which you'll do things their way and three during which you'll do things the way you have been doing them.* At the end of these trial periods see if there are any changes in your school performance and the way you feel about school. If there are positive changes, are they the result of less pressure from your parents, more work on your part? Discuss this together.

Every person is average in some way just as every person is extraordinary in some way. During your school years you should give yourself permission to be both, but understanding that your performance may be uneven, that your skills and interests are likely to change frequently as you develop a clearer sense of what you want to get from your education, who you want to be, and what you're willing to do to get there.

Facing Up to the Fear of Success

My mom went to public high school for gifted kids in New York City. She came out of there thinking being smart and working hard was what was expected of you, that it was no big deal to routinely get 97's and do independent studies and read college-level books in tenth grade. For me, it's different. We live in a farm community in the Midwest. I'm supposedly "gifted." You know what that means in my school? I get pulled out of class three times a week for the privilege of doing extra work in a gifted class. I have to make up the other stuff I miss. I lost two of my best friends because they honestly think I make them look bad in their parents' eyes. I'm scared to do my best because all my intelligence has gotten for me so far is a screwed-up social life and a load of extra work.

Susan De P., age seventeen

Being exceptionally good at anything during junior and senior high school can be just as problematic as convincing yourself it's OK to be average or just as stressful as failing courses can be. The payoffs for being very smart, very competent, or very successful are a mixed bag. Adults tend to give you lots of attention, admiration, and praise for your abilities. Kids, on the other hand, can give you a hard time, and your social life can suffer if the people you want to be friendly with don't happen to value your kind of intelligence, if they think it makes them look bad when they're compared to you, if they're afraid of getting labeled because they hang out with you, or if they assume you're "too good for" them and wouldn't be interested in sticking around with them anyway. (If this describes you to a T, you might want to contact Mensa, which is an organization for people with high IQs. You can get information about it from your school counselor. Mensa members must take a written test to be accepted, and there are Mensa chapters all over the United States and in other countries. Once you're in, you're a member for life and you may find many people there who have had to deal with the same things you're dealing with.)

If you're a really superior athlete you may have a different set of problems. Rather than losing friends or not being accepted by many kids because of your exceptional ability, you'll probably have so many so-called friends you won't be able to tell who likes you for yourself and who likes you for your athletic skills. You may have a lot of hangers-on, or groupies. If college scouts are after you, some of the other kids who aren't such hot properties may be jealous or resentful and take it out on you by bad-mouthing your accomplishments or making it seem like it's not such a great thing to be courted by the college teams. All of this can erode your self-confidence, make you suspicious of your real friends, and make you wonder if the effort you've put into your sport has been really worth it.

There are other stresses associated with being really good at anything in school. Whenever you achieve something, and reach a goal that you've worked very hard for — whether it's winning the fifty-meter breaststroke at the state swim championships, whether it's getting a full scholarship to college, whether it's winning the poetry contest at school — that goal is behind you. The focus of your life changes because what's done is done and it's time to go on to something else. That is often very scary and you may feel depressed, or like you've lost someone really close to you. Some students refuse to try for any other major goals once they've tasted success because they worry that any future achievements won't measure up, or, worse, that they'll fail totally.

It's not unusual to be afraid to be too good; in fact, it's more normal than abnormal. It takes a lot of guts and self-confidence to stand out in a crowd when the payoffs may not be the kinds you'd hoped for. Even the kids you think are exceptionally talented can suffer from self-doubts and outright fears. The bottom line is that everyone loses out if you make it hard for each other to show your stuff and feel good about it.

Homework

Homework is part of the job of going to school. Sometimes it's challenging and interesting but sometimes it's like medicine you have to take when you're ill — unpleasant but necessary if you're going to improve. For some students homework isn't an issue. They do it automatically, as part of a daily routine like brushing teeth. Others make not doing homework the focus of each day, but refusing to do homework can lead to a lot of unnecessary stress and strain.

If homework is a bone of contention between you and your parents and teachers, here's a list of *nine things you should know about homework* that may help you come to a meeting of the minds.

1. *Not doing homework often uses up as much time and energy or more than doing it would have.*

2. *Doing your homework is an acquired skill: the longer you do it the better you get at it, and the easier it becomes.*

3. *The point of doing homework is doing it yourself.* Don't crib from friends or let your parents do the work. The idea of homework really isn't just to get the grade; it's learning how to do the assignment, where to go for information, how to develop an argument, and so on. That's why letting someone else do the work for you is a copout. All you're learning is how to copy, and a Xerox machine can do that without having to spend six years in school.

4. *Homework isn't meant to be a recreational activity.* You don't have to pretend that doing homework is your favorite hobby. Nobody expects you to feel that way, not even your teachers!

5. *Homework isn't supposed to be a punishment.* Homework is an extension of the learning process. If your teachers routinely use it as a form of punishment, then something is seriously wrong in your class, and your parents and the school principal need to know about it.

6. *Homework can be a social event.* Study groups or studying with a friend and doing homework together are valid as long as you're serious about getting the work done before you start to socialize.

7. *Homework can be done on the phone.* Parents tend to get upset by this. You could point out to them that it's better to do some form of homework than none at all, and that just because you're doing it on the phone doesn't stop you from thinking! On the other hand, be honest with yourself at this point; sometimes studying with a friend on the phone produces no learning at all.

8. *Homework can be done while a TV, radio, or stereo is*

on. Many of us can concentrate better with background "noise" from the TV, radio, or stereo than in total silence. But if you're glued to *Dynasty* or dancing to DeBarge don't pretend that you're doing homework.

9. *Doing homework shouldn't dominate your life.* If you find the homework so hard that you consistently need to stay up past one in the morning to get it done, or if you get obsessive about it because you're worried about being perfect, talk to your teacher and try to figure out why this is happening.

If you're conscientious about homework assignments and do them correctly, good things tend to happen: you learn (sometimes in spite of yourself), your grades go up or stay up, your teachers and parents are usually satisfied. You can use that last fact as a negotiating tool to get privileges, "Mom, you said if I did my homework early I could go to Carrie's house after dinner." "Since all my homework's done can I take the car tonight?"

If you choose not to do your homework, your parents will probably want to know why. They have radar when it comes to noticing changes in your study habits (if you suddenly switch from a doing-homework to not-doing-homework routine) and tend not to believe you when you say you don't have homework (even if it's the truth). Parents may take away your allowance, ground you, and punish you in all sorts of inventive ways if you don't do your homework. Some will say they're doing this "for your own good." Others will say, "I'm not paying all these school taxes to have you waste your time and the teachers' time by not being prepared!" Though these remarks may reflect how your parents really feel, they're more likely to be gestures to try to reconnect with you and get you reacting and talking to them. Many parents monitor their teenagers' homework as a last-ditch effort at keeping some control over you. Parents and teachers realize that no one can *really* make you do your homework if you're determined not to.

Cheating

There are as many ways to cheat as there are students in a school, and all of us have been tempted to try at least one of them. This doesn't mean you're doomed to a life of dishonesty or juvenile detention. It may mean you're experiencing some school pressure that you really can't handle right now, or that your friends cheat and you do it because they expect you to, or that you're in the mood to court danger and you're gambling that you won't be caught. On the other hand, it could just mean that you're looking for an easy way out of having to deal with academic responsibilities.

Cheaters are usually not organized enough to be prepared for what they're supposed to do at school, and cheating is an attempt to hide this fact. Cheating is more than just copying someone else's test answers, making "crib sheets" for exams, agreeing to "fix" sports events, or faking illnesses to avoid making class presentations. Cheating is an attitude, a way of pretending you're doing what's expected of you without actually doing it. It's a habit that, like any other, can get out of control and blind you to other options when you're faced with a pressure situation.

All kids should have a chance to explain a first offense without being afraid that an ax will fall on them from parents and teachers. It's possible that you cheated because you have a full-time, after-school job and literally fell asleep studying the night before the test. That kind of situation is understandable, even if your decision to cheat was less than admirable. But if you've been caught cheating in every academic class and have been warned three times by the principal and now you've been caught again and will be suspended, your offense is in a different league from the first-timer's.

If you're a habitual cheater or have to struggle with yourself not to cheat, we'd like you to answer the following questions as honestly as you can. Do you use cheating in place of thinking because you think you're too dumb to learn? Are the risks of cheating less scary to you than the possibility that you might fail something? Is cheating just a bravado thing for you that has nothing to do with how well you're really understanding and learning your schoolwork? Do you cheat in an effort to be perfect so you can please your parents? Do you think cheating is OK since you see your parents cheat occasionally too?

Cheating is not OK. It's destructive in the long run, even if it means you ace a test today. Cheaters end up living a number of lies and have big gaps in their knowledge where the cheating was substituted for learning. Cheating also gives you a reputation. True or not, "once a cheater, always a cheater" can haunt you in later years, long after you've kicked the habit and gotten your life organized enough not to need cheating as a crutch.

If you feel pressures that make you turn to cheating as a solution, ask for help. Don't equate that need for help with being a loser or a lame-brain. Kids who ask for help with problems have strength of character, maturity, and insight — a better set of identifying traits than the labels that will be tagged on you if you're known as a cheater.

Teacher Troubles

You can be sure of one thing during your school years: you won't like every teacher you have, and not every teacher will like you. All teachers aren't created equal, and there are bound to be clashes, misunderstandings, and less than terrific communication from time to time.

Most teachers are supportive of students — they're on your side when you need them, they bend over backward to spend extra time with you when you ask, they do the best they can with limited supplies and textbooks, and try to keep you interested, motivated, and actively involved in learning. Most teachers care very deeply about their students and want them to succeed.

However, it's possible that you'll have a bad teacher. Some don't have a good grasp of the subject material they're assigned to teach and don't know how to teach it. Others are totally inflexible. There are teachers who'd rather be doing something else but can't find another job. Teachers may be biased against certain types of people and prejudge them, some are outright bigots, and some may be verbally or physically abusive or vindictive to such an extreme that they may go to great lengths to make life hard for the students they dislike. *Such teachers are a very small minority.* But the fact that they exist at all means you should have the information about how to cope with them, just in case.

If you have a poor teacher who doesn't know the subject well enough to really teach it, you have a few options, all of which require a lot of effort on your part. Talk to students in different sections of the same class and see what they're reading and learning. Try to do the work they're being assigned, to supplement your own. This means you must be *really* motivated to begin with and willing to do the equivalent of an independent study. Ask that teacher for extra-credit work. Instead of saying "I need this because I'm not learning enough" (which, though true, could be interpreted by the teacher as a threat or a slap in the face) say, "I'm really enjoying this class and I'm interested in learning more about subject XYZ. Could you please suggest some additional things I could do to give me an even deeper undertanding?" This approach is good for two reasons: if the teacher doesn't have the information at hand, he or she can make some inquiries, do some research, and in the next day or two give you a reasonable project to do, saving face at the same time. It also is complimentary (even if you are telling a white lie about liking the class) and doesn't set you up as an enemy.

You can borrow the notes and handouts from someone who has already taken the class with another teacher, compare them to your own, and fill in gaps in your own knowledge that way. If all else fails, you can always ask to be transferred out of the class. The trouble is that by the time you realize your teacher is awful, you may be too far into the term to be allowed to switch.

Inflexible teachers make rules, state requirements, and won't budge. They may refuse to make allowances for individual differences, tend to grade on rigid curves, and rarely give credit for class participation, good attitude, or improvement when it's time to tabulate students' final grades. Teachers who prejudge students are the types who don't like kids who dress in unusual ways or wear their hair in outlandish styles, who think that athletes are "dumb jocks" with limited capacity for academic success, who believe boys are always smarter than girls. Teachers who prejudge their students make learning a struggle. If you're prejudged, you start out with a strike against you. Your accomplishments may be suspect ("A kid like that must have cheated on the exam," one teacher said of a Merit Scholar who happened to have his hair cut in a buzz and was fond of wearing motorcycle jackets and muscle shirts).

Teachers who are inflexible and/or prejudge students can be confronted about their behavior. Here's what you can do:

1. *Make certain that what you think is happening really is.* Have you been doing your work? Are you sure your behavior and performance in class are up to par? Are you sure you're not creating hassles with the teacher rather than the other way around?

2. *Keep a diary of the times you think the teacher has treated you unfairly.* Include in it any work you think deserved higher grades, descriptions of class discussion and how you participated (as well as what other kids participated), and whether you volunteered answers in class but didn't get called on.

3. *Talk to other kids who are like you and who have had the teacher in the past.* Did they have the same kinds of hassles?

4. *Find out about the teacher's reputation in school.*

5. *Talk to the teacher.* If you say, "Could you please explain to me why I received this grade," and do it in a way that doesn't look like a threat or an act of defiance (you may have to do a good acting job) it shows you're a concerned student. If the teacher refuses to talk to you, you have additional evidence for your case against him or her; if the teacher agrees to discuss it with you there's the possibility for changing prejudgment into fair judgment.

6. *If you can't talk to your teacher directly, consult your school counselor.* A counselor can serve as a negotiator in whatever conflict is going on between you and the teacher. A counselor can also help you explore your feelings about having these things happening to you and may help you come up with constructive solutions.

7. *Ask your parents to contact the teacher and arrange a*

conference. Sometimes teachers ease up when they know your parents are interested and involved, and things can improve for you.

8. *If that leads nowhere, contact the principal and ask if you can be switched to a different class.*

9. *File a grievance with your school administration and school board and get legal help.* These are measures of last resort, to be used only if you are absolutely convinced you are in the right.

Some teachers go a step farther than the ones we've been discussing, and are blatantly bigoted or verbally or physically abusive. These are very ugly things for you to have to deal with and also very tricky things to prove. If you feel you have been mistreated by a teacher because of your race, sex, creed, or color or have been abused in any manner, follow the directions above and get legal help. You must be able to prove your allegation, and that means you'll have to keep track of what's said and done to you and when, whether other kids get similar treatment or it's just you who's singled out. You'll need to involve your parents as well as a lawyer.

No student should have to tolerate any of these kinds of abuses. There is a series of handbooks published by the American Civil Liberties Union — *The Rights of Students, The Rights of Teachers,* and *The Rights of Young People* — that is available in public libraries and in bookstores and that can give you a framework for how to proceed should you need to.

Flunking
and Other Facts of Life

It's possible to make it through school without ever getting a failing grade. But most kids have at least one failure to their credit, and some flunk routinely. What does a failing grade mean? It all depends on the circumstances. There's a big difference between a "one-shot failure" and the "predictable, perpetual flunk."

Let's look at the "one-shots." You failed a pop quiz you weren't expecting and hadn't studied for. You failed a test be-

cause you'd been absent for a week and didn't really understand the material the teacher sent home for you to do when
you were sick. You failed a major exam because there'd been a
crisis in your family, you were distracted and hadn't been able
to concentrate on your work for some time.

It's possible to have legitimate reasons to fail occasionally. Most teachers realize this, will ask you why, and offer to
help you pull your grades back up to par. Parents may not be
so calm. They may be afraid of what "failure" means for your
future. Since they rarely have your and your teachers' perspective, set them straight. Show them the papers on which
you've received better grades in that course, show them the
notes you take in class, tell them about the things you've
learned so far, and help them see your failure for what it is: a
product of an unusual situation.

However, failing grades mean something very different if
they are the "predictable, perpetual" variety. It's pretty difficult to fail everything, or to fail frequently. It takes a lot of
concentrated effort. It can become the ultimate challenge, even
a life-style. When school is The Enemy for some students,
they show their disdain for it by refusing to learn. They can't

seem to get recognition in school by the usual routines, so they make people stand up and notice them by failing. Sometimes their friends don't think it's OK to be a good student, and in order to prove that they're really part of a group they do their best to be the worst students they can possibly be!

If you fail perpetually, ask yourself "Why?" That may be one of the most difficult questions you'll have to answer because it means examining your self-image and the payoffs you get from what you're doing in school. If you fail classes because it's the cool, "in" thing to do in your group, ask yourself whether you have the courage to be a leader rather than a follower.

If you have the ability to learn and even a tiny bit of desire, you're shortchanging yourself by being a follower in a group that's probably going nowhere. But it's not easy to buck the tide, break out of an image, and substitute new habits for old ones. If your friends make fun of you or give you a hard time, tell them, "It takes more guts to be the first of your group to try something than the last," or "I'm a risk-taker and I know the odds both ways. I'm going for the better odds." You'll never know which way you like best until you try both.

If you fail a lot of courses but think you've really been trying and want to do well, something else may be going on that you need an adult's help with. You may be disorganized or have poor study habits. Some schools offer after-school or Saturday courses to help you improve your study skills and teach you how to take tests. You might be having trouble because of physical problems. Believe it or not, two very common reasons kids fail are poor eyesight and poor hearing that have never been properly diagnosed and treated. Another reason may be that you're not eating properly, because if you're run-down all the time you won't have the energy to pay attention in school or to study. Alcohol and drug abuse also are common factors in school failures because substance abuse impairs a person's ability to concentrate, memorize, or do complex thinking.

You also might have perceptual problems that make it extremely hard to read: some students see their letters reversed or upside down (a *d* looks like a *b* or *p*), which is one symptom of dyslexia. Often teachers don't know you have such a problem unless your school has the staff people to test you for it. If this situation describes you and you haven't been tested, get your parents to request such a test. You can get special help to learn to read more efficiently and you will probably see a marked improvement in your grades as a result.

What if you're not failing classes, but school is a downer and everyone is on your case about your attitude? It's possible that you've got an "attitude problem" that acts like a concrete wall that nothing can penetrate, and that prevents you from taking the chances that might get you turned on to learning. Your trademark is apathy and you drive teachers crazy. A teacher talks, you don't respond. A teacher challenges, you ignore that challenge. You may be the brightest, most creative kid in the class but no one knows it. You're probably labeled an "underachiever."

You can get rid of that label if you're willing to try to get something you're interested in included in what you do at school. Andy P., a sophomore in a large inner-city public high school that had a very rigid English curriculum, was required to read *Gulliver's Travels*.

> I hated it and I couldn't plow through it. I read *Mad Magazine* all the time and I knew darn well what satire was. I also am a good artist; I take graphic arts. I asked the teacher whether I could pass without doing the satire unit and she said, "No." Normally I'd have let it drop but she *dared* me to come up with a better project so I could pass. I don't know why, but I really reacted to that. I told her I'd draw my own satire, like in *Mad*, and I'd try to base it on *Gulliver's Travels* even though I couldn't get it read. So I skimmed the book for stuff to draw and I got interested. I really got involved. I ended up with a project as big as a comic book. I got an A (which no one could believe), I was written up in the school paper (which no one could believe either), and I used the project as part of my art portfolio the next term. I was really surprised at what I could do and could even like to do.

Sometimes all you need is a little effort on your part plus a willing teacher to turn things around and crack the wall.

Dropping Out

It'd be great to be able to say that no student should ever have to drop out of school. But that's not realistic and it's not true. Teenagers who have to deal with crises of such seriousness in their families that they're needed as caretakers or wage earners, and kids who must leave home for reasons of personal safety are justified in dropping out, not necessarily forever, but as a temporary measure.

Most dropouts don't fit that description. You may quit school because of the experiences we've been discussing in this chapter: failures, attitude problems, impossible situations with teachers, hassles with parents, pressure from friends who are antischool. You may not know the consequences of dropping out, not the least of which is that during the course of a normal adult working lifetime the American male dropout will earn approximately *a quarter-million dollars less* than a high school graduate, and a female dropout will earn *40 percent less* than a high school graduate.

Dropping out doesn't have to be final, though. It can be a trigger for change, the shock to the family that gets your parents aware of your unhappiness and makes them realize they need to help you or get you professional help (counseling, job training, arrangements for alternative schooling). It can also be the dose of reality that you need. You may find being out of school is no picnic, and you may decide either to re-enroll or earn a G.E.D. (General Equivalency Diploma).

It's OK to give school a second chance. All it takes is a call or visit to your local public school administrative offices and they'll tell you what you need to do. They'll even explore options with you that you may not have known about when you were a regular student: work-study, the G.E.D. program we just mentioned, alternative schools, mentor programs, and so on.

Getting educated isn't easy. But its challenges, roadblocks, and surprises should give you the skills you need to become independent and capable of making your mark later on as an adult.

7.

Dating, Romance, and Love

"Love me tender, love me true," sang Elvis Presley in 1956, echoing a nearly universal desire. "Will You Love Me Tomorrow" was the pointed title of a 1961 hit by the Shirelles, whose song hinted at the sure-you-love-me-now-when-you're-in-my-arms-and-want-sex, but-what-happens-afterward dilemma. More recently, Pat Benatar sang about romance in a different perspective in "Love Is a Battlefield," while Air Supply's "Lost in Love" portrayed still another view of what love is all about. Other rock hits like "Bye Bye Love," "Breaking Up Is Hard to Do," and "Where Did Our Love Go?" have focused on the flip side of love and romance.

As the popularity of these songs suggests, love and romance are both fascinating and anxiety-provoking topics. Searching for love — in all the wrong or right places — is an activity that most teenagers are concerned about. What to do if you think you've found love, how to tell real love from counterfeit versions, how to handle breaking up, and how to survive the dating scene until Cupid's arrow strikes are the topics we'll consider in some detail in this chapter.

Dates and Dating

It's bad enough that I never know if I'm kissing right. Now that I have braces, I'm doomed to a dateless life for two years, I just know it.

Megan G., age thirteen

I took a girl I really like to dinner and the theater. I wanted to impress the heck out of her. We had a lot to drink. When I took her home I threw up on her kitchen floor. She made me clean it up. My reputation is shot.

Paul Z., age eighteen

Have you ever seen that Mel Brooks film, *High Anxiety?* That's me before a date. I can never just have fun. I have to look perfect. I have to do everything right. It's like I'm always watching myself. I wish I could be more natural.

Courtney F., age sixteen

Is the perfect date a myth? Are dates as important as we all seem to think? Is it possible to have a good time and not date? Will life ever be the same after a break-up? How do you know who'll make you happy? How can you learn to behave the right way on a date? Can you ever live down a social goof? Believe it or not, your parents and grandparents struggled with these kinds of questions, and your children and grandchildren probably will too.

When You First Start to Date . . .

Learning about dates and dating takes time. It's a gradual process, a lot like learning to play a musical instrument. At first it feels awkward. You have a general idea of what's involved but the results may be tentative, even awful. But you keep at it and one day you get it right. Things flow. You don't have to think much about it. You can relax enough to enjoy the process and the result. Whether it's music or dating, practice makes perfect, even though you may hit lots of wrong notes along the way and you can never predict the outcome no matter how prepared you are.

When you first start dating you may feel like you're on a roller coaster — flying high one moment, scared to death the next. Because things are new to you and you have no points of reference to determine how you're doing or what might happen next, you may feel confused and wonder how you'll ever manage a social life with the opposite sex. There are three simple things you can do to improve the odds you'll have fun on a date.

1. *Find out where you'll be going and what you'll be doing.* If you show up dressed in jeans and your date's parents are

taking you to a fancy restaurant, that's disaster. If you're counting on a romantic night and end up going to a ball game with twenty other people, you might be angry and disappointed. Knowing the plans ahead of time lets you psych yourself for the kind of date it will be. You can bone up on the ball team's statistics, learn in which order you use the silverware at a fancy dinner. Such preplanning can improve the chances that you'll be able to participate fully in the date and not feel like a misfit.

2. *Find out if you're going out alone or with other people.* If you're very nervous about a date — especially if it's your first or second time out with the person — it may be easier to double-date or go with a group of kids. You won't have as much of a chance to talk one-on-one with your date, but you probably won't feel like you're under miscroscopic examination by your date, either. On the other hand, you might not like the other kids, or you might feel like someone else is trying to horn in on your date. But if you know the format of the date ahead of time, at least you'll have one less element of surprise to deal with.

3. *Tell your date what you'd really like to do.* Sometimes the biggest stumbling block to having fun on a date is not saying what you mean, what you like, or what you hope for. No, we're not talking about being a spoiled brat who's only out to get his or her own way. We're talking about caring enough about yourself to be honest and direct. That's not a guarantee that your date will change the plans — if tickets to a concert by a group you hate have already been bought and can't be exchanged, that's life — but it does set the stage for an honest relationship if you're going to keep seeing each other. Of course, that implies you'll give your date the chance to state his or her preferences to you!

Tough Questions, No Easy Answers

"I've been on a lot of blind dates this year. Nothing has clicked so far. Is there something wrong with me?"

Blind dates are often risky. There's probably nothing wrong with you. Sometimes the "chemistry" of two people doesn't blend well and it's nobody's fault. But it's also possible that you may be just a little too particular about what you want in a date. Have you been willing to have fun, even if your dates didn't turn out to be perfect physical specimens with enchanting personalites? Sometimes you accept a blind date but you "know" ahead of time that it won't work, and then it doesn't. It can be that you have an "I dare you to entertain me" attitude and you come across as critical or snobby.

You can usually salvage a blind date — even if the person doesn't take your breath away and give you instant romantic fantasies. Don't expect miracles in the first place; that way you'll be able to enjoy little things. Did you share any laughs? Did you go someplace fun? Did you get to eat some good food? Giving your date points for the small things that went right can actually change your original reaction and may even make you recognize potential in the relationship.

> *"I keep getting turned down for dates. Even when I manage*
> *to get a date, something seems to come up and it gets can-*
> *celed. What can I do to improve my social life?"*

No, you don't have to sign up with an escort service. You need to take a good, hard look at the kinds of people you're asking out. Do you know them from classes or do you just use the Chinese restaurant method — "I'll try one from Column A and two from Column B"? Do you pick your dates from the group of kids who are on the rebound from romantic breakups, or who are *so* popular they're booked weeks in advance? In other words, do you set yourself up to fail socially?

cathy®   **by Cathy Guisewite**

How do you do your asking? If you say, "I may not be perfect, and you might not consider me the best catch, but do you want to gamble and go out with me?" you don't exactly present yourself in a good light. Don't put yourself down when asking someone for a date.

If you're a guy, don't be too macho or too aggressive. Few girls like the "Me Tarzan, you Jane" approach. If you're a girl, don't be coy and cutesy or act dumb or helpless. Not too many guys like girls who play those roles. Be yourself, look for a date with similar interests, pretend you have self-confidence, and your chances for getting dates will probably improve.

> *"I turn down a lot of dates because I'm ashamed of my family. I don't want anybody to pick me up at home and see how I live and how my parents act. I don't want kids to think I'm like my folks."*

Many of us have imperfect home lives. Tight finances, parents who have problems, obnoxious brothers and sisters are a few of the hurdles that have to be cleared. You're stuck with your family, but you don't have to let them ruin your social life.

One easy way of dealing with this situation is to meet your date at another location the first time or two that you go out. If you like your date, and you plan to keep on dating, you can tell him or her about your situation at home.

You should realize that if someone asks you out, they want to be with you, and you won't lose points if your parents aren't like the people on "Family Ties" but more closely resemble Miss Hannigan in *Annie* and Scrooge in *A Christmas Carol.* If you're very worried about what a date might think, you might try approaches such as "I'd like to prepare you for what might be going on at home when you come to get me," or "My family is a bit unpredictable and I think you should know what you might have to deal with when you pick me up." This sort of remark can ease the surprise factor. Actually, a date will probably see much less that's wrong than you do. Don't let your home environment hinder you — if a date cares about you, the only thing that should matter is you. Look what happened to Cinderella.

"I want to go out with a girl who's in a wheelchair. But I don't know where I could take her or what she'd be able to do. I'm also worried about what my friends will think. Could you give me some suggestions?"

Go for it. Ask her out but tell her what you're worried about. She'll have the answers that you don't have. Your friends may think you're brave, or crazy, or adventurous, or they may not think anything's unusual at all. If you like the girl and they're really your friends, they'll be on your side. It may be that you're doing something they'd like to have done but didn't have the self-confidence to try.

"I met the most incredible guy at my Nautilus workouts. We got along right away and he's now my training partner. I feel a lot more for him than friendship and want to ask him over to my house for dinner and maybe date him. But he's black and I'm not and I think my parents will freak. Should I invite him anyway?"

Interracial dating can be problematic if you come from a family or community that advocates sticking to your own kind. The sad truth is that life can be made very hard for you and your date if that's your environment — you can practically count on hearing racial slurs, people may question your sanity and values, and you may be ostracized from your family and prior social group. This can happen if people who come from different religious backgrounds date, too.

While it may be worth trying to discuss this with your parents or one or two of your best friends — after all, they may be more supportive than you think — only you can answer the question for yourself. If the disadvantages don't outweigh the advantages, go ahead and begin to date. The bottom line is that you're two people who really like each other and enjoy each other's company. Even if the disadvantages seem horrendous, you may decide to encourage the relationship. It *is* possible that together you can overcome people's preconceived ideas. It's also possible that your dating won't cause any problems at all. But you'll never know until you try, and you may live to regret it if you don't try.

"I've been dating one guy for three months now and he's only kissed me a few times. Am I doing something to turn him off?"

The best way to find out is to talk to your boyfriend about this. He may think he's showing you a great deal of respect by having such restraint. You may have a reputation of being a "hands off" girl that he doesn't want to test. He may be afraid of being rejected if he makes sexual advances. On the other hand, you may be giving him subtle signals that physical contact is off-limits: do you resist cuddling, hugging, hand-holding? Do you giggle uncontrollably when he moves close to you? If you want your relationship to get more intimate, are you willing to make the first move and kiss him the next time you're alone together?

Sit down with him and talk, talk, talk until you uncross your signals.

"My figure is a real drawback. Guys come on like I'm Miss Super Seductress. I hate to always be fighting them off and saying, 'No.' "

It's unfortunate that your dates treat you that way, but your problem isn't unique. In our culture, physical beauty and ample endowments can pose many problems with dating, just as physical imperfections can.

If you've been dealing with guys who can't see beyond your measurements, you need to be very assertive. It's more than just saying "no." It's an attitude that sets limits and says, "I'm more than the sum of my physical parts." It may be that guys *assume* you're more experienced than you are because you look more mature. It may be that you're only going with really high-power guys who are very popular and used to getting their way. Sometimes you have to tell a date, point-blank, "I don't like being treated as a sex object." You could also say, "I'm sorry to have to bring this up but I've had some bad experiences fending off guys and I don't want to get into hassles with you. Please don't assume things about me. Ask me first; I won't get mad." Don't worry if the guy acts the innocent or looks offended. Setting limits helps assure an equitable dating relationship, not one based on cat and mouse games.

"I'm always concerned that my friends won't approve of my dates. I think I may be asking the wrong girls out for the wrong reasons — just to impress the guys!"

You may be absolutely right. When you're not so sure of your own worth and your own attractiveness, having a group of friends who agree with you and applaud your choice of dates is very comfortable.

As you get more mature, you begin to trust yourself more. You know your tastes better and you have a backlog of dating experiences to use as a yardstick regarding what's fun and pleasurable for you and what isn't. It sounds as though you're at that juncture in your dating life now. Eventually, when dating turns into romance or even love, you won't care who approves of your choice as long as the two of you are happy.

Love

"There's this girl I'm dating who I really like a lot. How can you tell when you're really in love?"

"My boyfriend and I have a terrific relationship together and we both love each other very much. Is there any way to be sure our love will last?"

"What's the difference between love and infatuation?"

Love is one of the most difficult emotions to define. This is partly because we use the word to mean many different things. When someone says, "I love fudge brownies," or "I love horses," it clearly isn't quite the same as loving another person. To complicate things even further, there are many different types of person-to-person love. How you love your parents or grandparents, for example, is very different from how you feel about a boyfriend or girlfriend with whom you're in love.

Adults often assume that teenagers aren't capable of *really* being in love, but this assumption just isn't true. Love is not bound by a person's chronological age any more than bravery or intelligence is. On the other hand, many teenagers (and plenty of adults, too) can be fooled into thinking they're in love by a condition called infatuation, which is a powerful but short-lived emotional state of attraction to another person that is, in a sense, a counterfeit version of love. Social psychologists have found that it often isn't possible to distinguish between infatuation and love while they're happening — most of the time, you can only tell that it was infatuation after it's over. This is partly because both infatuation and love in early stages result in a blurred objectivity that overlooks the faults or weaknesses of the person to whom you're attracted. In addition, because both infatuation and falling in love give you a major emotional high — a sense of being on top of the world — you may not be a very objective observer of your own behavior or feelings in either situation.

Despite these problems, there are some practical pointers that may be of help in distinguishing between love and infatuation.

1. Infatuation doesn't have much staying power; it's likely to wear thin after a few months. In contrast, real love doesn't end after a lifespan of only two or three months.

2. With infatuation, once the initial rush of emotions is over, the more time you spend with the other person, the less interesting he or she seems to be.

3. When problems arise, infatuation often fades away. In contrast, real love takes most problems in stride and may even be strengthened by such experiences.

4. Infatuation is often a self-centered feeling, while real love is more a matter of concern for your partner's happiness and well-being.

5. Infatuation is usually marked by jealousy and possessiveness. With real love, the partners are so certain of their feelings — and so trusting of each other — that jealousy is unnecessary.

6. Infatuation is often an acting-out of a fantasy about what

love should be in which the fantasy is more important than reality. Real love doesn't require illusions to keep it going — the reality itself is enjoyable, so the lovers can be themselves.

7. Infatuation is sometimes mainly a matter of physical attraction, with good looks and sex being the primary ingredients. If you don't enjoy each other's company when you're not having sex, it's a pretty certain sign that your feelings (while passionate) *aren't* love.

Real love is a give-and-take proposition in which caring and respect come to the forefront. In order for this to occur, it is usually necessary for a person first to have a firm sense of his or her own identity. This means that if you're pretty insecure about who you are as an individual or still groping around to find out who you want to be, it's not too likely that you're really ready for a mature love relationship. While it is true that some people try to discover their identity through love, love can't really be a substitute for a person's individuality, as this comment from an eighteen-year-old girl indicates:

> When Jimmy and I were going together, we were *sure* we were in love. Unfortunately, as the months went by I found that I was only thinking of myself as a part of him, not as a person in my own right. It was like I'd submerged my identity in our relationship — ignoring my friends, my family, and my interests — all so we could be the "ideal" couple. When I found out he was cheating on me, I was heartbroken at first. Then I finally realized that our love was doomed right from the start, because I wasn't really ready to be in love and still be myself. It's for sure that I won't make that same mistake again.

Not all love relationships are the same. Some start suddenly, with a head-over-heels, love-at-first-sight beginning. Others develop slowly and unexpectedly — sometimes even when two people don't like each other much at first. Still others occur when one or both people are in a state of "love readiness" and are looking for someone to fall in love with because they see love as a rewarding, desirable thing. Love readiness is also common when a person is on the rebound from another relationship that's just broken up. The wish to replace the ex-lover in this situation is partly a matter of wanting to prove that you're attractive and desirable and partly a reflection of wanting to have the security that romantic companionship offers.

Love relationships also have different styles. Some are stormy, with an almost constant flip-flop of emotions: ecstasy one moment, arguing and accusations the next. Other love relationships are mainly based on physical attraction, with an intense sexual magnetism as the predominant feature. (Both of these styles suggest a love that isn't likely to last very long.) Others are based on a more levelheaded approach to love, with less intensity and excitement at the beginning but a greater chance of gradually developing into strong bonds of commitment. And, while it may be surprising, there are many instances in which love is simply an outgrowth of warmth, affection, and mutual caring and does not include dramatic fireworks or never-ending series of crises. Love can also take on a more playful, casual style, although lovers in this type of relationship are less likely to have a strong sense of commitment to each other. In addition, some love relationships blend the above-mentioned styles in various combinations.

Being in love can provide you with a deep sense of security and well-being, but it can cause some problems, too. Here is a rundown of eight common love problems couples encounter.

1. You may not be completely sure your love is being returned. Repeatedly asking the person you love "Do you love me?" isn't the answer to this predicament, since you won't really know if the answer you get is genuine or forced. In love, as in most other things, actions speak louder than words. By the same token, it is perfectly reasonable to prefer not being in the dark, so having an in-depth conversation with your partner in which you explain your uncertainties and ask for an answer is certainly OK.

2. You may be worried by doubts about your love. Doubts about a love relationship are perfectly natural. As the initial thrill of being in love disappears, each lover typically begins to notice the other's flaws and suddenly comes to the realization that the lover isn't perfect. So what? Expecting perfection isn't realistic. Learning to accept each other's imperfections is a necessary step in forming a foundation for a stable, lasting love. (On the other hand, waking up to realities about your lover or your relationship that you can't live with is also completely legitimate. After all, it's better to break off the relationship than to be trapped into something you don't want with someone you no longer enjoy.)

3. *You may be puzzled by one-upmanship and other kinds of game playing in your relationship.* The best way to deal with this is to avoid getting entangled in these games yourself, since it almost always takes two to play. This means don't keep score about who's done what for whom, don't try to get even for something that's bothering you, don't complain to other people about how your lover treats you, don't try to make your partner jealous, and don't sulk about what's bothering you, expecting your lover to read your mind.

4. *You may find yourself lying to your partner, or wondering if your partner is lying to you.* If this occurs, it's time to take another look at whether your relationship is really intact. Deceptiveness is one of the most reliable early-warning signs of trouble between lovers. The only way to handle this situation is to talk it out (without recriminations) to get to the bottom of why it's happening. If it can't be stopped, it's time to hit the road. Trust is one of the most important elements in a relationship.

5. *You may feel smothered by your relationship.* This can happen for several different reasons. If your lover is very domineering and you don't speak up for what you want, you may constantly find yourself giving in to what he or she wants to do. Similarly, if the two of you spend so much time togther that you're prevented from pursuing your own interests and having your own identity, you may get that smothered feeling. Finally, some people unintentionally become too dependent on their lovers, developing a virtual inability to deal with the world without the lover's advice or help. These situations can generally be prevented or dealt with by establishing enough space in your relationship to allow you and your lover to lead

your own lives and do your own thinking. Occasional time out from your togetherness will probably help your love grow and develop.

6. *You may get frustrated by unsuccessfully trying to change certain things about your partner.* While it may not be too difficult to help your lover change in some ways that you'd like — for instance, to learn to be a better dancer — there are other types of change that you can want your partner to make that are nothing more than wishful thinking. If what you'd *really* like is to have your partner undergo a personality transplant — becoming witty, talkative, humorous, and romantic — when what you've actually got is a boring, wimpy, inhibited nerd, forget it. No matter how much you think you can help this transformation, you probably can't, so you need, instead, to decide "Can I live with what I've got, or is it best to find someone else?" Trying to mold someone into your ideal image is something you really should try to avoid.

7. *You may be worried because you have fights.* Relax. Unless you're fighting on a day-by-day basis or unless the fights turn into cruel, vicious encounters, you should realize that verbal fighting or arguing is a normal part of love. (*Physical* fighting among lovers is something else entirely; except in unusual circumstances, it's a dangerous practice.) In verbal fights couples can let out their tensions, frustrations, hurts, and angers, which is a good deal better than carrying all this garbage around locked up inside you. In effect, fair fighting can clear the air, even if it temporarily causes unhappiness.

8. *Your relationship seems to be stuck in a rut.* If boredom sets into your life, it isn't useful to try to blame it on your partner. It also isn't necessary to decide you've got to try hang-gliding off the Empire State Building together in order to bring some excitement into your relationship. Accept responsibility yourself for identifying where the problem is and what you'd like to do about it. For example, if all your afternoons are spent hanging out at MacDonald's with your lover, you might try to get a little variety by taking up some sports activity together (for example, roller-skating, swimming, tennis) or even volunteering together to work at a local hospital or nursing

home. If, on the other hand, your relationship is spent mostly in making out with your lover, it may be helpful to break the monotony by spending more time with a group of friends. Even a steady diet of pizza gets boring after a while.

The 20-Point Checklist for Improving Love Relations

It shouldn't be surprising that love isn't always perfect, but it also shouldn't be surprising that people don't know much about love. If you think about it, most of us spend more time learning how to drive a car than learning how to love. For those who are interested, though, we offer the following practical pointers.

— Be realistic in what you expect from your partner and your relationship. Looking for perfection is always going to leave you dissatisfied.

— Long-lasting love comes in part from building shared interests and enjoying them together.

— Don't assume that sex is the most important part of a love relationship.

— Try to express your affection regularly to your partner; don't assume that it doesn't need to be said.

— Be direct and honest in communicating your feelings to your partner. This is one of the best ways to develop trust. Keeping your feelings hidden will eventually undermine any love.

— Avoid being too critical of your partner. Whenever possible, try to see things from his or her point of view.

— Don't try to take responsibility for making your partner happy, because you can't do it by yourself.

— Be willing to compromise.

— Be willing to listen to criticism.

— Be willing to assume responsibility for your own actions instead of blaming them on somebody else.

— Be attentive to your partner's needs, but don't try to guess what they are. Your guesses are likely to be wrong at least half the time.

— Don't give up when problems occur; try to talk these situations over to come up with mutually acceptable ways of coping.

— Don't force your partner into compromising his or her values or becoming something he or she isn't.

— Be sensitive to your partner's feelings.

— Be willing to admit your weaknesses and uncertainties.

— Remember that a love relationship should be a two-way street, so be sure to share decision-making responsibilities.

— Don't let your love relationship obliterate your relationships with others, or your own sense of identity.

— Keep your promises (and don't promise what you can't deliver).

— Help bring new interests and perspectives to your relationship.

— BE YOURSELF.

Finally, don't let yourself fall into what we call the "love fallacy" — the mistaken idea that once you've found love, it will last forever and ever on its own. Few loves are likely to last a lifetime even under the best of circumstances. Without hard work and much creative energy put into the act of loving and being loved, the fragile thing we call love is likely to wither and die.

Breaking Up
Is Always Hard to Do

Well, almost always. There may be a time when you're going with someone you discover you really don't like very much — and heading for the exit, even if it means sitting at home listening to your tape collection every Saturday night for three months, seems better than the prospect of trying to save a terminally boring relationship.

Most of the time, though, deciding how and when to end a romance isn't easy at all. For one thing, you may be unsure of whether the problems you're having with your relationship are correctable or not. If a solution *could* be found, things might work out all right — so you wonder how to decide if you've both tried hard enough, if you're giving up too soon, or if there's just no possibility of salvaging the good feelings you and your partner once had together. You also may be tempted to stick with a somewhat stale relationship because (a) it's all you've got; (b) there don't seem to be any immediate prospects for a new romance on the horizon; and (c) there's a prom coming up (or a big party, or a junior class trip, etc.) and you can't bear the thought of going with someone you hardly know (or going by yourself, in an uncoupled state). As if these considerations weren't enough, there is the additional complication of worrying about how breaking up will affect your boyfriend or girlfriend — after all, most people don't just walk away from a romance with complete disregard for their partner's feelings.

Keeping these things in mind, you can see that breaking up is likely to be an emotion-wrenching event that occurs after a lot of soul-searching. While you might occasionally get blindsided by a boyfriend or girlfriend who announces "I've had it" out of the clear blue sky, most of the time there will be plenty of early warning signs when a relationship is going on the rocks. For example:

— Spending time together starts to get boring.
— You each start criticizing the other a lot.
— You fight frequently, often over trivial matters.
— Your girlfriend (or boyfriend) doesn't look as attractive to you as she (or he) once did.
— You stop thinking about your future together.
— One or both of you lies to the other a lot.
— One or both of you starts making excuses to avoid your being together.
— Your boyfriend (or girlfriend) seems less sensitive to your feelings and desires.
— Signs of tenderness become scarce.

If these warning signs don't lead to enough repair work to restore the luster to your romance and you decide that breaking up is the best thing to do, you might want to keep these hints in mind:

1. *Don't feel guilty for deciding that the relationship wasn't right for you any longer.* Even if it lasted for a long time and consumed a lot of your energy, bringing an end to one particular romance isn't a sign of failure — it's more likely to be a sign of growth.

2. *Don't try to put all the blame for the break up on your soon-to-be ex-partner.* In every relationship we've seen, both partners' attitudes and behaviors have something to do with the outcome. Besides, assigning blame is a useless game. There are two sides to each romantic story.

3. *Don't broadcast the gory details to your friends, no matter how interested or sympathetic they may seem to be.* Being a blabbermouth in this situation is wrong for a number of different reasons. First, no one will believe that your version of what happened is entirely objective and fair. Second, hanging your dirty laundry out in public makes you seem inconsiderate and immature. Third, the more you are a motormouth on this topic, the more it tempts your "ex" to tell all sorts of scandal about *you.* Stop and think about whether this is what you want to happen. Instead, you can just tell your friends, "We really had something going for a while, but it just didn't work out for either of us."

4. *Don't be afraid to let yourself go into mourning for a while for the now-dead romance.* It's perfectly natural to feel discouraged and depressed when a breakup occurs, especially if the relationship was one of long standing and deep affection. Still, people are sometimes astonished to find that they don't feel like being the life of the party just after a breakup has occurred. While you might have thought that breaking up would be a big relief and give you a sense of newfound freedom, you may actually find that you're more than a bit short-tempered, uncertain of your attractiveness, and embarrassed a bit in social situations. Give yourself a few weeks to get over the emotional hurt, and don't be surprised if you find yourself getting teary-eyed when you least expect to. (Even guys cry

during or after a breakup.) The good news is that these down feelings generally disappear in short order — in just a few weeks you'll probably be back in the swing of things none the worse for wear.

5. *Don't keep living in the past.* One seventeen-year-old kept reading and rereading love letters from his former girlfriend every night for months, desperately trying to think up ways to get her back again. This isn't a very useful strategy — in those cases where a broken-up romance resumes, it's usually because of a spontaneous chain of events, not by some carefully planned operation. Besides, the more you live in the past, the less you'll notice about what's going on *now*. This will only drag out the hurt feelings.

6. *Don't be afraid to be friends with your ex.* Just because you've broken off a romance doesn't mean that your friendship has to end, too. It may simply shift to a different kind of interaction — *if you let it.* But realize that it can lead to awkward feelings and situations, such as jealousy over new lovers.

7. *Don't put down your ex's new dates; it makes you look petty and jealous.*

8. *Don't try to date your ex-partner's friends in an attempt to stir up your ex's jealousy and get him or her back.* It will make you look foolish and it won't work.

9. *Don't give up on love.* You haven't lost your one chance in life.

One Last Word about Dating, Romance, and Love

Sharp-eyed readers have probably noticed that this discussion has hardly even mentioned sex. This isn't an oversight or an attempt to dodge a sensitive issue. Instead, because questions about sexual matters are of such interest and importance to most teenagers, the topic requires an extensive discussion in its own right. The next chapter, which is devoted entirely to sex, will provide you with some important facts to think about.

8.

Straight Talk about Sex

We live in a society where sex is almost everywhere. Turn on the radio and you may hear Madonna singing "Like a Virgin," the Pointer Sisters doing "(I Want a Man with a) Slow Hand," or Motley Crue describing a quickie sexual encounter in "Ten Seconds to Love." At the movies you might have seen *Risky Business*, in which a teenager temporarily turns his home into a sex-for-sale emporium while his parents are in Europe. Television offers steamy daytime soap operas and nighttime fare that includes movies on topics like rape, incest, and homosexuality, as well as shows like "Dynasty" and "Dallas" that feature seductions, affairs, and other sexual goings-on. The best-seller list is heavily populated with novels featuring torrid sex in every imaginable combination.

Given this reality, it's no wonder that teenagers, like most other people, think about sex with some frequency. And that's certainly reasonable, because one of the most interesting parts of adolescence is becoming aware of your sexuality. Unfortunately, though, sex is also a confusing topic to many of us, bringing us to the point of this chapter.

We won't preach to you or try to tell you what's sexually right and wrong here, although what you learn should help you in your personal sexual decision-making. Instead, our purpose is to present you with facts — lots of facts — that cover a wide range of topics about teenagers and sex.

A Preliminary Note about Personal Values and Sexual Decisions

No matter what your age, you may have a certain degree of uncertainty about sex. Is it right to have intercourse with someone before you're married? Should you have sex with someone if you're not in love? Is it wrong for a teenage girl to use birth control, because that indicates she's planning to have sex? Is masturbation bad for you?

These questions and others like them can't be answered by using any simple formula. Each of us brings a framework of values to analyze such questions, including values learned from our families, from our religion, from our friends, from the media, and from our life experiences. In part, sexual decisions are outgrowths of how we judge the relative importance of these values and how we resolve the conflict they may create.

Sometimes sexual decisions don't get made this way — by thinking about values — but instead get made impulsively or on the basis of ignorance or guilt. For example, if you're talked into having sex by someone who says "If you really love me, you'll prove it," your decision may really be a way of dealing with your own guilt and uncertainty about the relationship — "How else can I show I love this person?" This sort of decision-making is much more likely to be regretted later on. And since all of us have to live with our sexual decisions, we should take an active role in making sexual choices rather than just letting the choices "happen."

There's no timetable for any of this; different people mature at different rates, and whether or not you are physically mature may have little or no bearing on whether you think you're emotionally mature enough to handle a full-blown sexual relationship that includes intercourse, or whether you choose to express your sexual feelings in other ways. What you've been taught to believe in terms of moral values may, however, have a bearing on your choices just as what your friends are doing and thinking may have an impact on what seems OK to try sexually and what doesn't. If you decide to have intercourse you will do so understanding that, as with anything in life, there are potential risks that need to be considered and balanced against the more appealing and positive sides of the activity. And whatever your sexual choices may be, we also hope they will be made in a way that doesn't hurt anyone.

Four Brief Points about Sex in Modern American Society

1. *Contrary to what you might think from portrayals in Hollywood's movies, NOT every other teenager besides you is already sexually experienced.* Often, those who talk the loudest do the least — so bragging friends may be exaggerating or even fantasizing about their sex lives.

2. *Sex is not the most important thing in the world — even to teenagers.* According to a recent survey, adolescents rate many other factors as more important to romance than sex. (This doesn't mean that sex can't be a great deal of fun — it can. But recalling this fact can help keep things in perspective.)

3. *Be wary of any sexual information you learn from friends.* There's a good chance they may have their facts wrong.

4. *It's perfectly normal and natural for you to feel confused or ashamed about sexual thoughts, sexual feelings, sexual body parts, and sexual acts.* Many of us do. We hope this chapter will help change some of those negative feelings.

Puberty

Before we move on to discussing various types of sexual activity and sexual feelings, it is helpful to understand the biological process called puberty. Puberty isn't a disease — it's a normal part of everyone's development in which the body undergoes a gradual series of changes from the physically immature state of childhood to a physically mature form. As part of this process, puberty leads to substantial growth, the appearance of "secondary sex characteristics" (like a boy's facial hair and deepening voice and a girl's developing figure), and the ability to reproduce.

Despite what you may think, puberty isn't a sudden

event that happens overnight. The changes of puberty occur gradually, with the entire process typically lasting from two to six years — although you may not even be aware of some of the earliest changes happening in your body. This is partly because the blueprint for each person's puberty development was actually set before birth, when the brain was programmed by chemical messengers called hormones for a later awakening of the centers that start the process of puberty. Before any visible changes of puberty occur, these brain centers begin to function in their preprogrammed fashion, secreting hormones that act on a small acorn-sized organ located just beneath the brain — the pituitary gland — that in turn sends its own hormones to begin the final growth and maturation of the sex organs.

As a result of these inner chemical events, which you cannot feel at all, the reproductive organs — the testes in males, the ovaries in females — begin to enlarge and function in an adult manner. The hormones made by these reproductive organs, which were produced in only small amounts during childhood, begin to be produced in much larger quantities. Over time, this increased production leads to the physical changes of puberty that you can measure or see.

In males, the major hormone made by the testes is called testosterone, the so-called male hormone. (This is technically a misnomer, because females also make testosterone in their bodies, but only in much smaller quantities.) In females, the major sex hormone made in the ovaries is estrogen, the so-called female hormone. (Males have small amounts of estrogen, too.)

The gradual rise in the levels of these sex hormones eventually triggers an accelerated rate of growth in the long bones in the body. This is known as the adolescent growth spurt, which you may recognize if you (or a friend) suddenly shot up by three inches in height over a summer. Curiously, this growth spurt usually occurs about two years earlier in girls than in boys (on average, about twelve versus fourteen years old). One result of this difference in the timing of puberty between the sexes is that many girls are taller than boys their age from about eleven to fourteen. If you're worried or self-conscious about height, though, you can relax — by mid-adolescence this height difference tends to reverse itself as males catch up and typically go on to become taller than females.

As with all of the changes of puberty, there is a lot of variability in the timing of the adolescent growth spurt from one person to another. This means that a boy who is 5′ 3″ in the eighth grade may be a six-footer by his junior year in high school, while another boy who is already 5′ 11″ in eighth grade may not grow to be much taller. (If you're wondering how tall you'll be as an adult, although there's no sure-fire way of knowing, you may get a clue from your parents' heights. Height is one characteristic that often depends on heredity.)

Another interesting fact about the adolescent growth spurt is that it doesn't always start at the same time in all parts of the body. For instance, the feet often start to grow four or five months before the lower legs, so if your feet suddenly seem too big to you, you may be pleasantly surprised in another few months to find that they "fit" your body proportions better.

There are a number of other physical changes during puberty of which you should be aware. For one thing, differences in hormones between the sexes lead to differences in body composition and build. This is because testosterone, which is much higher in boys than in girls from mid-puberty on, helps to build up muscle in the body, whereas estrogen (which is much higher in girls) leads to an increase in a layer of fat just beneath the skin. In addition, rising hormone levels also trigger an increase in skin oil production that can cause acne, which accounts for the fact that grade-school children generally don't have problems with pimples, while teenagers do. Another effect of rising hormone levels in both sexes is an in-

crease in body hair, particularly in the underarm region, on the arms and legs, and in the pubic region.

There are several other notable changes during puberty that deserve a bit more discussion. For example, the process of female breast development is often a source of anxiety and jealous comparisons. Breast growth can start anywhere from the age of eight to age fourteen, and *when* it starts is not an indication of how large a girl's breasts eventually will be. In addition, because there's a great variability in the length of time it takes for complete breast development once it's begun, you can't predict at thirteen or fourteen or fifteen what size your breasts will be by the time you're eighteen or nineteen. However, even if you're dissatisfied with insufficient breast development, you can't increase your bust size by exercise or using special creams (even if they claim to have hormones in them) or mechanical devices. Companies that advertise such products are just taking advantage of your anxieties. Furthermore, you should realize that medical experts agree that breast size has nothing to do with sexiness or sexual responsiveness.

We should also note that some teenage girls are troubled by just the opposite problem — having breasts that they feel are too large. Many of these teenagers are very self-conscious about their appearance and resentful of the fact that males often presume that they must be "oversexed" — or at least always interested in sex — because they're so well endowed. Dealing with such assumptions constantly can make a female feel more like an object than a person. In addition, some females with large breasts develop physical difficulties because of their breast size. For example, very large breasts can cause a great deal of pressure on bra straps and can also create problems with running or other sports activities. As a result, surgery to reduce the size and weight of the breasts is sometimes required. (In fact, this is one of the most common forms of breast surgery performed in the U.S.)

Another biological change in girls during puberty is the beginning of menstruation. Menstruation is a flow of blood from the lining of the uterus that occurs about once a month in females from puberty until their late forties or early fifties. (The lining of the uterus sheds because a pregnancy hasn't occurred; during pregnancy, the fertilized egg, or ovum, becomes attached to the inside of the uterus in a process called implantation.) Contrary to what you might think, the amount of menstrual flow is usually quite small — on average, there is a total of only four to six tablespoons of fluid over the four or five days that a period lasts.

Some girls begin to menstruate as early as eight or nine, while others don't start getting periods until they are fifteen or sixteen. Menstruation usually begins only after breast development has gotten well underway and after the peak growth spurt has occurred. In America, the average age at which menstruation begins is about twelve and three-quarters, but girls who have very low body fat levels (because of rigorous physical exercise, like long-distance running or serious ballet dancing involving hours of training and practice a day) often don't begin getting periods until much later. In fact, there's absolutely no reason to worry about not having begun getting periods before the age of sixteen; after this, a medical checkup may be warranted.

When a girl first starts having periods, they may be quite irregularly spaced, coming at forty-five- to ninety-day intervals or even longer, rather than every four to five weeks. This is not an indication of any sort of physical problem. Such irregularity will most likely change in a year or two. The important thing to remember, though, is that menstruation is a signal that a girl is capable of getting pregnant. This isn't an academic observation — it's a major point to keep in mind if you're going to be sexually active, because teenagers can (and do) get pregnant at the age of thirteen or fourteen even if they think they can't.

Several other points about menstruation should be made here. First, no one can tell when you're menstruating — you don't look any different, you don't behave differently, and there are no changes in your stamina, your intelligence, your attractiveness, or your personality. Second, while some females have cramps either just before their periods start or in the first day or two of flow, most aren't hampered at all in their activities. (If you find that you're having severe cramps around the time of your period, it's advisable to see a doctor, because these can now be treated fairly easily.) Third, menstruation is nothing to be ashamed of or embarrassed by. It's a completely natural, normal, healthy process that is a hallmark of being feminine and growing toward maturity. As Gloria Steinem noted in her 1983 book *Outrageous Acts and Everyday Rebellions,* if men could menstruate, "Men would brag about how long and how much. Young boys would talk about it as the envied beginning of manhood. Gifts, religious ceremonies, family dinners, and stag parties would mark the day."

One other aspect of puberty for females is generally overlooked. Because of the increase in estrogen levels in their bodies, girls begin to experience vaginal wetness frequently during puberty. This wetness, or lubrication, is a result of normal secretions inside the vagina. While vaginal wetness is sometimes a result of sexual excitation (whether from day-dreams, reading something sexy, watching a sexy movie, or sexual activity), it can occur at other times, too. Sometimes awareness of vaginal wetness causes teenagers to feel ashamed or embarrassed, but it is a natural reflex response of the body that isn't really too different from having saliva in your mouth.

As we already mentioned, puberty tends to start some-what later in boys than in girls. The size of the male sex organs begins to increase gradually from about the age of twelve until seventeen, and sperm production — which begins during childhood — becomes fully established, so fertility is present. In addition, during puberty boys begin to experience wet dreams (sometimes called "nocturnal emissions"). Wet dreams are simply a reflex response of the body in which ejac-ulation (sperm spurting out of the tip of the penis) occurs while a boy is asleep. Usually, but not always, he may have been having a sexy dream at the time this reflex occurs. The reason this is called a wet dream is that the boy is often awak-ened by a wet spot on the bed after he has ejaculated. While about half of all fifteen-year-old boys and three-quarters of all eighteen-year-old boys have had wet dreams, many of them were never told that this would happen — so they're surprised or worried when it occurs. As a result, they may be afraid a nocturnal emission is a sign of some illness or abnormality, whereas actually it's just a healthy reflex that is a completely natural part of growing up.

Teenage males also find that they get erections much more frequently than they did when younger. These erections are sometimes a result of sexual daydreams, but can also occur at absolutely inopportune times — like when you're standing on the cafeteria line at school, or when you're in church, or when you're wearing a tight-fitting swimsuit. Needless to say, this can be something of an embarrassment unless you're able to think of a way of covering up until the bulge in your pants has subsided. In any event, it's helpful to realize that all males have had similar experiences, and it's a completely normal thing.

Three other aspects of male puberty should also be mentioned briefly. One is that increased testosterone levels in the body cause the voice box (larynx) to grow larger. As a result, the boy's voice gets lower in pitch — but before this happens, there may be an awkward period in which the voice seemingly jumps from alto to soprano to tenor and back in the same sentence, and squawks and breaks become a source of considerable embarrassment. This deepening of the voice can occur as early as twelve or not until seventeen or eighteen.

The second change that should be mentioned is the growth of facial hair in boys, which is also dependent on testosterone. Generally, around the time a boy is thirteen or fourteen facial hair begins to grow at the corners of the upper lip with a fuzzy, fine-textured appearance. As it spreads over the mustache area, the hair begins to become coarser and somewhat darker. Six months to a year later, hair begins to appear on the upper cheeks and just below the lower lip. Finally, hair growth spreads along the lower jawline and appears last of all on the chin. (One practical note to keep in mind: most boys can't grow a very respectable beard until they're eighteen or somewhat older. Sorry, but there's no way to change this.)

Finally, many adolescent males (about 60 percent, according to medical surveys) have a period of time in which their breasts become prominent or enlarged. This condition, which is called gynecomastia, is a result of the rapid increase in hormones occurring during puberty. In most cases, it will disappear within six months to a year, but it can be a major source of embarrassment and concern. Seeing your breasts become enlarged doesn't mean you've got cancer or you're homosexual. And although this is usually just a temporary condition that will go away spontaneously, if it persists, it can be corrected by plastic surgery.

Masturbation

Masturbation is a fancy-sounding word for sexual self-pleasuring — touching or rubbing your own sex organs to produce sexual arousal. Because masturbation has been misunderstood and strongly condemned in the past, when it was sometimes called self-abuse, it has continued to this day to be a source of guilt and fear for some people.

Doctors once thought that masturbation was provoked by an improper diet (chocolate, oysters, gravies, coffee, alcohol, ginger, and salt were among the foods thought to be the most common culprits). "Improper" physical stimulation brought on by activities such as riding a bicycle, rope-climbing, or even running a sewing machine were also thought to bring on masturbation. And in the early 1900s, if you were a child whose parents suspected you of masturbating, you might have been sent to bed wearing metal mittens or even a straitjacket to prevent you from touching yourself "down there."

Today, these ideas are recognized as completely outdated. Numerous scientific studies have shown that masturbation is a common activity in all age groups — including those of young children and adults as well as teenagers. In fact, it's now regarded as a natural, healthy act rather than a sign of weakness or instability. Reflecting this attitude, recent surveys show that four out of five adolescents approve of masturbation. And among teenagers who masturbate (about 85 percent of males and 75 percent of females) a majority do so at least once a week — hardly what you'd call a "rare" activity. Nevertheless, some worries about masturbation still linger on in the minds of many teenagers, as if to say "anything that's this much fun has *got* to be bad for you." Here, then, are some facts to set these worries straight.

1. Contrary to old wives' tales you may have heard, masturbation does not cause insanity. It also won't make hair grow on the palms of your hands.

2. The idea that masturbation is unnatural doesn't make much sense if you consider that it's commonplace in the animal kingdom (where not only monkeys and apes engage in this behavior, which you can see for yourself at any zoo, but other animal species as diverse as porcupines, elephants, dogs, and even dolphins do, too). It might also interest you to know that masturbation is almost universally found in various human cultures, from the most primitive to the most technologically advanced.

3. Masturbation doesn't prevent the development of healthy sexual functioning — it actually helps people learn how to respond sexually. Many sex therapists now believe that it is those people who have *never* masturbated who are more apt to have sexual problems as adults.

4. Contrary to a big worry many teenagers have, no one can tell by looking at you if you masturbate or not.

It's now clear that masturbation can serve many useful functions such as relieving sexual tension, providing a safe means of sexual experimentation, combating loneliness, or improving sexual self-confidence, as these two comments show.

> I first discovered that touching myself could be very arousing when I was thirteen years old and really didn't understand much about sex. I used to masturbate while I looked at pictures in *Playboy*. Now that I'm seventeen and going with a girlfriend, I still masturbate occasionally when I get real tense or when I haven't gotten together with my girl for a while.
>
> *Jim R., seventeen*

> I had never even thought about masturbating (in fact, I wasn't even sure what the word *meant*) when I was fourteen, but I was reading this really sexy book that gave me a warm, tingly feeling in my crotch. I started rubbing myself as I was reading, and pressing my thighs together, and the next thing I knew I had an orgasm. I think it was about two more years before I figured out that this was what they meant by masturbation. What a surprise *that* was!
>
> *Sally M., eighteen*

It is also important to realize that masturbation isn't for everyone. People who choose not to masturbate shouldn't feel that there's something wrong with them. No matter what the reason for such a decision — be it religious, personal, or something else — the important thing is that all persons must have the right to make and hold to those sexual decisions that are right for them. Since it's not unusual for teenagers to feel that masturbation is something to be ashamed of — as one sixteen-year-old boy put it, "Every time I do it I promise myself it'll be the last time" — it's also important to know that if this is how you feel, you should either stop masturbating (so you'll stop feeling guilty) or talk with someone who can help you deal with this sense of shame. If you're uncomfortable because you're afraid you're the only one in the world who masturbates, think about the fact that statistics show that most of your friends probably do it too.

ONE NOTE OF WARNING ABOUT MASTURBATION

In recent years, word has been spreading among teenage boys that the intensity of sexual arousal during masturbation can be increased by hanging oneself to temporarily cut off the oxygen supply to the brain. As a result, thousands have tried hanging themselves for short periods (using a rope or a belt, and keeping a chair nearby so they can get down from their self-imposed "hanging") — and dozens of deaths have resulted. This is no laughing matter at all ... what happens is that with the brain deprived of oxygen, a person's coordination is disrupted, and even the easiest physical tasks (like climbing onto a chair and removing a noose from around your neck) can be almost impossible to do. There are many more ways to get sexual thrills than to take a chance on snuffing out your own life. DON'T EVER TRY THIS DANGEROUS, SENSELESS ACTIVITY.

Making Out and Petting

Masturbation may be something you do in private, but most sexual activity, like dancing, takes two to tango. The range of erotic possibilities with a partner is much more varied (and usually more interesting) than those things you can think up and do by yourself.

The possibility of getting into a sexual situation with a partner sometimes provokes anxiety and alarm rather than pleasant anticipation. This is most true for younger teenagers — perhaps understandably — but can apply to people of any age. Concerns that are commonly mentioned include (a) being embarrassed, (b) being shy, (c) believing that sex is bad, and (d) worrying about not measuring up to the partner's expectations. It's interesting to note that while teenage girls are somewhat more cautious in moving into sexual situations, partly because of the added risk of becoming pregnant, boys and girls share almost equally in the above concerns.

It's perfectly natural to be a bit nervous about any kind of sexual play with a partner. For one thing, most new experiences cause us to be uncertain and on guard because we aren't dealing with familiar territory. When it comes to sex, you are not just likely to be nervous about yourself (Does my breath smell OK? Did I use deodorant? Am I attractive to my partner?) but you'll probably have some questions and concerns about the person you're with, too. Are they having a good time? What are they thinking? Can you trust them to stop when you want to stop? These and many other questions will bounce through your mind, sometimes leaving you so busy wondering and worrying that you may not be able to really recall all the details of what just happened. Relax a bit, though — this won't last forever. As you gain a little more self-confidence and familiarity with such sexual interaction, you'll be able to put most of these concerns into the background. To assist you in sorting through some of the problems you may have, we'll answer a number of questions about making out and petting before we discuss sexual intercourse in the following section.

How old should you be before you start making out? What's the right age for a girl to let a boy touch her vagina, or to touch a boy's penis? There are no precise guidelines as to what you should "do" sexually at a particular age or after a certain number of dates. Just allow yourself to do what you feel comfortable doing, despite pressure you may get from your partners or friends. If it doesn't seem right and it doesn't seem comfortable, leave it alone.

If a boy gets very aroused sexually, doesn't he need to get release so he won't damage his body? If levels of sexual excitement get really high for any length of time in either sex, there can be a feeling of achiness in the pelvic area or groin if there hasn't been an orgasm. But boys aren't in any more need of release of sexual tension than girls are, and in both sexes, if the need is great enough, the body takes care of it with orgasm occurring during sleep. In other words, boys don't require any special services from a sexual viewpoint to prevent physical problems.

Can you get so carried away when you're making out or petting that you can't control yourself? The idea of getting so swept away by passion that you do something you really don't want to do is more myth than reality. Sure, you can get so carried away on a trip to a store that you "accidentally" shoplift something. But don't confuse poor judgment, lack of responsibility, and giving in to an impulse with getting carried away. On the other hand, if you know from experience that you have a lot of trouble controlling your impulses, it might be most advisable to stay away from sexual situations until you've gotten somewhat more mature.

Can a girl get pregnant from giving a boy a "blow job"? Using the mouth, lips, and tongue to stimulate the penis is known in slang terms as a "blow job," although usually a sucking or licking motion is used — it's not like playing the saxophone. No one can get pregnant from this activity even if the boy ejaculates in his partner's mouth. (Many girls prefer to have the boy withdraw his penis just before ejaculating, as they find the taste of semen unpleasant, but others find it a turn-on or at least find it tolerable and do it because their partners enjoy it.)

I get real embarrassed when my boyfriend wants to kiss my vagina. Is that normal? Many girls find having their sex organs licked or kissed by their partner very arousing. Others are so concerned about vaginal odors or vaginal cleanliness that they are, as one sixteen-year-old girl told us, "totally grossed out by the experience." Many older teenagers of both sexes say that it can take a while to get used to the idea of oral sex, but that it's worth the wait because they find it a very gratifying form of sexual play. Some women find it easier to be comfortable with this activity if they bathe or shower before sexual activity, being sure to wash their genitals with soap and water. Realizing that oral-genital contact is no less hygenic than mouth-to-mouth kissing also helps people get comfortable with this type of sexual activity. Perhaps the most important ingredient, though, is for the girl to feel that her partner is doing this because he genuinely wants to, not just because he thinks it's expected of him.

What's the right way to touch a girl's vagina to turn her on? There really isn't any "right" way to have sex. Good sex isn't a matter of pressing the right buttons at the right time. Different types of touching — firmer, lighter, rubbing, stroking, teasing, and so on — are best for different people, and even the same person may prefer a different touch at different times. Instead of trying to figure out what's "best" for your partner, the easiest thing to do is ask her! Let her tell you or show you what she finds pleasurable and arousing. (Exactly the same thing applies to how girls should touch a boy's penis — there isn't *one* right way of doing it.)

Sometimes when I'm making out with my girlfriend, I have fantasies about other girls. Is this normal? The answer to this question actually applies to both sexes. It's very common for people to fantasize about sex with someone other than the person they're with *right in the middle of sexual activity.* It seems to be a way of adding to your arousal, and it doesn't mean that anything is wrong with you if it happens. Of course, sexual fantasies can occur at other times too — either deliberately brought to mind, in a sort of private sexual video, or as a kind of offhand daydreaming. Having sexual fantasies is perfectly natural, even if the things you fantasize about are things you'd never dream of doing in real life. (This isn't really surprising, since people who fantasize about what they'd do if they robbed a bank and got away with a million dollars aren't criminals, either.)

How can a girl tell if she's had an orgasm? Orgasm refers to the peak level of sexual arousal and its release in a rapid series of muscular contractions followed by a wave of relaxation sweeping over the body. In other words, it's a powerful feeling of pulsations that sort of explode into a warm, relaxed state. It can occur with any type of sexual activity, not just with intercourse — in fact, many people have their first orgasm by masturbation. Most females describe orgasm as beginning with feelings of intense warmth or tingling in the genital area that seem to spread across the body, followed by a brief sensation of throbbing in the vagina or pelvis that lasts for ten or fifteen seconds. Immediately after orgasm, a sense of complete body relaxation sets in. However, orgasms come in different sizes and shapes — some are bigger, longer, more noticeable ones, while others are smaller, quieter, and less intense — so if you're looking for a feeling like Christmas and the Fourth of July all wrapped into one, you may be disappointed.

Going All the Way

You've probably already asked yourself, "Will I or won't I?" when you've been thinking about sexual intercourse. This may have been either just a theoretical question, because the opportunity may never have arisen, or it may have been a practical necessity because of a relationship you've been in. Or, instead, it may have been a challenge to yourself — something you viewed as a test of your maturity or your courage, or your ability to keep up with the other kids in your crowd. Perhaps you've already decided to wait until you're married or older. Whatever your reasoning in response to this question has been before, it may be enlightening to learn a little more about sexual intercourse before making up your mind.

First, let's consider a few mechanical aspects. Sexual intercourse involves inserting the penis in the vagina and moving it back and forth to produce pleasurable sensations for both partners. Usually, the penis needs to be erect (hard) for insertion to be possible. A variety of positions can be used for having intercourse, including some that involve sitting or standing, but the most common positions are lying down, with either the male or female on top, and both partners facing each other. Intercourse can last anywhere from a few seconds to an hour or more, but most often it lasts for just a few minutes.

If a girl has not had intercourse before, she may have a thin tissue membrane called the hymen partially covering the opening to her vagina. (Often, though, the hymen has been broken or stretched at an early age by exercise or by inserting a finger or tampon in the vagina.) Contrary to what many people think, even if the hymen is still intact, the first intercourse experience is not likely to be painful or marked by a great deal of bleeding. In fact, the excitement of the experience is frequently so great that little if any discomfort is felt.

> The first time I had intercourse, I was expecting the worst. In my mind, I thought it was going to be this big, painful ordeal — and that I'd just have to grit my teeth and get it over with. It wasn't like that at all. In fact, I can truthfully say I really enjoyed it and didn't feel anything more than a momentary sense of pressure.
>
> *A sixteen-year-old girl*

> The first time was a real surprise to me. I was expecting it to be terrible, but it wasn't like that at all. In fact, it was kind of nice.
>
> *An eighteen-year-old girl*

On the other hand, there are also people who feel that their first experience with intercourse was a letdown. One seventeen-year-old girl told us, "I felt like, that's it? That's what everyone's saying is so terrific? I couldn't understand what all the fuss was over — the whole experience was about as exciting as having someone stick his thumb in your mouth and poke it around."

One of the questions we've been asked most often by sexually inexperienced teenagers is "How do you learn how to have intercourse?" Everybody learns a little differently, as these answers from teens suggest:

> My girlfriend and I just learned from each other.
>
> *A seventeen-year-old boy*

My partner was older and more experienced than I was, so he sort of did all the work.

A sixteen-year-old girl

I tried to read a lot about it, which really didn't help. Then one day I was into this heavy makeout session with a girl that I liked a lot and she asked me to make love to her. I told her I really didn't know what to do, so she showed me.

An eighteen-year-old boy

I just sort of followed my instincts and did what came naturally. It was no big thing.

A seventeen-year-old girl

Sometimes, to be certain, an inexperienced couple may have to try to have intercourse several times before they get it to work, as this eighteen-year-old boy's recollection suggests.

"When my girlfriend and I were both seventeen, we decided that we wanted to make love, so we went to a motel one Saturday night. We were both so nervous that we giggled at everything we did and couldn't get aroused at all. We wound up mad at each other until we realized that it was our tension that was causing the trouble. In a sense, it may have been that we were too *deliberate* about the whole thing — planning it so carefully and all — because the next weekend, after a few more planned attempts had failed — when we weren't really trying to do it, we found that it all fell into place."

The first experience of intercourse can be a very positive one, with a sense of intimacy, happiness, and satisfaction, or it can be a source of worry, disappointment, and guilt. Many people regret having had their first intercourse with a partner they didn't really care for. Others feel used. Others are elated at having proven to themselves that they're really grown up, or at having been successful at such a mysterious undertaking. Still others are simply relieved that they've gotten it over with and aren't virgins any longer.

Unfortunately, while some sexually experienced teenagers are pleased with their responses, our research shows that about one-third of this group are disappointed and dissatisfied — making up a group that we call "unhappy nonvirgins." Typical complaints include one or more of the following items: (1) sex hasn't measured up to their expectations; (2) sexual problems prevent them from enjoying themselves and sometimes cause them severe anxieties; (3) sex becomes a sore spot in their relationship ("You're not really interested in *me*, you're just interested in my body"); (4) pregnancy scares (or an actual pregnancy) or worries about sexually transmitted disease override any pleasure that comes from sex; and (5) they find that they feel too guilty about their sexual activity. Because of these and similar reactions, it's important to realize that sex isn't always the perfect thing you may *think* it's going to be before you've tried it. So you need to ask yourself, "Am I prepared to cope with problems or disappointments if they occur?" If not, you're probably not ready to have sexual intercourse just yet.

Everything You Ever Wanted to Know about Birth Control (but Might Have Been Afraid to Ask)

If you're going to be responsible about your sex life, you've got to begin by being prepared for avoiding unintended pregnancy. The only way you can accomplish this is if you know the pertiment facts about birth control. (If you've already decided that you'll cope with this problem by not having sexual intercourse, that's fine, but it's still advisable to read a little farther because: [a] it never hurts to be informed, and [b] there's no telling when you might change your mind. Changing your mind is nothing to be ashamed of, but having sexual intercourse without using any birth control is really playing with fire — and *you're* the one who may get burned.)

What is there to choose from if you're sexually active? Adolescent males really only have one choice available to them — the condom (sometimes called a rubber, safe, or prophylactic). Condoms are thin sheaths of latex rubber that come rolled up in plastic or foil packages. In order to be effective, the condom must be unrolled onto the erect penis *before* intercourse begins. It works by preventing sperm from entering the vagina, and if it is used properly and consistently, it is very effective in preventing pregnancy from occurring. In fact, if condoms are used in combination with another birth control method, such as foam or a diaphragm, the combined method is as effective as the pill.

Condoms are convenient — they can be bought without a prescription and are easily carried about without being noticed. Condoms are safe since they have no negative health effects at all. They are easily accessible at drugstores, at family planning clinics, and in some areas, from coin-operated vending machines in men's rooms of gas stations or bars. Condoms are also especially helpful because they provide considerable protection against many sexually transmitted infections. Furthermore, by using the condom, a male shows his partner that he is willing to take some responsibility for their sexual activity — which is not a matter to be disregarded. There are a few drawbacks to condoms, though. For one thing, some males complain that the condom causes decreased sensitivity during sex. Sometimes, too, using an unlubricated condom may be uncomfortable for the female. In addition, even though condoms are tested rigorously during the manufacturing process to detect leaks, if a condom gets torn (by a fingernail, for example) it loses its effectiveness.

Many teenagers have heard a lot of jokes about condoms and are worried that using this birth control method might make them seem "old-fashioned" or "out of it." Nothing could be further from the truth. Pretending you're too sophisticated to use a condom is really giving away your *lack* of sophistication about sex . . . and nothing can drive this point home more dramatically than an undesired pregnancy. In fact, condoms now come in a wide variety of designer colors and shapes, including some with ribbed surfaces to provide additional sexual stimulation during intercourse. And lubricated condoms may actually make intercourse more comfortable for some couples when vaginal dryness is a problem.

The birth control choices for adolescent females may seem a bit bewildering at first, but it really boils down to a question of "the pill or not the pill." Before discussing these options, we'd like to offer a few comments on birth control methods we think teenagers should *avoid*. Most doctors agree that IUDs (intrauterine devices: small plastic objects that are inserted inside the uterus and then worn continuously) should not be used by teenagers except in the rarest circumstances because they have been linked to serious health problems, physical discomfort, and subsequent fertility difficulties. Rhythm methods (which involve having to determine which are your fertile days by various techniques, such as measuring your morning temperature) are simply too unreliable, with failure rates from 20 to 40 percent. The same can be said for withdrawal (having intercourse without using any contraceptive device, but having the male withdraw the penis from the vagina before he ejaculates), which is apt to be frustrating to both partners, as well as chancy, since it has a failure rate of about 25 percent.

In contrast, the pill is a spectacularly effective birth control method. Not only does it have an effectiveness rate of about 99 percent in females who use it consistently, but also the much publicized side effects of the pill that create health problems for some women who use it are practically nonexistent in teenagers. In fact, compared to the health risks of pregnancy for a teenager, the pill is a real winner, with about the only problems being minor ones such as skin rashes, mild nausea, breast tenderness, or slight weight gain. (However, because the long-term effects of birth control pills have not been fully studied, it is advisable to stop taking them temporarily after having used them for three years or so, waiting for several normal menstrual cycles to occur before restarting the pill.)

Birth control pills require a prescription and a good memory. They have to be taken every day for three weeks beginning on the fourth day after menstruation begins. If one pill is missed, *two* pills should be taken the next day. If more than one pill is missed, it's quite possible that the birth control effectiveness will be reduced for that month's cycle, so an alternate form of contraception must be used. Many people who use the pill find that it's easiest to take them at the same time each day — for instance, when they brush their teeth before going to bed at night — in order to develop a routine that guards against forgetfulness. It's not necessary to go into a panic if you're an hour late in taking the pill, though, since timing it down to the minute isn't necessary at all.

Here are several comments we've heard from teenage girls who've used the pill:

— I was surprised to find that I really didn't feel any different once I started taking the pill. At least, not *physically.* I guess you'd have to say that I felt a lot more secure, a lot more protected, not having to worry about getting pregnant.

— Once I'd been using the pill for a couple of months, I noticed some definite benefits. First, the cramps I usually got right before my periods disappeared completely. My pimples cleared up, too. And, best of all, I felt more relaxed and spontaneous about sex — it wasn't like gambling every time my boyfriend and I made love. I think this definitely contributed to more sexual pleasure.

— I wasn't having any problems with the pill when I was sixteen, but I heard a scary TV report saying that there were a lot of health problems with it, so I decided to stop. Well, I guess I shouldn't have done that, because I accidentally got pregnant soon after — and *then* I found out the health risks they were talking about applied to women over thirty-five, not to teens!

Nevertheless, the pill is not for everyone. For instance, it's not particularly well suited to someone who is sexually active only once in a while. And some teenagers with health problems (such as diabetes or high blood pressure) are best advised to choose a different birth control method, because the pill can sometimes cause these problems to worsen. In addition, because getting the pill requires a medical prescription — which may be either too expensive or too embarrassing for some teenagers — it is useful to take a look at other contraceptive options that are available.

The diaphragm (DYE-uh-fram) is a dome-shaped cap

made of thin, soft rubber stretched over a flexible rim. It is *always* used in combination with a contraceptive cream or jelly, which must be put inside the rim of the diaphragm just before its use. The diaphragm must then be placed inside the vagina, positioned so that it blocks the mouth of the cervix (the entrance to the uterus, or womb) *before* sexual intercourse occurs. It should be removed six to ten hours after intercourse; if it is removed sooner, it is possible that live sperm in the vagina may reach the cervix and swim up into the uterus.

Because diaphragms come in different sizes, it is necessary to be fitted for one in a simple, painless examination done by a doctor or nurse. After the fitting is completed (in a minute or so), the girl is shown how to insert the diaphragm and how to check the position of the rim to see that it's in the proper place.

The effectiveness of the diaphragm is not as high as that of the pill, although it is still a useful method of birth control. (As previously mentioned, using the diaphragm in combination with a condom results in a degree of effectiveness quite similar to that of the pill.) This is partly because the protection provided by this birth control method depends on the regularity of its use. If someone leaves her diaphragm at home and unexpectedly finds herself in a sexual situation, she runs the risk of getting pregnant no matter how diligently she's used her diaphragm in the past — unless she has an alternate method of birth control available or abstains from having intercourse. Since many people seem to think, "Just this once won't make a difference," it's not so surprising that this situation can lead to a very unhappy ending.

The drawbacks of the diaphragm are (1) insertion can be difficult for some females; (2) stopping the action to put it in place can break the mood of a passionate moment; and (3) the cream or jelly used with the diaphragm causes irritation in about 5 percent of users.

Another approach to birth control involves the use of spermicides, or vaginal chemical contraceptives. These products — which include foams, jellies, creams, and tablets or suppositories — contain an ingredient that kills sperm. Although all of these products must be put inside the vagina *be-*

fore having intercourse, the exact instructions for insertion and the timing of use vary from brand to brand. For this reason, you must be certain to read the instructions for each product carefully and follow them exactly. The effectiveness for spermicides is good (like the condom or diaphragm) but not spectacular (like the pill). Failures can occur if the product is improperly inserted, if the time limits of product effectiveness are not followed closely, or if the product has become outdated. (You can check the last point by looking at the expiration date stamped on the outside of the spermicide package before you use it.) One little-noted benefit of spermicides is that they seem to provide some protection to females against certain sexually transmitted diseases such as gonorrhea. In addition, you can get spermicides in drugstores without a prescription and you will probably be pleased to find that they are reasonably inexpensive. One word of warning, though — don't confuse so-called feminine hygiene products with spermicides. Even though they may be displayed side-by-side on the same shelf with spermicides in a drugstore, feminine hygiene products have no birth control usefulness at all. The primary drawback of using spermicides is that they are often a bit messy. In addition, as previously mentioned, they cause vaginal burning or itching in a small percentage of users.

A variation on the spermicide theme is the newest entry in birth control methods to reach the market, the so-called contraceptive sponge. Sold under the trade name "Today," this one-inch-by-two-inch round spongy product is soaked with a chemical that kills sperm and also blocks sperm from entering the cervix. This disposable-after-one-use product is inserted into the vagina before intercourse after dampening it with about two tablespoons of water and squeezing it gently to activate the spermicide in the sponge. Many users say that it is easier to insert than a diaphragm, making it particularly suitable for a relatively inexperienced teenager who may be somewhat unsure of how to position a diaphragm. Furthermore, since the sponge doesn't require a prescription, it doesn't take a trip to the doctor's to get started in its use. Finally, the sponge is consistently rated as convenient because (1) users don't feel its presence; (2) it can be inserted hours before sexual activity or at the last minute; and (3) once it's inserted, it provides contraceptive protection for a full twenty-four hours — no matter how many times a user has sex. At present, it appears that the sponge is pretty much like condoms, diaphragms, or other spermicides in its birth control effectiveness.

Two other options will be mentioned briefly here, although they should not be regarded as primary forms of preventing unwanted pregnancies. The first is the so-called "morning-after" pill, which consists of high doses of female sex hormones (estrogens) taken *after* unprotected intercourse in order to stop pregnancy from occurring. While the effectiveness of this method is high in terms of achieving the desired result (working in more than 96 percent of cases if it's timed right), use of the morning-after pill is often accompanied by undesirable side effects such as nausea, vomiting, and breast tenderness. The method works best when it is used as soon after unprotected intercourse as possible (preferably, within the first twenty-four hours); after three days have gone by, it is far less likely to be successful. This birth control method can only be prescribed by a doctor. *However, only you can alert a doctor to the fact that you've had unprotected intercourse — no matter what the circumstances or reason — so you need to act fast to obtain this type of help.* (You cannot wait for a pregnancy test to let you know if you're pregnant — by the time a pregnancy test turns positive, it's too late for the morning-after pill.)

Another alternative is abortion. Obtaining an abortion — a topic discussed in detail in Chapter 13 — is far simpler today than it was in the past. However, deciding if you want an abortion once you're pregnant is much more complicated and emotionally nerve-racking than it may seem on the surface. And abortions, although safer than pregnancies for young people, are not without their physical risks. For these reasons, we again repeat that *no one should rely on abortion as her primary means of avoiding pregnancy* — instead, we urge everyone to make informed, deliberate choices of responsible ways of handling their sex lives so as to avoid unwanted pregnancies before they start.

What You Should Know about STDs

Most people prefer to avoid thinking about unpleasant subjects. You may be tempted to skip this section as soon as you discover it's about infections that are spread by sexual contact. But if you're smart, you'll read on — *carefully* — because learning about STDs (sexually transmitted diseases) is an important part of being knowledgeable about sex and being able to prevent such infections, or knowing what to do if you think you might have been exposed. One reason this is particularly important for adolescents is that many of the STDs have been spreading like wildfire in the teenage age group in the 1980s — in part, because of ignorance about their warning signs and how they can be transmitted.

Let's start by recognizing that there are many myths about STDs that you may have heard. Here are a few examples, along with the facts you need to correct the misinformation conveyed by each myth:

Myth 1: *It's easy to catch a sexual infection from a toilet seat or a drinking fountain.*

Fact: *STDs almost always are a result of intimate physical contact.* While it is theoretically possible to catch such an infection from a toilet seat or water fountain, the odds against this happening are much higher than the odds of your winning $10,000,000 in a lottery.

Myth 2: *You can't catch an STD from someone if you don't have intercourse with that person.*

Fact: *STDs are spread by a variety of forms of sexual contact, not just intercourse.* Oral sex, touching your partner's sex organs, and even kissing can be the source of a sexually transmitted disease. Being a virgin *doesn't* mean you're immune from this risk.

Myth 3: *Nice, clean-cut kids from good families don't get STDs — they only occur in people who don't wash properly or who are very poor.*

Fact: *You can't tell by someone's grooming and appearance, or even by the person's pedigree, whether someone has an STD or not.* Contrary to the popular misconception, persons with an STD won't be drooling saliva down their chin or have scabs all over their body. Since rich and poor alike are affected (should we say, *infected?*), you can catch an STD from someone who drives a Porsche just as easily as from someone who drives a beat-up Chevy. While appearance isn't foolproof, there are some telltale physical signs you can be alert for in intimate situations — such as blisters or sores on or near the sex organs, or a puslike discharge from the penis or vagina. These should flash an immediate warning to stop what you're doing *right away* and have your partner seek medical attention. Remember, however, that the absence of visible abnormalities doesn't always mean that no STD is present. One more thing to keep in mind — even *nice* kids can have STDs.

Myth 4: *If the symptoms of an STD disappear by themselves, no treatment is needed.*

Fact: *Wrong, wrong, WRONG.* If the symptoms of an STD disappear, the STD is *not* over — instead, it's probably moved deeper into the body, where its impact on a person's health may be even more serious. Getting appropriate medical testing and treatment is particularly important in this circumstance — especially since a person can still spread the infection to his or her sex partners while they may mistakenly think things are all right.

Myth 5: *Once you've had an STD, you can't get it again.*

Fact: *STDs aren't like measles — you can get reinfected.* In fact, if the person you caught the infection from hasn't been treated properly and cured, you may even catch it twice from the same person.

Now, having set the record straight on these myths, it's time to discuss the more common STDs and their symptoms.

Gonorrhea is a type of STD that's been around for more than forty centuries but has become more widespread in recent years. There are about two million new cases each year in the U.S., with approximately one-quarter of these occurring in teenagers. Gonorrhea is relatively easy to detect in males, since it usually causes a puslike discharge from the tip of the penis along with painful, frequent urination within a week of becoming infected. The majority of females with gonorrhea don't have *any* symptoms, however, and when symptoms occur (such as vaginal discharge, burning or pain with urination, or abnormal menstruation) they are often so mild as to be overlooked. This is particularly troublesome because untreated gonorrhea in females can cause serious complications, including permanent sterility (being unable to become pregnant). In addition, females who have gonorrhea but don't realize it may unwittingly transmit their infection to their sex partners, which can cause more than a little embarrassment and hard feelings between lovers. Fortunately, gonorrhea is easily tested for in either males or females by taking a culture (a simple, painless procedure done by a doctor or nurse using a cotton swab) and then trying to grow the gonorrhea bacteria in a laboratory. Treatment is a large dose of Penicillin G, which is almost 100 percent effective.

Syphilis, which affects males more than females, is fortunately relatively uncommon today, accounting for only about 80,000 cases a year in the U.S. The earliest sign of syphilis is a painless sore (called a chancre) that typically occurs on or near the sex organs but can sometimes occur in other areas such as on a finger, on the lips, or in the mouth. (This doesn't mean that you need to panic every time a sore appears on your body, though.) The chancre usually begins as a reddish pimple that ulcerates and forms a round sore surrounded by a pink rim. Untreated, the sore heals in about four to six weeks, giving the false impression that the problem has gone away. Instead, what happens next is that the infection passes into a stage called secondary syphilis, which can start up to six months after the chancre heals. Common symptoms in this stage include a pale red rash on the palms and soles, sore throat, fever, and aching joints. If the disease is still untreated, a quiet (latent) stage occurs where the infection invades tissues such as the spinal cord and brain; in the most devastating stage of late syphilis, serious heart problems, eye problems, and even brain damage can occur. Syphilis is usually diagnosed by blood tests (although it can also be detected by examining fluid from a chancre under a special kind of microscope) and is effectively treated with penicillin.

Genital herpes is an STD that has attracted a great deal of attention in recent years both because it is very common (more than half a million new cases each year) and because it is incurable. It is caused by the herpes simplex virus and it usually shows up as clusters of small painful blisters on the sex organs. The first episode, which is usually the most severe, is typically accompanied by fever, headache, painful urination, and tenderness in the groin. The blisters burst within four to six days and form reddish wet sores or ulcers, which heal within another week or so. However, when healing occurs, the herpes virus actually burrows into nerves near the base of the spinal cord, where it remains in an inactive state. Repeat attacks of genital herpes occur — sometimes only once or twice, but sometimes dozens of times — and are annoying not only because of physical discomforts but because during these attacks the infection is contagious: that is, it can be passed to a sex partner. Genital herpes is particularly problematic for females for two reasons. First, it can be transmitted to a newborn baby at birth, causing death or serious damage to the baby's brain in many cases. Second, in some women genital herpes seems to be linked to the later development of cancer of the cervix (the lower part of the womb). Although genital herpes can be detected by blood tests or by cultures, there is no known cure at present. A drug called acyclovir has been found useful in lessening the pain and duration of early genital herpes attacks, however, and in some cases appears, at least partially, to prevent frequent recurrences.

Recently, another type of STD that is very similar to gonorrhea but caused by a bacterium called *chlamydia*, has been found to be increasing at an alarming rate. Especially widespread among sexually active teenagers, where it is estimated to involve 10 percent of males and 20 percent of females, chlamydia infections are troublesome because the symptons are often mild, so the disease may be overlooked. Since this STD can cause fertility problems and eye infections, and can be transmitted to infants at the time of delivery, it is attracting considerable attention. Fortunately, when detected (by a culture test) it is easily treated by antibiotics such as tetracycline. About 30 percent of people who have gonorrhea also have a chlamydia infection at the same time.

Pubic lice, or "crabs," are tiny parasites that attach themselves to pubic hair and cause intense itching. Although "crabs" are usually transmitted by sexual contact, you can also catch them from sheets, towels, or clothing used by a person who is already suffering from this infestation. "Crabs" are more of an embarrassing annoyance than a health problem, and can usually be taken care of by using a cream, lotion, or shampoo sold under the trade name Kwell. Simple soap and water will not get rid of this problem.

There are a number of other STDs that sexually active teenagers risk catching. *Genital warts* — dry, usually painless grayish-white warts with a cauliflower-like rough surface — were once thought to be relatively harmless, but are now known to be both infectious and possible forerunners of certain types of cancer. *Infections of the vagina* (which often produce a frothy discharge, an unpleasant odor, and itching) are commonly, but not exclusively, transmitted by sexual activity. *Hepatitis B*, an infection of the liver, is another example of a disease that can be sexually transmitted or can be due to other causes. *AIDS* (acquired immune deficiency syndrome), which is a condition in which the body's ability to fight off certain rare types of cancer and infections is impaired, is found predominantly among male homosexuals, but can also be transmitted by intimate heterosexual contact. AIDS is particularly frightening because there is no cure for it at present and it seems to be almost invariably fatal.

Fortunately, some very practical guidelines are available to help you minimize the chance of catching an STD or spreading it if you've already caught it. *Read these guidelines carefully* — they may come in handy sometime.

1. *Be informed.* Knowing about the symptoms of STDs can help protect you against exposing yourself to the risk of infection from a partner and help you know when to seek treatment.

2. *Be observant.* Knowledge alone isn't enough. Believe it or not, looking is the best way of discovering if you or your partner has a genital discharge, sore, rash, blister, or other sign of sexual infection. (Needless to say, this can't be done in the dark, no matter how romantic you think darkness may be.) If you see a suspicious sore or blister, don't be a hero about it and don't try to give your partner the benefit of the doubt — pull away from any and all sexual contact (*even kissing*) and insist that your partner be examined. While "looking" may

seem cold and crass to you, remember that you don't have to announce why you're looking or use a magnifying glass to get a proper view. In fact, a good, close look can often be obtained in the preliminaries (getting undressed, giving your partner a massage).

3. *Be selective.* Putting it simply, having many different sex partners increases the risks of STD. Having sex with someone you don't know is also risky — you don't know if you can trust your partner or who he or she has been with in the recent past.

4. *Be cautious.* Use of a condom will definitely lower the chances of getting an STD. Using foam or jelly will also reduce the female's risk of getting gonorrhea. Urinating soon after sexual intercourse helps flush invading organisms out of the system and may help reduce the risk of STD slightly. However, it's important to realize that none of the above steps are foolproof, so if you think you've been exposed, promptly contact a doctor for advice.

5. *Be honest.* If you have (or think you *may* have) an STD, tell your partner. This can avoid spreading the infection and will alert your partner to watch for his or her own symptoms, or to be examined or tested. Likewise, if you're worried about your partner's condition, don't hesitate to ask. It's foolish to put your health at risk just to protect someone else's feelings, and if you can't be honest with each other, you probably don't have a great relationship anyway.

6. *Be promptly tested and treated.* Quick diagnosis and treatment reduces the risks of complications of an STD. However, don't assume that one treatment will always work perfectly — sometimes it doesn't, and additional medicine is required.

What You Should Know about Homosexuality

Being sexually attracted or turned on by people of the opposite sex is called heterosexuality. Being sexually attracted or turned on by people of your same sex is called homosexuality. In everyday language, heterosexuals (males attracted to females, females attracted to males) are sometimes called "straight," while homosexuals (males attracted to males, females attracted to females) are often called "gay." People who are sexually attracted to either males or females are sometimes called "bi," which is an abbreviation of the term *bisexual*. Since few topics are as poorly understood as the nature of homosexuality, we will spend a little time here clarifying matters for you.

To begin with, there are many misconceptions about homosexuality that most of us have heard at one time or another. One example of this is the notion that most homosexual men like to wear makeup and dress in women's clothing. Actually, very few homosexuals act this way — such cross-dressing is, in fact, more common among heterosexuals than among homosexuals. Another misconception some people have about homosexuality is that you can catch it from someone else, sort of like chicken pox. Again, this idea is completely nonsensical, with no basis in fact at all. Still another wrong impression is that homosexuals hang around schoolyards looking for young children to lure into sex. In fact, most child molesters are heterosexual, yet homosexuals have been unfairly thrust into the "bad guy" role because of past prejudice and misunderstandings.

Most people have had the experience, at one time or another, of feeling strongly attracted to a person of their same sex — a friend, a teacher, a coach — and wondering whether this means that they're homosexual. This confusion may be compounded by the fact that there's no easy way of describing exactly what they feel for this person, or even by the fact that they have dreams about this person — dreams that may take on sexual overtones, and thus may cause more than a little guilt or embarrassment. If this has ever happened to you, relax — it's a perfectly natural experience, and by itself it doesn't mean that you're homosexual at all.

Why do concerns about homosexuality provoke such strong reactions in us? In part, it's because homosexuals are very much in the minority in our society. (Current estimates suggest that 10 percent of males and 3 percent of females are homosexual.) Another reason is that most people are afraid that homosexuals are psychologically abnormal, although research studies in the last twenty years have proven that this is *not* the case. But because it used to be believed that homosexuality was a form of mental illness, and because many people still consider homosexuality a form of sinfulness, it is not difficult to understand why it is still misunderstood. In fact, one sign that many people are actually frightened of it is the continued use of derogatory terms like *queer, fag, fairy, homo,* and *lez* to label homosexuals negatively.

Although a minority of adults are homosexual, substantial numbers of children and adolescents have at least some exploratory sexual experiences with a person of their same sex. While these may be either childhood "games" like the "let-me-look-at-yours-and-you-can-look-at-mine" variety or more "serious" (that is, less gamelike) experimenting with masturbation in late childhood or early adolescence, both of these forms of same-sex activity are harmless, ordinary phases of growing up that do not automatically direct a person into a homosexual life. In fact, the great majority of people who have had such experiences go on to become full-blooded heterosexuals who marry and have children, even though many of them may have wondered when they were in their teens if they were really homosexual or if something was "wrong" with them.

Why, then, do some people become homosexual while others move into a heterosexual life? The most truthful answer is to say that scientists don't really know. But this doesn't just mean that no one knows what "causes" homosexuality — no one knows what "causes" heterosexuality either. Despite dozens of theories over the years, no simple solution seems to apply. However, what *does* seem clear is that (1) homosexuality isn't inherited, (2) homosexuals haven't just "chosen" to be that way, and (3) homosexuals are not all alike any more than all heterosexuals are alike.

Some homosexuals say that they discovered that they were gay in childhood, sometimes as early as age five or six, while others didn't recognize this aspect of their personalities until adulthood. The most common pattern for gay males, however, is to come gradually during the teenage years to awareness of having a same-sex preference. This awareness is *not* just a matter of "I feel real nervous around girls" or of having those "socially awkward blues." Instead, it is apt to be a deeper-seated sense of being different and of being attracted to male bodies and images as physically, sensually desirable. (This isn't the same as saying, "I like the way a male's torso looks when it's well developed," because lots of heterosexual males have this same reaction.)

In just the same way, teenagers who don't enjoy dating by the age of sixteen or who haven't fallen in love by seventeen are not necessarily destined for a life of homosexuality. It could very well be that they haven't found a heterosexual partner who appeals to them as yet, or it might also be that they are preoccupied with other interests or activities. This is quite natural — after all, all teenagers don't mature physically at exactly the same time, and they don't all mature in the romantic side of their lives at the same time either. This is that wonderful part of life known as individuality — it's not something to be ashamed of or worried about.

Nevertheless, many adolescents do worry about whether or not they're gay and feel like they don't have anywhere to turn to discuss this sense of confusion. This is because (1) everyone seems to expect them to fit automatically into the world as a heterosexual, (2) there isn't *really* anyone they'd feel comfortable talking to about this, and (3), it's such an embarrassing, worrisome topic. This sense of isolation and inability to get answers to very personal concerns is apt to heighten the anxiety that a teenager feels in this situation.

While we want readers to understand clearly that having had some sexual contact with a person of your same sex doesn't automatically mean you're homosexual, we also want to say very plainly that there's nothing *wrong* with being homosexual, either. Homosexuals are not all swishy, effeminate male hairdressers or interior decorators as you typically see them portrayed on TV or in the movies. They include truck drivers, doctors, lawyers, professional football players — in fact, people in all walks of life. Likewise, female homosexuals (sometimes called lesbians) are not typically masculine in appearance or interests. In fact, they may have fashion model looks, or just plain features, and range in occupation and interests from waitresses to secretaries to airline pilots. For these reasons, you should see right away that you can't judge whether or not you're homosexual by how you look or how you walk or how you talk. Similarly, you can't really judge whether you're homosexual or not on the basis of your worries about relations with the opposite sex, as this comment from a nineteen-year-old boy shows.

> When I was fifteen or sixteen, I was always in terror of girls. My palms broke out in a cold sweat if I even talked to a girl over the phone, and the few times I went out on dates I was in a virtual state of panic. As a result, I guess, I started to think that I might be a homosexual, and the more I looked at myself in the mirror and the more I inspected my mannerisms, the more I convinced myself this must be the case. In fact, all through my high school experience I thought I was pretty much destined to a homosexual life. Then I got to college and met a girl I really liked. She was as shy as I was, I guess, but I soon realized that being shy is *not* the same as being gay.

In other instances, of course, some teenagers become firmly convinced that they really *are* homosexual and are comfortable in accepting this sense of themselves. Even though they may confirm their discovery by positive responses to sexual experiences with partners of the same sex and by feeling closer and more comfortable with homosexual friends than with heterosexual ones, they may be very reluctant to tell anyone else about this. This may force them to lead a make-believe existence, pretending to be heterosexual — interested in heterosexual relationships, planning on eventually getting married — while they really feel, deep inside, that they're something else entirely. Some homosexuals spend much of their lives hiding their inner sense of themselves from others, which is called "being in the closet." Increasingly, though, today's improved climate of acceptance of homosexuality is encouraging many younger homosexuals to "come out of the closet" — that is, to reveal their homosexuality to others.

Coming out is sometimes a long-drawn-out process of self-disclosure that starts slowly and tentatively with telling your best friend (and waiting to see the reaction that provokes) before telling other close friends and finally family members and other acquaintances. Other people have found that coming out can be easiest if it's done quickly, even though a lot of thinking and planning may have gone into the decision about where, when, and how to tell parents and friends. There is no single approach that's best for everyone. We suggest, however, that if you have good, open communications with your parents (if your parents are reasonably tolerant and open-minded) talk over your feelings with them sooner rather than later. In contrast, if you have trouble talking to your parents or have reasons to believe that they are strongly opposed to homosexuality, it might be best to wait until you've moved away from home before coming out to your family. Even with these guidelines in mind, you can't really predict how parents and other family members will react, as these comments from homosexual men and women in their early twenties show.

> My father is a minister, and I was sure that he would be so embarrassed and upset on learning of my being gay that he would cut off my college money and never want to see me again. As a result, I didn't come out to my parents until this year, after I'd graduated from college and got a job. I was totally surprised by how accepting and supportive my parents both were when they learned the news. Now I wish I'd been open with them earlier, because it would've made my life a lot less complicated.
>
> *A twenty-two-year-old male*

> I was constantly worried about being "found out," so I finally decided — around the age of eighteen — that I had to let my parents in on my secret. What a mistake that proved to be! They've spent the last four years trying to send me to doctors for a "cure" and trying to bribe me into dating girls. They simply can't understand who I am and how I feel — or they don't want to.
>
> *A twenty-three-year-old male*

> Having come out to my parents at nineteen, I can't offer any good advice on the subject. They still feel, deep down inside, that their daughter has somehow gone wrong, but they've been trying to accept the situation as best they can. They let me bring my girlfriend home to visit, but there's so much tension on those occasions that we've decided to give up on that activity.
>
> *A twenty-two-year-old female*

Given the mixed experiences that homosexuals have about the coming out process, and recognizing that in many instances announcing to the world that you're homosexual may cause you to be discriminated against in matters such as jobs or housing, it's important to not make any impulsive decisions about coming out to others but to think things through carefully.

One final word about homosexuality. Not everyone who is homosexual accepts these feelings or is happy about this aspect of their lives. If this type of dissatisfaction affects you or someone you know, you should realize that help is available. There are psychologists and sex therapists who specialize in working with homosexual people who want to develop heterosexual interests and downplay or eliminate their homosexual feelings. And there are also therapists who specialize in helping homosexuals develop more acceptance for their own situation.

Talking with Your Parents about Sex

My mom makes it sound like the world is composed of rapists, perverts, and "nice" guys — those are the ones who don't want more than a kiss before getting married. She's living in another age. I can't talk to her about sex at all.

A fourteen-year-old girl

It really surprised me when I discovered that I could talk with my mother about sex. I mean, I didn't think she'd be too open-minded on this topic and I didn't want to be lectured to. Well, I wasn't. Our conversations about sex have been useful and informative.

A sixteen-year-old girl

I've never been too comfortable talking with my parents about sex because it's so obvious *they're* not comfortable. But since they're so uptight, how do I find out what I want to know? It's not in *Playboy*, you know.

A fifteen-year-old boy

As these remarks show, it isn't always easy to talk with your parents on a topic as potentially loaded as sex. This can be true even if you generally communicate well with your parents, and if lines of communication between you are already strained, talking about sex may seem like an impossibility. After all, *both* of you may be embarrassed or uncomfortable on this topic. You may be worried that anything you ask about will lead your parents to jump to unwarranted conclusions — "How can you even *consider* such a thing, Susan; you know that you'll get a reputation as a tramp!" You may even be fairly certain your parents won't have an answer to your questions. Despite these hesitations, many teenagers tell us they wish they *could* communicate with their parents about sex. If this applies to you, the following pointers may be of some help.

1. *Approach the subject gently.* Most of the time, it's not going to be helpful to plow right in to this subject. Instead of asking, "Mom, do you think masturbation is bad for you?" you might start by first finding out if your parents have a few minutes for discussion. Then tell them you want to talk about a sexual topic — this way you won't catch them completely off guard, as this announcement of the topic gives them a chance to gather their wits about them. (If they suddenly remember that they've got an errand to run, don't be too worried; it's simply a way for them to save face while they figure out what to say. But make sure they do talk about it later.)

2. *Be up-front in stating that you don't want to hear a lecture.* Some parents get more than a little flustered when their kids ask them about sex. They may react defensively by pulling out one of their standard lectures ("The Dangers of Teenage Sex" is a favorite one that you may have heard before). If you can let your parents know that you'd like to have a *conversation* instead of sitting through a lecture, you may cut this one off at the pass. Remember, though, if you've previously had several useful conversations about sex with your parents and they haven't turned them into lectures, skip this item entirely — they've already got the point.

3. *Try not to hit your parents with a big, difficult question at the front end of your conversation.* Working into a meaningful dialogue can take some warm-up time. If you start your conversation with the Big Question, whatever that might be ("Is it

OK for a fifteen-year-old to use birth control pills?," for example), you're likely to provoke an overreaction from your parents instead of a reasoned, thoughtful response.

4. *Avoid using slang terms about sex when you're talking with your parents.* Otherwise, they may be so uncomfortable with the words you're using that they can't really deal with the contents of your questions or comments. (However, if your parents use slang in talking to you, you can probably do it too.)

5. *Show respect for their opinions, even if you disagree or think their ideas are old-fashioned.*

6. *If you can't find out what you want to know from your parents, find someone else you can talk to.* Depending on what you need to know about, your family doctor, or a trusted schoolteacher, or even another relative may be of some help. You're far less likely to gain accurate facts from friends — the odds are high that they don't know much more than you do.

Teenagers and Sex: A Concluding Note

The personal sexual decisions facing all teenagers today are far from easy. And there's unquestionably a lot of pressure to become sexually experienced so you can feel mature, accomplished, and "in the know." But at the same time, it's important to recognize that it's perfectly all right to say "no" — and sometimes saying "no" can be the most mature, intelligent decision a teenager can make.

> I was going with a boy I liked a great deal, but he kept pressuring me to have intercourse with him. I had decided in my own mind that if our relationship hinged on having sex or not, it wasn't exactly what I wanted. And I stuck to that decision. It's a good thing I did, actually, because when he started dating another girl in my class, he told all his friends as soon as they made it together.
>
> *A seventeen-year-old girl*

> This may sound a little unbelievable, but I turned down a chance to have sex with this girl I had been dating be-

cause I wasn't really prepared to make a *commitment* to her. I know my friends would probably laugh, but I feel better about sticking to my own values and doing what I think is right.

A sixteen-year-old boy

Some experts have suggested that sex may be the most intimate form of communication possible. If it becomes just another thing to do, like eating pizza or going to the movies, its meaning and its value will have been diminished.

9.

Drugs and Alcohol — What You Don't Know *Can* Hurt You

If a modern-day Rip Van Winkle awoke today after a forty-year nap, one of the most puzzling changes he'd see would be the widespread use of drugs by American teenagers and young adults. In fact, many researchers, educators, and government experts believe that the extent of drug use in our society has reached epidemic proportions — and that, like an epidemic, drug use takes a terrible toll on the health and well-being of those affected. Teenagers are squarely in the middle of this epidemic. Not only do larger numbers of teenagers today use drugs than in the past, today's adolescents begin using drugs at a younger age than ever before. Given this reality, it's no wonder that many teenagers say, "Since almost everyone is doing it, what really can be wrong?" "What can be so bad?"

If there was a guarantee that (1) drugs would give you a pleasurable experience, (2) drugs wouldn't cause any health problems, (3) drugs wouldn't interfere with your social, psychological, and academic growth, and (4) drugs wouldn't make you dependent or addicted, then it would be quite sensible to use them from time to time for their recreational value. Unfortunately, though, no such "ideal" drug exists — and no matter what your friends may tell you and what you might want to believe, there is simply no guarantee that if you use drugs for "only" recreational purposes (to "have fun" or to "relax") that nothing bad will happen.

176

A True Story

(Only the Names Have Been Changed to Protect the Innocent)

Danielle, who was fourteen, and her boyfriend Larry, who was fifteen, were on their way to see Sting perform in a concert they had been wanting to see for months. On their way to the stadium, an older kid was openly selling marihuana (he was saying, "Get your good grass here; wonderful weed for sale," sounding just like a hot-dog vendor at a baseball game). Larry and Danielle stopped and watched him make three or four fast sales. When Larry finally pulled out his wallet and bought four loose joints, which he gave Danielle to put in her purse, they were immediately collared by a plainclothes policeman. Not only were they brought to the police station — which made them miss their concert — they both wound up being convicted on drug possession charges, which became a permanent part of their police record.

What happened to Larry and Danielle is no rare occurrence. Like it or not, possession of illegal drugs is a criminal offense. Teenagers who are caught — and there are tens of thousands each year who fit in this category — become part of the criminal justice system, with their futures jeopardized because they have an arrest record. Some will be sent to jail — at times, for startlingly long sentences — and others will be sentenced to residential treatment programs. Later on, they will be excluded from many companies and jobs if they have a police record — even if it goes back to an impulsive act when they were younger. Ask yourself this question: Can a few minutes of chemical pleasure be worth the possible future consequences?

The matter of legality seems like a minor issue compared to the more disturbing aspects of drug use. If you like drugs, if you find they produce pleasant sensations or excitement in your life, if they make you feel important and "cool," isn't it likely that you'll want to use them over and over to enjoy these wonderful experiences? Logically, whatever positive effects a drug might have are likely to lead to frequent use, which typically creates a state of drug dependency (you feel that you need the drug and miss it if you don't have it) or, even worse, a state of addiction (your body is hooked on the drug and has withdrawal symptoms if you don't get it regularly). The trouble is that almost everyone is certain that *he or she* won't get hooked on drugs — "No sweat, man, I do coke when I want to fly, but *I'm* in control of it." Why, then, is Mercury Morris (a star running back with the Miami Dolphins of the NFL) serving a twenty-year prison term for crimes committed in order to feed his cocaine habit? Why did the movie star John Belushi overdose and die in 1984? Why do thousands of teenagers become addicted to heroin each year? *Not* because they were in control of the fun they were having with drugs, but because the dangerousness of what they were doing wasn't apparent to them until it was too late.

> The story I want to tell is really a short one, and I'm telling it so other kids will wake up to what's going on out there with drugs. I have a twin sister who's locked up in a psychiatric ward right now, where she's been for more than a year and a half, because we both thought it was so cool to do drugs with our friends. Without realizing what was happening to us, we got in heavier and heavier, and finally she just flipped out. Now she just sort of sits there and stares off into the distance. She won't talk and won't move anywhere — and my friends *still* use drugs because they think it can't happen to them. Wise up. Drugs are for fools.
>
> *A sixteen-year-old girl*

Assuming that you or your friends have been using drugs for a while and that you've been lucky enough to avoid any problems and have a good time, there is still no guarantee that sometime in the future you won't become caught in a "no win, no exit" labyrinth. There simply is no guarantee that anyone who uses drugs will escape all the consequences. This doesn't mean that if you smoke a single joint of marihuana once in your life, just to see what it's like, that you'll be scarred forever — but there are always risks associated with drug use that it pays to be aware of.

Fact: *Drugs can interact with your personality and/or your body's chemistry so as to produce permanent damage or death.*

Admittedly, neither happens frequently to occasional drug users (as opposed to addicts). But even if the statistical risk is one in a thousand and you become the one, your life literally can end before you've really had a chance to live. This is not as remote a risk as you would like it to be. You probably either know someone who has "lost it," "freaked out," or "blown it." Maybe a friend or an acquaintance has heard about one of these tragic tales. Alcoholics Anonymous estimates that there are more than 20,000,000 alcoholics in the United States and the government estimates that there are at least 2,000,000 drug-dependent persons in the population, too. Clearly, then, getting hooked on a drug that you *think* you can control is easier than you might imagine.

Would you ever use drugs to prove to your friends how mature you are? Do you think that if you turn drugs down, your friends will think you're afraid to try them? Do you worry that your friends will desert you if you refuse to join in their drug use? These are questions that only you can answer for yourself. But remember, it's best to think about these issues when you don't feel any pressure to use drugs. Trying to grapple with these questions at a party where everyone is smoking pot or snorting coke is a little like trying to decide if you want to have surgery while you're lying on the operating room table: not only is it a bad place to try to think clearly, you might make a decision you regret later on. And instead of trying to come up with your answer without any help from others, you might try discussing this topic with your closest friends and family if you value their opinions.

When you're grappling with the question of "Do I or do I not use drugs?" you might also ask yourself what is the most important goal of life? Those who believe that happiness alone is the answer simply live for the times when they can feel good, when they can escape from boredom, frustration, or pain. Many of these people see nothing wrong with popping pills, swallowing booze, sniffing some powder, or injecting something that produces an immediate sense of euphoria — even if it's short-lived. But is this really the answer to life? There is another consideration that we think is infinitely more important and gratifying — *self-respect*. What is self-respect? Simply stated, self-respect can be achieved only when a person acts responsibly and does what he or she thinks is right. Self-respect is elusive because it must be earned the hard way — it cannot be bought on a street corner for five bucks. Those who have self-respect know they can maintain it and make it grow based on their actions rather than by relying on artificial pharmacological means. Like designer clothes, drugs may be a badge or status symbol, but the act of taking a psychoactive substance really proves nothing other than that you merely want to conform and may be too weak to assert yourself and say "no." The really tough decision you face, the do-I-or-don't-I-use-drugs question, is ultimately a test of your self-respect.

What Do I Say if I'm Offered a J?

If you've decided you want to stay drug-free, or even if you're in the midst of thinking about this question, it can be quite helpful to learn some quick comebacks to help you deal with situations in which someone offers you drugs. If you're prepared ahead of time, it's less likely that you'll be embarrassed or caught unaware. You might want to consider some of the following possibilities:

— "No thanks, I don't need drugs to get high; I get high on living."
— "I had a bad reaction to that stuff last year, so I've sworn off it for now."
— "I have a rich uncle who's leaving me a million dollars in his will if I stay clear of drugs. You can understand *that*, can't you?"
— "Sorry, but I'm in training, and that stuff is no good for me."
— "I'm taking some prescription medication that wouldn't mix too well with that. Doctor's orders, you know."
— "I promised my girlfriend (boyfriend) that I'm going to stay straight."
— "I'm already flying — if I take anything else, I think I'll go into orbit."

— "Have you checked how pure that stuff is? I heard a lot of it's been contaminated with some heavy chemical junk."

— "Can't do that tonight because I'm having a urine test at the doctor's tomorrow."

— "I'm driving some friends (or my date) home, and I promised them I'd stay clean."

— "I've got a big swim meet (or other sports event) coming up this week and I don't want to mess with my bod."

— "Sorry, but it's against my religious beliefs."

— "No way. I just read a study that shows that stuff cuts down your sex drive."

— "Thanks, but I'm giving blood at the Red Cross tomorrow and they won't take me if I use that junk."

Maybe best of all, though, if you can be comfortable with it, is simply saying, "Thanks for the offer, but I don't use drugs."

Do I Help
the Ones I Love?

One of the toughest situations you may ever face is deciding what to do when a close friend or relative gets so involved with drugs that you sincerely are scared for their safety or survival. We're not talking about trying to push your own values onto someone else or trying to make a friend see eye-to-eye with you on the question of whether or not to smoke pot. The question is — if you have valid reasons to believe someone's life or health is in jeopardy — what can you do about it? Can you make a difference?

> My best friend got pretty heavily into doing drugs when we were fifteen years old, although I never really got hooked on them myself. Once he started on coke, he began to get sort of screwed up about his life, and he was stealing stuff to feed his nose. That was where I started to get pretty worried about him — but I never said anything, and now he's in the pen doing ten to twenty on a burglary

and drug possession rap. I guess if I'd tried to get him to stop it might have made a difference.

Barry T., age seventeen

I'm not too proud to admit it, but a couple of years ago I really got my head messed up with drugs. I was doing it *all* and never thought it would hurt me. I'd probably be either dead by now or pretty much of a zombie if my boyfriend hadn't pushed me into getting help to get the monkey off my back.

Sarah L., age eighteen

Not too long ago, my eighth grade sister was running around with a crowd of druggies and, like an idiot, she joined right in. I could see what it was doing to her, so I finally sat her down for a long talk. I told her that I loved her so much and was so worried about her that if she didn't quit on her own I'd tell our parents what she was doing. Fortunately, my approach worked and she stopped — which was a good thing, because one of her drugged-up friends was paralyzed for life when she tried to do a high dive into an empty pool just last month.

Archie T., age fifteen

What if you're confronted with the difficult question of how to deal with a friend or loved one who's heavily involved with drugs? First and foremost, you need to examine the facts and determine whether the situation is sufficiently serious to warrant *any* action on your part. To assist in making this decision, ask yourself the following sorts of questions:

— Is the person's health being jeopardized by his or her drug use?
— Are there clear-cut personality changes that I can see as a result of this drug use?
— Is there criminal behavior — such as stealing, dealing, or even engaging in prostitution — caused by the need to get drugs?
— Are the person's goals and ambitions being destroyed by drug use?

If the answers to the above questions are all "no," it's possible that you're overreacting and exaggerating the potential problem your friend may have. You may not approve of your friends' getting drunk every Saturday night, or lighting up a joint at parties, but if they're seemingly in control of their lives and not endangering anyone else by their actions (for instance, by driving when they're under the influence) then you're probably best off simply talking things over to give them your viewpoint — but going no farther. Likewise, if you have suspicions or guesses about drug use patterns, but no facts, don't barge in like a police detective making an arrest — you might be wrong, and it could cost you a friendship.

If, on the other hand, your friend or loved one's drug use involves potentially life-threatening drugs like PCP (angel dust) or LSD (acid), it's another story entirely. These drugs can produce permanent psychological damage, even if they're only used once or twice. And injected drugs, such as heroin, can lead to death by overdose. The bottom line here is that if you know your friend is into these drugs, *something* has got to be done — or you may end up carrying a huge burden of guilt if something happens and you didn't bother to try to help.

The next logical question you need to consider is this: Do I care enough about my friend or relative to try to get them to quit? If your brother, sister, father, or mother is the person who is abusing drugs (including alcohol), you really don't need to justify your actions, no matter how radical or heroic they may be. It is normal and natural to want the very best for your family, and it is also understandable that you have a vested interest in wanting to keep your family safe. In addition, you certainly are entitled to try to avoid being embarrassed or humiliated by the behavior of any of your family members.

If it's a friend you're concerned with, however, you really have to ask yourself whether this person is so important to you that you're willing to withstand the many insults, manipulative ploys, and even outright outbursts of anger that your attempts at getting them to get off drugs will bring. Certainly, there's no easy way to quantify just how much you care for someone else — so this usually has to be a decision based on your gut reactions. Being sure of the depth of your concern for and commitment to this friend is important before proceeding because it's almost a certainty that your affection and sincerity will be questioned. Most people who are hooked on drugs suffer from distorted thinking patterns (Alcoholics Anonymous calls this "stinking thinking"), so your friend may think that you're out to get them busted, to take away their fun, or to hurt them in some other way. A favorite druggie ploy is to question the motivation of anyone who tries to get them to stop. "Why are you so worried about *me?*" you may hear. "Get your own act together — but get the hell out of my face!" Another common response is "Don't be so uptight about things; I'm just using drugs to relax a little. What's wrong with that?" Still others may say, "Look, everyone knows that drugs are safe if you know what you're doing. I *really* appreciate your concern, but I'm just having some fun, OK?" And be prepared for the friend who reacts to your attempts to help by accusing you of being a narc. Your answer here is easy, though. "I care enough about you that I will do whatever I can to help you or even force you to stop."

Think about what happens if you permit yourself to be manipulated into the conspiracy of silence. By remaining silent you are really showing that you didn't think your friend or loved one's drug abuse was important enough to do anything about, *or* that you simply didn't care enough to become involved. Silence has only one meaning for the drug-dependent person — he or she can continue to do what he or she has already been doing. Should something horrible happen, you will be left to agonize for the rest of your life over why you didn't do your damnedest to stop your friend or relative from harming him- or herself or hurting someone else. The amount of guilt and personal self-disgust can become consuming. Try to think how you would feel if you attended the funeral of someone you loved who died because you turned your back on helping him or her in that person's time of desperate need. Try to think about what you would like your friend to do if your situations were reversed — if *you* were dangerously hooked on drugs and couldn't see how you were being harmed. In the final analysis, the most tangible proof of how much you care for someone is how willing you are to stick with that person and help, rather than abandon him or her, when the going is toughest.

Suppose that you've decided you're going to try to get a friend or loved one to kick the drug habit. Here is a list of specific strategies you can use:

1. *Confront the person with your concerns.* Unless you're willing to discuss the drug issue honestly and directly with your friend or loved one, there is little chance that you'll be able to accomplish anything. Plan what you're going to say carefully, taking into account the fact that most people who are into drugs more than casually use denial to downplay the seriousness of the situation. For example, they may point to someone else who seems to be worse off than they are to "prove" that they're still in control, or they may try to blame all the problems they're having on factors other than their drug use. Another common ploy: even your closest friends may try to con you into thinking that nothing's wrong — that they're not even using drugs anymore. "Oh, I *was* doing that, but I stopped last week," they might say. "You're absolutely right, that stuff is no good for you." Don't be taken in by this kind of performance.

2. *Stop your own use of drugs.* This can be one of the most effective ways available of getting your message across. It is your persuasive way of saying, "I care enough about what you are doing to yourself to stop because it may make it easier for you to stop. I also know that if I continue to use, even though I may not be in as much trouble as you, you will say I'm hypocritical." Furthermore, once you stop, you become a responsible role model for your friend or loved one.

3. *Don't assist your friend or loved one in getting or using drugs.* It may be obvious, but refusing to lend your friend money or your car is tangible evidence that you won't stand by idly as they continue to destroy themselves with drugs. Likewise, don't let yourself be a patsy for your friends by providing alibis for them or giving them your homework to copy to cover up for the fact that they haven't done it themselves. Finally, to be consistent, you must refuse to go with them to buy drugs and refuse to be around them while they're using or while they're high.

4. *Threaten to notify a respected friend or relative of the*

drug abuser's. The person you will tell, in all probability, will be devastated by the news but is not likely to do anything rash or radical. The drug abuser will probably plead with you not to do this because he or she doesn't want to cause the person any unnecessary pain, which gives you a great opportunity to say, "If you *really* felt that way, you'd stop using drugs before I have to tell them." In other words, the threat becomes an incentive to abandon the self-destructive behavior. If the threat doesn't produce any action, you'll need to actually carry out your plan — behavior that itself may be beneficial because the drug abuser may stop his or her drug use at the urging of both you and the other person.

5. *If the above steps haven't worked, enlist the help of the drug abuser's other close friends.* Peer pressure can be a powerful influence on anyone's behavior, and getting a group of close friends together to confront the person who is abusing drugs can accomplish several things. First, it conveys a clear message — "We all know what you're doing to yourself" — which can be pretty hard to deny. Second, it's a powerful statement of caring, which in itself can convince a person of the importance of giving up drugs. Third, as a group you can more easily and effectively provide a support network to assist you in stopping the use of drugs. In one instance, five friends got together and chaperoned their drug-using buddy one by one, around the clock, for three solid weeks until they were certain he was drug-free. It was the friends' dedication and group unity that got him over the worst part of it, the ex-drug-user said later.

6. *Threaten to notify a third party who has the power to act decisively.* This is not a step to be taken impulsively, but if circumstances are really serious and you haven't been able to help by using any of the previously mentioned strategies, you need to consider this as a possible option. You could, for example, talk with a school guidance counselor about your friend's drug problem. (If you first approach this without naming the person, you can find out how the guidance counselor plans to handle the situation. That way, you're not jeopardizing your friend's well-being by putting him in the hands of someone who's just going to report him to the police or toss him out of school.) Another possibility is to talk with your

friend's employer, who may be able to put the worker in a drug rehabilitation program. If your friend is really on a self-destructive course or is clearly endangering others (for instance, if you know that he or she is driving while high on drugs, or if you know he or she is dealing to younger kids) then you even have to consider speaking to someone who has the official power to institutionalize the individual unless he or she stops all drug use immediately. If this sounds like a drastic remedy — *it is*, because it's a super-serious problem.

It's not easy, or pleasant, to take any of the steps we've mentioned above. But by getting involved in a responsible way, you just might save somebody's life or at the very least, help him or her salvage it from drug oblivion.

Drug Facts You Should Know

Today's teenagers need to have accurate facts at their disposal about a wide variety of drugs. Here is a summary of current information on illicit drugs that are most frequently used and abused by teenagers.

Alcohol

Alcohol is sometimes overlooked as a drug of abuse for several reasons. First, companies that manufacture beer and liquor spend tens of millions of dollars for advertising that projects an image of drinking as a sociable, pleasurable activity — a way to relax. Those commercials that show good friends enjoying a thirst-quenching brew after a hard-fought basketball game, after work, while lolling on the beach, or on a date at a fancy restaurant all carefully create the idea that drinking is fun. Unfortunately, what is left out of these commercials is the darker side of alcohol use: the people killed by drunk drivers, the lives ruined by alcoholism. A second factor that prevents most people from thinking of alcohol as a drug is its easy availability. After all, just walk down the aisle of most supermarkets and you'll find dozens of brands of beer and hundreds of bottles of liquor and wine right there alongside of the ketchup and Rice Krispies. Go to almost any wedding or party and alcohol will be served. Surely this can't be a *drug* that is being used so widely? The third reason most people don't think of alcohol as a drug of abuse is that it's legal for adults. If it's legal, that must mean it's safe, right? Unfortunately, though, statistics show that 1.5 *million* teenagers are problem drinkers, with half of them — three-quarters of a million teenagers — believed to be full-blown alcoholics. Clearly, then, alcohol *is* an abused drug.

As a drug, alcohol is a powerful depressant to the central nervous system, meaning that it disrupts the normal workings of the brain and many of the body's reflexes. The precise effects depend on the amount of alcohol absorbed into the bloodstream, which in turn reflects the amount of alcohol consumed, the rapidity with which it is taken, the weight of the person, and the amount of food in the stomach (alcohol is absorbed more quickly when the stomach is empty).

One or two drinks taken slowly — over an hour or more — won't affect most people beyond making them feel relaxed and possibly a little light-headed. (Note, however, that there are three sets of circumstances where this may not be true: 1. If a person has little or no experience with alcohol, he or she can get very tipsy from even one or two drinks. 2. If the "drink" is not a standard one-ounce shot of liquor — for instance, if a person drinks a four- or five-ounce scotch-on-the-rocks — the effect will not be that of one drink, but will reflect the actual alcohol content consumed. 3. If alcohol is mixed with other drugs, its effects may be exaggerated [scientists call this "drug potentiation"].)

Larger amounts of alcohol, or even two drinks chugged rapidly, begin to affect judgment and physical coordination. Typically, boisterous behavior, slurred speech, "tipsy" balance, and slowed reaction time begin to appear. (Note that these effects are less likely with two or three drinks in a person who weighs more than 170 pounds and who is eating food while he or she is drinking.) With four or five drinks consumed in an hour, people invariably become drunk, although they may protest that they're feeling fine and perfectly in control of their actions — and they may even seem to be walking and talking normally to someone else, particularly if the other person has been drinking, too.

Some teenagers get into contests to see who can consume the most alcohol in a short time period — sometimes, in fact, the alcohol isn't simply chugged down; it is actually funneled directly into the stomach. Drinking escapades of these kinds are not harmless examples of youthful exuberance — there are literally hundreds of fatalities each year from these sorts of alcohol binges. The reason is that with very high blood concentrations of alcohol, the part of the brain that controls breathing is affected, so that sometimes breathing stops entirely. Even at nonfatal levels of high alcohol intake, the brain can be short-circuited to such an extent that a person blacks out and loses consciousness. While it may seem funny when someone blacks out at a party from drinking too much, and someone says, "Oh, let them sleep it off," there is actually some danger to leaving the person alone in this situation: it would be far better to try to wake him or her and get the person on his or her feet to walk off some of the effects of the alcohol.

Chugging contests and blacking out aside, the biggest danger of teenage alcohol use is unquestionably the problem of mixing drinking and driving. *Even when you're not drunk, a few drinks affect your driving coordination, reaction time, and judgment.* Ask yourself: "Would I want to fly somewhere in a plane with a pilot who's just had three drinks in the last two hours?" Of course you wouldn't, because you know full well that it would be a risky situation. There's no question that driving on a turnpike, or trying to make a turn on a busy intersection on a rainy night, or even trying to judge the distance of an oncoming car, is just as difficult as flying — and by driving when you've been drinking, or riding with someone else who has, you are endangering your own life and that of others. In avoiding auto accidents, even a few hundredths of a second in the time it takes a driver to brake the car can make all the difference in the world. And the average driver who's had three drinks in the last two hours will be *35 percent slower* in his or her driving reflexes than when he or she is not drinking. If they've had even more to drink, worrying about the speed of their reflexes is almost silly — their judgment and coordination are so impaired that the risk of being in an accident is considerable.

The million and one half teenagers who are abusive drinkers may not be as likely as older people to see the health effects of heavy alcohol use right away, but over time they may develop numerous serious health problems. Alcohol abuse causes several kinds of liver damage (both cirrhosis and alcoholic hepatitis) as well as irritation and bleeding in the stomach, pancreatitis, alcoholic heart disease, and brain damage. In addition, heavy drinking disrupts normal sex hormone production in both males and females and is likely to cause major difficulties in sexual function. Furthermore, alcohol abuse also contributes to infertility in both sexes, lowering the sperm count in males and sometimes blocking ovulation in females. And even moderately heavy drinking by a pregnant woman can cause a series of problems with the developing baby, including growth deficiencies before and after birth, facial abnormalities (especially involving the eyes), damage to the brain and nervous system, and mental retardation (this is called the fetal alcohol syndrome).

If heavy drinking is suddenly stopped after a person becomes physically dependent on alcohol, full-blown symptoms of withdrawal appear. In the mild form, these withdrawal symptoms include shakiness, irritability, restlessness, trouble sleeping, anxiety, sweating, and a rapid heartbeat. About one-quarter of the time, there will also be hallucinations during withdrawal (hearing voices or seeing things that aren't really there), but these usually clear up within a week. In more serious cases, suddenly stopping the use of alcohol causes seizures ("rum fits") or a condition called d.t.'s (delirum tremens: *delirium* means confusion and disorientation, like the person not knowing who he is or where he is; *tremens* refers to the tremors, or shakes). Although d.t.'s don't happen very often in teenagers, they may occur in those who have been regularly using barbiturates or tranquilizers along with large amounts of alcohol. *D.t.'s are a life-threatening condition that requires immediate emergency medical attention.*

Marihuana

Marihuana, also known by names such as "pot," "grass," "weed," "Mary Jane," "hash," "Maui Wowee," and "Acapulco gold," is the most widely used mind-altering substance in America other than alcohol. It is also illegal. Because marihuana is widely available, comparatively inexpensive, pleasant to use, and relatively safe from a health viewpoint when compared to other illicit drugs, it is the first street drug most teenagers are tempted to try. First-time users often don't feel much after smoking pot, but with repeated use it usually produces a thirty-to-sixty-minute "high" marked by a sense of relaxation, an alteration of a person's sense of time (time seems to pass more slowly), and feelings of happiness and pleasure. In addition, most users say that while they're high on pot their sensory awareness seems increased — they see colors more vividly, hear sounds more perceptively, taste and smell things more clearly, and are more aware of the textures and temperatures of things they touch than when they're not high. Marihuana also makes people hungry, thirsty, and sleepy (the so-called "marihuana munchies" are named for the craving to have something to nibble on while high).

Marihuana is *not* an addictive drug, although those who use it heavily over time (every day or almost every day) can become psychologically dependent on it — that is, they begin to feel that they must smoke marihuana in order to be able to perform their everyday tasks or just to feel good about themselves. Early claims that marihuana was completely safe have now been disproved by hundreds of scientific studies, but the early arguments by opponents of marihuana of dire health consequences have also been shown to be greatly exaggerated.

If marihuana is used *occasionally* — less often than a few times a week — negative health effects are relatively few. Anxiety attacks (panicky feelings and hyperexcitability) occur in 1 or 2 percent of users; "flashbacks" (recurrences of the marihuana high without using the drug) are even less frequent. The greatest physical danger seems to be that driving and other machine-operating skills are impaired because of decreased alertness, visual distortion, slowed reflexes, and difficulties with coordinating complex reactions.

Most people don't realize that marihuana use is just as dangerous to driving as driving while drunk. Many people who are high feel that they're completely in control of themselves — in fact, they may even think that their reflexes are *better* than they usually are, because their time sense is distorted. But tens of thousands of auto accidents and thousands of fatalities occur annually because of people driving while high on marihuana.

> I was driving back from a pizza party we had for a friend who was moving away from town. Judy, Sally, and Joan were with me, and we had all shared a few joints of pot while we listened to music and reminisced about our lives. As I was going through town just after midnight, I looked up at the flashing red light that seemed to be blinking so slowly, like a clam opening and shutting, and the next thing I knew, a truck coming in the other direction smashed into us. It was horrible — Sally, who was sitting next to me in the front seat, was killed. Judy and Joan were both severely burned. But all three of us were sitting there giggling when the police and ambulance pulled up, because we were stoned out of our gourds. If we hadn't been high, Sally would still be alive and that damn accident wouldn't have happened — I would have stopped for the flashing red light just like I always do. If only someone had warned us about driving when you're high.
>
> *A seventeen-year-old girl*

In contrast to the occasional use of marihuana, heavy use (four times a week or more over a period of months or years) is another story entirely. To begin with, the active chemical ingredients in marihuana accumulate in the body over time, particularly in tissues such as the brain, the testes, and the liver. Studies have shown that sperm production is lowered by long-term heavy marihuana use, and levels of the major male sex hormone, testosterone, can be depressed. Because testosterone plays a major role in controlling both sexual maturation and physical growth (such as height and muscle development) during puberty, younger teenagers may be particularly vulnerable to this effect. Recent studies also suggest that heavy marihuana use can disrupt normal menstrual function in females, and it has also been found that the active chemical component of marihuana enters the bloodstream of the developing baby if a pregnant woman uses this drug.

Long-term heavy marihuana use also damages the lungs and lowers resistance to infection. Since marihuana smoke has many of the same ingredients as tobacco smoke, some experts feel that prolonged, heavy use may lead to lung cancer. Many scientists have also found evidence suggesting that very frequent marihuana use leads to the so-called "amotivational syndrome," marked by lack of ambition or motivation, withdrawal from social interactions, and passivity. Dr. Kenneth Blum, president of the National Foundation on Addictive Diseases, notes, "The resultant lethargy, social and personality deterioration, and drug preoccupation may be comparable to the skid row alcoholic's state." Several high school coaches we interviewed agreed that kids who get heavily involved with marihuana usually lose interest in both their studies and their sports activities, even when they were previously exceptionally talented and competitive athletes. One college admissions officer put it this way: "The largest category of students who flunk out or drop out in their freshman year on our campus is the potheads. The funny thing is, when we try to warn them about what's happening, it quickly becomes plain that they don't even care." Even in heavy marihuana users who don't fit this description, it is clear that the marihuana high interferes with a person's ability to function in tasks requiring memory, concentration, organized thinking, or quick reaction times, a handicap that can create difficulties at school, at work, or in sports activities.

On the other hand, it is now fairly certain that early reports of brain damage due to heavy marihuana use were in error (the damage found was probably due to drugs other than marihuana). Likewise, there is little evidence to support claims made in the 1970s that heavy marihuana use causes a high rate of serious psychiatric problems in teenagers.

Despite the weight of scientific findings to the contrary, many young adults believe that marihuana is a "perfect" drug — cheap, fun, and safe. But the cost can't be measured in terms of what a joint or two sells for when getting caught with pot can put *you* in the joint. And before deciding just how safe marihuana is, consider this conclusion of the prestigious National Academy of Sciences: "What we know about the effects of marihuana on human health justifies serious national concern." This doesn't mean that marihuana is more dangerous than most other street drugs (it isn't), and it doesn't mean that smoking one marihuana cigarette in your life will put you in the hospital (it won't), but the point of this discussion has been to provide you with the facts you need about marihuana, whatever your decision about your personal use may be.

Cocaine

Cocaine ("coke," "snow," "Big C," "Charlie," "powder") is clearly the "in" drug in the 1980s. Although teenagers are not as likely as adults to plunge nose-first into regular coke use because of its expense, it is estimated that there are four to six million cocaine users in America today, including one out of every ten teenagers. This situation is a marked change from the 1970s, when far fewer adolescents had experimented with this drug.

Cocaine is extracted from the leaves of a coca plant and can be either inhaled ("snorted"), smoked, or injected. It produces a temporary — twenty- to thirty-minute — high marked by euphoria, a sense of power, and intense alertness. To some, it is the "ultimate high," giving users feelings of supreme competence, mastery, and perfection. Its appeal also comes partly from its reputation as the "Rolls Royce" of drugs (partially because of its use by celebrities, models, and sports figures) and its supposed effects as a sexual stimulant. This mystique is also a byproduct of its somewhat glamorous past: Sigmund Freud wrote a detailed study of cocaine as a mental energizer and the fictional but widely admired Sherlock Holmes used cocaine regularly to combat depression and lethargy.

Cocaine is also popular for a number of other reasons. For one thing, it is easily concealed and requires little or no drug paraphernalia to use, thus decreasing the risk of detection. Detection is also made difficult by the fact that snorting cocaine is quick and, unlike smoking marihuana, has no telltale odor. Even when high, the cocaine user isn't likely to be recognized by others because the drug doesn't cause slurred speech or trouble with walking or physical coordination; furthermore, coming down from a cocaine high doesn't typically cause drowsiness. Finally, cocaine has been surrounded by so many myths about its safety that many people mistakenly believe that it's a drug that's completely safe. These myths include the notion that cocaine must be safe because: (1) it was once put in Coca-Cola (it was, but in such small quantities that its physical effects were minuscule); (2) it's been used by Peruvian Indians for centuries and it hasn't harmed them (actually, the Peruvian Indians don't use cocaine; they chew the leaves of the coca plant); and (3) it's been tested and approved by the FDA — the U.S. Food and Drug Administration (while cocaine *is* approved for limited medical use as a topical anesthetic, its use as a recreational drug is another matter entirely because it's not taken in the same doses or in the same way).

While ten years ago many medical experts thought that cocaine was a fairly safe drug, renewed research interest on this topic has revealed some startling facts about the supposed "safety" of coke. Once again, the safety of this drug is partly related to the frequency of its use, with occasional users having relatively few health risks of consequence. The immediate effects of cocaine on the body are stimulation of the nervous system, a faster heart rate, an increase in the breathing rate, a widening of the pupils, and a slight increase in body temperature. Immediately after the cocaine high is over, the user generally "crashes" — experiences a reaction of irritability, restlessness, and a craving for more cocaine. Cocaine overdoses, although relatively rare, can lead to hallucinations, seizures, coma, and even death.

Frequent use of cocaine, or using cocaine by freebasing or injection, is quite another matter. Both freebasing (smoking a purified extract of cocaine) and injecting cocaine increase the speed with which users will become addicted to this drug, although almost everyone who uses it on a daily or almost everyday basis will gradually develop a powerful addiction. And even those users who avoid a true addiction by resisting the temptation to use the snowy-white powder with quite so much frequency are apt to pay a high price. According to Dr. Mark Gold, the researcher who runs the 800-COCAINE hotline service that had received over one million calls by August 1984, among regular cocaine users the following problems occur: depression (83 percent), anxiety (83 percent), irritability (82 percent), problems sleeping (82 percent), chronic tiredness (76 percent), lack of motivation (66 percent), fighting and violent arguments (66 percent), difficulty concentrating (65 percent), severe headaches (60 percent), loss of sex drive (53 percent), loss of friends (51 percent). In addition, many heavy cocaine users complain of difficulty with sexual functioning; chronic runny noses, sore throats, and upper respiratory infections; and financial difficulties brought on by the high expense of supporting the coke habit. Most teenagers who get heavily into this drug turn to stealing to support their expensive drug needs, while others start dealing drugs in order to feed their own noses.

Cocaine may seem like a supersophisticated way to bring a little excitement to your life, but what few people realize is how strong a lure this seemingly innocent powder can become. As one teenage tennis star now says ruefully, "The day I first did a line of coke was the start of the end for me. Coke made me feel so good so easily that I quickly got into doing it every day. Within six months, my professional tennis career was busted, I had spent over $50,000 buying, and most of my friends had deserted me. The only thing that saved me from myself was getting arrested and put in a drug rehab program. But even now, months after I've stopped, I still get intense cravings to freebase, and I'm not sure that I can stay clean. That's a terrible thing to say, isn't it?"

Amphetamines

The amphetamines, like cocaine, are stimulants. Known in street lingo as *speed, pep pills, bennies, dex, crank, splash,* or *crystal,* these drugs are particularly dangerous because of their high addictive potential. Occasional use of amphetamines when they're taken by mouth doesn't seem to have particularly serious consequences. The major effect of the drug is to heighten alertness and overcome fatigue — which leads some students to use them when they're trying to stay up all night to cram for a test — although complex judgments can be negatively affected (leading to difficulty in scoring well on an exam; one student user told us she had written an entire history exam on two lines of a blue examination booklet, not realizing what she had done). When injected or inhaled, amphetamines cause more intense sensations, sometimes described as a "flash" or "rush." If mixed with other drugs or taken in excessive doses, "mainlining" (taking the drug intravenously) can result in hyperactivity, poor impulse control, hallucinations, irrational (sometimes destructive) behavior, and occasionally a condition in which the "speed freak" is unable to move or speak. Dozens of cases have been reported in which teenagers have committed murder while on an amphetamine buzz; in some instances druggies have killed their friends because of the extreme suspiciousness and hostility that amphetamines sometimes produce in users. Death due to overdose can also occur.

Amphetamine addicts or abusers are also susceptible to a number of other effects, including a sizable risk of suicide. Brain damage and heart problems both can occur, damaged blood vessels are common, and liver disorders are frequently seen. Severe weight loss and malnutrition, thought disorders (especially paranoid delusions — feeling "someone is out to get me"), and disturbances of sexual function round out the unpleasant picture of this condition.

Fortunately, amphetamine use among teenagers seems to be on the decline. Nevertheless, the high risks of "speed" are not to be ignored.

"Downers"
(Depressants: Tranquilizers and Sleeping Pills)

The barbiturates — drugs like phenobarbital (Luminal), secobarbital (Seconal), and amobarbital (Amytal) — are an important part of the street drug scene. Widely available and relatively inexpensive, they are used either alone (to reduce anxiety, to "relax," to slow things down) or in combination with other illicit drugs to tone down their excessive stimulant action. Barbiturates are dangerous any way you look at them. To begin with, they are the drugs most commonly used to commit suicide. Accidental deaths due to the combination of alcohol and barbiturates are not unusual (the two drugs act together to produce a more profound effect than just the sum of taking each one separately). The barbiturates are also highly addicting.

Barbiturate use typically produces symptoms that are very similar to being drunk: slurred speech, sluggishness, difficulty walking, impaired mental capabilities, irritability, decreased attention span, and reduced physical coordination. Over time, the frequent user of barbiturates builds up tolerance to the intoxicating effects of the drug, requiring higher doses to get the same effect — but because the amount of drug that can be lethal doesn't change, even very frequent barbiturate abusers risk a fatal overdose. Barbiturate addicts have full-blown withdrawal reactions that commonly include nervousness, fearfulness, vomiting and stomach pains, tremors, insomnia, and excessive sweating. In severe cases, these withdrawal reactions can progress to include generalized seizures, delirium, coma, or death, so medical care is strongly advised.

Methaqualone, previously sold under brand names such as Quaalude, Sopor, and Parest, is another kind of downer that enjoyed some popularity among adolescents ten years ago because it was supposed to be a sexual stimulant. The truth is that methaqualone actually *impairs* sexual performance, although because it may lower sexual anxieties, some users report feeling sexier when they use the drug. Like barbiturates, methaqualone is addicting and dangerous, although many teenagers seem convinced the drug is innocuous, in part because it's so readily available. Especially when methaqualone is mixed with alcohol, marihuana, or heroin, death can occur either as a result of the heart stopping or because breathing ceases. Chronic abuse of this drug typically produces impaired coordination, unsteady walking, inability to concentrate, memory problems, poor judgment, and flat emotions. In late 1983, legitimate U.S. drug companies agreed to stop manufacturing this drug completely because of its high abuse potential, but since most of the methaqualone reaching the street was illicitly produced, this dangerous drug will continue to be available for years to come.

In contrast to the above-mentioned depressant drugs, tranquilizers such as Librium and Valium are less widely used by teenagers and are somewhat safer. Valium, in particular, is used in the drug subculture to treat complications of drug experimentation, such as a bad LSD trip. It is also sometimes used to ease the letdown after a long bout with stimulants such as amphetamines or cocaine. Rather than giving a true high, Librium and Valium leave their users feeling "spacy," "floating," or "mellow." While these drugs have high abuse potential, they are not usually addictive. But like the other depressants, Librium and Valium are particularly dangerous when mixed with alcohol.

PCP (Phencyclidine)

PCP ("angel dust," "hog," "superweed," "monkey dust," "goon," "elephant tranquilizer") is difficult to classify because it can act either as a depressant, a stimulant, or a hallucinogen, depending on how it's taken and the dose used. It comes either as a crystalline powder or as capsules and tablets in a variety of forms, and is sometimes mixed with other drugs such as barbiturates, heroin, LSD, and amphetamines. Although it was originally taken by mouth, it is now most often smoked or snorted. Despite its widespread availability, PCP is one of the most dangerous drugs being used today.

PCP causes bizarre effects that often include a tendency toward violence, impulsive behavior (including self-destructive acts like suicide), and an intense sense of depersonalization, in which the drug user feels that he or she is outside his or her body, or is being controlled by some external person or force. People high on angel dust have walked off roofs of tall buildings thinking they could fly like Superman; turned viciously on their friends, sometimes killing them; and used autos like Sherman tanks attacking enemy lines. PCP used in low doses sometimes produces a sense of elation and feelings of power and intense sensory awareness, but it also commonly causes paranoia, distorted vision, hallucinations, muscle incoordination, and flashbacks. (Flashbacks are experiences that occur months or years after using a drug, in which parts of the sensory hallucinations of the drug "high" recur suddenly and without warning — creating a disorienting and scary episode.) In high doses, PCP can cause seizures, coma, or extreme hyperactivity. All users risk having serious mental breakdowns from this drug, including sudden psychotic reactions that require hospitalization and intense treatment efforts. Unfortunately, these psychotic episodes have sometimes been permanent, leaving the drug user with a brain like a boiled zucchini.

Psychedelics

The use of psychedelics such as LSD ("acid," "the cube," "big D," "white lightning," "blue dots," "pink dots"), peyote, and mescaline — drugs taken from a small cactus that grows in Mexico and the southwestern United States, and similar substances (DMT, psilocybin) has been on the decline among teenagers in America in the last five years. While these drugs vary in their chemistry and specific actions, they all affect brain activity so that users are inundated by flooding sensations of color, sound, touch, and smell. In some cases, frightening hallucinations may occur (for instance, being eaten by giant spiders); in others, the hallucinations may take on religious overtones or seem to reach into the depths of the universe. These drugs are particularly dangerous because they break the user's contact with reality and can cause both abrupt or long-lasting psychiatric problems. Flashbacks can also occur and tend to be unpleasant and frightening. Because these drugs offer the promise of a cosmic, mystical vision of the world in which the user will attain instantaneous understanding of complex matters, users overlook the possibility of bad drug trips that can damage their minds or their bodies — sometimes on a permanent basis. In one case, a twenty-four-year-old student on an LSD trip tried to "conquer time" by drilling a hole in his skull; in another instance, a seventeen-year-old boy set his pet dog on fire while under the influence of acid. Clearly, underneath the promise of profound visions and insights coming from the drug experience, the psychedelics are dangerous drugs that *don't* offer a money-back guarantee.

Narcotics

The narcotics are a class of drugs made from opium, such as heroin, morphine, codeine, and related man-made compounds including methadone, Demerol, and Dilaudid. These highly addictive drugs all share similar properties and carry an extremely high risk to street users. Heroin ("H," "smack," "horse," "joy powder," "scag") is a white or brown powder that is used in a variety of ways. It can be inhaled ("snorted"), smoked, injected under the skin ("skin popping"), or injected into a vein ("mainlining"). However it is used, a tolerance to its effects develops rapidly so that more and more of the drug must be taken to get the short-lived pleasurable effects. This tolerance quickly leads to a state of physical dependence on the drug, with withdrawal symptoms such as runny nose, shaking, sweating, nausea, vomiting, abdominal pain, muscular aches and pains, chills, insomnia, and, occasionally, convulsions, occurring if the drug habit isn't "fed" on time.

The numerous problems caused by narcotic addiction affect almost every facet of life. From a health perspective, addicts are constantly exposed to a risk of a drug overdose because they can never be certain of the purity of the heroin they're using. (Most heroin sold on the street is actually 90+ percent other material, but occasionally a more potent form is sold, which can be lethal.) In addition, there are many risks that come from using improperly sterilized needles for injecting the drug, or sharing needles between users — these include hepatitis, life-threatening infections of the heart valves, blood poisoning, tetanus (lockjaw), and AIDS (acquired immune deficiency syndrome), which is currently running rampant among addicts and is nearly always fatal. As if these risks were not enough, narcotic addicts have a greatly lowered resistance to infections, problems with fluid in their lungs, and serious malnutrition.

Beyond these serious health problems, narcotic addicts face a huge number of other everyday hurdles. Because getting and using their narcotic becomes the major preoccupation of their lives, addicts usually become withdrawn and alienated, suspicious of everyone who doesn't do drugs with them. Interpersonal relationships suffer because the addict has little patience with the ordinary niceties of life, such as conversation, romance, or enjoying shared activities (unless they have to do with shooting up). Addiction also unmasks or exaggerates previously existing emotional problems and creates psychological problems of its own, including a generalized suspiciousness and sense of insecurity, and frequent bouts of depression. Ambitions and drive are left aside as the addict focuses all of his or her energies on getting drugs (which usually involves criminal behavior such as theft or prostitution because of the expense of the habit) and using them. In fact, most addicts quickly lose their interest in sex, food, and hobbies they've previously enjoyed, as everything in their lives fades into a drug-blurred background. Not surprisingly, few narcotic addicts are able to hold jobs or progress in school, and many wind up after a few years — if they manage to avoid, for that long, being arrested or dying from an overdose — as burned-out bodies who look ten or twenty years older than they really are. It's a frightening picture in every way imaginable.

Despite these facts, large numbers of teenagers continue to try narcotics as a lark, as a form of rebellion, or as a gesture of anger at themselves or at the world. Although they're all sure that *they're* not going to get hooked — that *they're* in control — it's only the very lucky ones who manage to avoid the quicksand trap of this slow form of committing suicide. One sixteen-year-old girl put it this way:

> I was so naive about using smack it was incredible. At fourteen I was snorting it and skin-popping once in a while, but as I got older I wanted more of a thrill. Shooting up gave me that thrill, all right, for a few minutes every day, but within six weeks I had tripled my dose and I was having the creepy-crawly jitters within ten hours of not having my hit. I went through all of my money in the first two weeks I was mainlining, and I soon found out that the only way I could buy my drugs was by turning tricks — you know, being a prostitute. I ran away from home to L.A., where I worked the streets at night to make money and shot up during my off-hours. On the day before my sixteenth birthday, I was picked up by the cops in a drug bust, so I turned "Sweet Sixteen" going cold tur-

key in a jail cell. Fortunately, my mother sent me to a residential drug treatment program, or I'm not sure I would have lived to see my seventeenth birthday.

Narcotics are extremely dangerous drugs, no matter what anyone else tells you. Avoid their use any way you can. If you're already using narcotics, or know someone else who is, get help right away — tomorrow could literally be a day too late.

Inhalants

Some children and teenagers inhale fumes from paint sprays, gasoline, dry cleaning solutions, airplane glue, lighter fluid, spot remover, or fingernail polish in order to get high. These readily available and inexpensive products produce a brief high, generally lasting only a few minutes, and while they may seem to be practically harmless — after all, they're legal — the truth is that their effects are more dangerous than you might think. The chemicals in these substances are toxic in high doses, so that repeated direct contact can cause physical injury. Some of these products are actually poisonous, and more than a hundred deaths a year result from their use. Other health problems such as liver and kidney damage, muscle weakness, neurological disorders, anemia, and damage to the heart have also been found to stem from inhalant abuse.

Older teenagers look down at glue-sniffing as a "babyish" thing to do but may become involved with another type of inhalant. This is a drug called amyl nitrite (known as "poppers" or "snappers" because it often comes packaged in glass pearls or vials, which give a popping or snapping sound when broken open). Amyl nitrite is now most commonly obtained not as a drug but in the form of room deodorizers under names like Bull, Rush, Kick, and Bullet. While it is reported to boost a person's energy briefly and to improve the intensity of sex, it causes headaches, nausea, and dizziness due to a drop in blood pressure and a slowing effect on the heart. It is not addictive, but it's definitely not healthy either.

Cigarettes and Tobacco

Probably the most underestimated addicting substance in our everyday lives is tobacco and its active chemical ingredient, nicotine. While it is clear that cigarette smoking causes lung cancer, heart disease, emphysema, and a host of other medical problems, it is also clear that tens of millions of Americans are so strongly addicted to cigarettes that they are unable to quit despite repeated efforts to do so. Let's put it another way — despite the fact that most smokers realize that the health hazards of cigarettes result in 300,000 premature deaths each year, they are so strongly hooked on tobacco that they continue puffing away. This has led many drug abuse experts to conclude that cigarettes may be even more strongly addicting than heroin. This is partly so because every time a person inhales a cigarette, it delivers a jolt of nicotine to the brain just seven seconds later. The effects of this bathing the brain in nicotine vary from person to person, but many smokers claim that it helps them feel less tense, increases their alertness, and helps them to concentrate.

From the health viewpoint, cigarettes are a complete disaster. Cigarette smoking has not only been found to cause lung cancer; it has also been linked with cancers of the mouth, tongue, larynx (voice box), esophagus, pancreas, and urinary tract. Smokers have more hardening of the arteries, high blood pressure, and heart disease than nonsmokers do. Smokers also are at high risk for developing serious lung problems such as emphysema and chronic bronchitis that can wind up crippling a person's breathing capacity to the point that he or she becomes an invalid. All in all, smokers have a significantly reduced life expectancy.

Years ago, smoking cigarettes may have seemed to be a grown-up thing to do. Today, with most people well aware of the above-mentioned health risks, it's no longer so cool or grown-up to smoke. In fact, as more and more offices, schools, restaurants, and other public places are banning smoking entirely — or limiting it to specific sections — and as more and more people are coming to a realization of the health risks and economic costs of smoking, smoking is being frowned on as a thoughtless, tasteless, messy, and harmful habit.

So-called "smokeless" tobacco, also known as chewing tobacco, is enjoying some heightened popularity these days among male teenagers. While smokeless tobacco doesn't lead to lung cancer or heart disease, it *can* cause cancer of the mouth and tongue and serious dental problems in long-term users, and it can also lead to nicotine addiction.

Ten Ways of Getting High without Drugs, Alcohol, or Tobacco

1. Look at a sunset on a clear, cool night.
2. Run a ten-kilometer race in a personal-best time.
3. Fall in love.
4. Listen to some good music through headphones.
5. Hike in the mountains on an autumn afternoon.
6. Get turned on to dancing.
7. Pump iron.
8. Walk barefoot along a secluded beach under a moonlit sky.
9. Help a handicapped person.
10. Be creative and find your own personal turn-ons. There are thousands of other possibilities.

10.

Eating Problems and Self-Image — The Broken Mirror

Americans have several national passions — football, base-ball, fashion, and food. We love to look good and we love to eat, but since there's a popular attitude that looking good means being lean and thin, we've developed two other pas-sions — the pursuit of thinness and dieting.

Young people observe and mimic adult attitudes and be-haviors. Because they do, many buy into the notion that if they're thin they'll be happy and have fewer problems than if they were heavy or even obese. We're constantly bombarded with the idea that certain styles and looks are more desirable than others. Teen magazines and adult fashion magazines routinely publish makeovers, and the "after" photos *always* look better than the "befores." There are an increasing num-ber of televised beauty peagants and bodybuilding contests that get us thinking about the ratio of fat to muscle that we'd need in order to look like Mr. or Ms. Olympia or Miss America. Exercise clubs, health spas, and diet centers run TV ad campaigns suggesting they can help you achieve that cer-tain look. In one, Cher tells you that she's not afraid of mus-cles, she's afraid of fat! A Quick Start Weight Loss ad shows a very skinny woman throwing her arms joyfully around her scale. Jane Fonda's workout tapes are still topping the video charts. Librarians in charge of teenage reading sections say they are often unable to keep up with the demand for books about diet and dieting.

The message that gets pounded into us over and over is that your body is the most important part of the image you project to others, and how happy, strong, and healthy you are depends on how little you weigh. This is far from accurate. The ads conveniently forget to mention that many of the spokespeople have had cosmetic surgery, or have had major struggles with eating disorders such as anorexia, the self-starvation disease, and bulimia, the binge-purge syndrome. The ads forget to tell you that for some people eating and exercise become obsessions that, instead of enhancing self-image, can do a lot to destroy it. They don't have warnings or disclaimers at the ends of the articles or ads — ATTENTION: *Success or failure as a person isn't measured by your weight or shape.* They don't tell you that it's not healthy to apply all your energy and passion in pursuit of a single goal to the exclusion of all other aspects of your life. Perhaps they should.

If you pursue the "thin is in" message you put yourself in a bind. People eat not just for nutrition, but because it's pleasurable. Eating out with friends is as much a part of our social lives as going to dances or sports events. But if you eat high-calorie foods like burgers, fries, and milkshakes you may end up feeling guilty because you don't want to get fat. If you start to feel guilty about eating you're likely to put yourself down for having no willpower. If you feel bad enough you may start to diet, even if you have no need to. If the dieting gets out of hand and you're not coping well with other stresses in your life, you could flip into anorectic or bulimic behavior patterns.

One of the reasons it's easy to get caught up in the quest for thinness is that during adolescence you spend a great deal of time and energy trying to develop your self-image into something you like and are comfortable with, and an equal amount of time learning to project that image to other people. Self-image includes your body image (how you think your body should look) as well as what you'd like to be and your opinion of yourself right now. Concentrating on staying thin fits right in with your already sharp sense of body image. If it's really important to you to be thin, and you're not, your self-image may go down a notch or two; if you succeed in being thin, your self-image may soar. But the shape of your body doesn't determine whether you'll be popular or not, successful or not. If you look like Madonna it's no guarantee you'll sing like her. If you body-build and learn to wrestle like Mr. T., it's no guarantee that you'll get a multimillion-dollar Hollywood contract.

Eating Is More Than Just Eating!

Eating is more than just a way to nourish your body and keep it in running order. It's a social activity that involves lots of habits, some good, some bad. When you're a young child your parents can control and monitor what, when, and where you eat. The dining table can be a place where your self-image begins to develop and gets reinforced by your family. It's also the place where problems can start. If your parents constantly tell you that "good children clean their plates," and that "food equals love," you'll clean your plate every time to show them you love them, whether or not you're hungry. But if *you* believe that "thin is better than fat" and they're telling you "food equals love" or even "fat people are always happy," you'll have some problems. If you eat to satisfy *them* you'll get fat, which will make *you* unhappy. Some really serious confrontations can occur as a result of different attitudes or appetites within families, and can eventually trigger an eating disorder in the person who feels out of synch with everyone else.

The older you get, the less control your parents have over your eating habits. Once you become a teenager, a number of circumstances that didn't exist before may now affect what, when, and where you eat and who you eat with:

1. You may buy several meals a week at school and eat out with friends instead of eating meals with your family.
2. You may have pocket money that lets you buy any kind of food you want, even "junk."
3. You may have developed tastes for exotic foods and try things your parents may never have even heard of, much less approve of.

4. You may eat in "pig out"–"diet"–"pig out"–"diet" cycles.

Your parents may not care for these developments. They may not want to let go of the job of feeding you (after all, providing you with nourishment was the very first thing they could do for you). They may feel that because you're assuming more responsibility for your own nutrition it means you won't need them for anything else either, and they may get scared but not know how to tell you.

Eating should be a pleasure, not an issue with a capital "I." It shouldn't cause family disharmony. You might want to share the following information with your parents if the topic of food and eating heats up. First of all, the idea that three meals a day are necessary for health isn't always true. Nutritionists say it's just as healthy (sometimes even more so) to eat five or six smaller meals rather than three big ones. Actually, when you have a hectic schedule as most teenagers do, snacking may have to take the place of regularly scheduled meals. Also, you don't have to clean your plate or eat when you don't feel like it just because "it's time." If possible, you should eat only when you're hungry (except if you're sick and the doctor tells you otherwise).

On the issue of junk food, sometimes "junk" is pretty good. For example, things that are often considered empty calories aren't so empty. Three slices of pizza have about 54 grams of carbohydrate, 25 grams of protein, 15 grams of fat, 450 calories — roughly the equivalent of a lamb chop, string beans, and a small baked potato. Most people junk out from time to time, even parents (and you may need to remind them of this fact).

If your parents turn eating into a personal issue, you might say any of the following things as a way to open discussion and negotiations,

"It's not fun to have someone monitoring every bite of food we eat."

"You *can* worry and get me professional help if my eating habits begin to interfere with my everyday life-style and cause me physical or emotional damage."

"I love you because of who you are, not because of what you feed me or give me. I hope that you love me for who I am, not for whether I accept or reject the food you offer me."

Try to make your parents understand that confusing eating with self-worth and self-image issues can lay the foundation for problems with obesity, anorexia, and bulimia. You might want to give them this chapter to read.

Mirror, Mirror, on the Wall, if I'm Fat I Won't Be Invited to the Ball!

There are many teenagers who are overweight and completely happy with themselves and their lives. This section of the book isn't about them. It's about people whose weight interferes with the quality of their lives and who find that it creates real problems for them.

What are the problems? The most frequent one is having to deal with incorrect, unfounded assumptions people make about you if you're overweight: that you're lazy or have no willpower or you don't care about yourself because if you did you'd lose those extra pounds.

Being overweight can make you feel different from your peers, not different in an interesting or creative way like Annie Lenox or Prince, but different in a way that makes you feel like the butt of a bad joke. Actually, there's not a lot of information available to you to prove your ideas about acceptable weight and body image wrong. MTV doesn't show too many overweight rock stars, male or female. Ads geared to the teen buying market — for fast food restaurants, soft drinks, clothing — use actors and actresses who are slender, acrobatic, cheerleader, or jock types to hawk their products. If overweight kids appear in teen magazines they are usually part of diet-plan makeovers. And although there are now modeling agencies for "big, beautiful women," teenagers are yet to benefit from this slowly changing social acceptance of *all* body types.

Heavyset boys are luckier than heavyset girls in one respect. Boys have many role models to look up to and pattern themselves after: ultra-heavyweight power lifters, football players, body builders, even sumo wrestlers. "Big" translates into "strong" in these examples, any or all of whom can be seen on weekend TV. In contrast, large women are glaringly absent from the airwaves, and if they are heavyset as are the Soviet women athletes, there is usually a negative remark made to the effect that they must be taking male hormones or steroids to get that big. Television doesn't give much coverage to sports in which bigger women are successful, like discus, shotput, and javelin throwing.

So if you're overweight you may start to believe you aren't as good as everyone else. In other words, you let the bad press about overweight people actually affect how you think about yourself. That, in turn, can affect what you really do accomplish or are willing to try to achieve.

When teenagers have problems, the adults they confide in may try to talk them out of the problems. That's why overweight teenagers usually hear two categories of advice from adults: the "forget it, in ten years it won't matter" kind, and the "you think you have problems? Wait till you're a parent — then you'll know what problems are" kind. If you've heard either of these, you'll realize they're not very helpful, though they may be well-meaning. What you need instead are some facts to help you answer the following questions:

1. Do I really want to lose weight?
2. Why do I want to lose weight?
3. How can I succeed at losing weight?
4. How will my life be different and how will I be different if I lose weight?

Don't Let Your Weight Determine Your Fate! Get the Facts Straight!

Did you ever find yourself saying, "I know this is going to be a lousy day," before it even began, and then you actually had a lousy day? This is one version of something called the "self-fulfilling prophecy." It means that we can make or break a situation in part because of our attitudes, in part because of what we actually do. It implies that we have a lot of control over the outcome of our own lives.

If you focus on your weight, you may make what you weigh the basis for negative self-fulfilling prophecies. A kid on a diet whose scale registers a gain of two pounds may get depressed and have a lousy day. Similarly, overweight teen-agers who don't really know how to lose weight and keep it off will persist in stepping on their scales daily, even though they know that this activity will trigger a series of really bad feelings about themselves. Being overweight, or just thinking you're overweight even if you're not really, can make you insecure and scared. It can prevent you from having self-confidence. It can make you cautious. It can make you feel undesirable, be afraid of dating, even cause you to doubt your sexual attractiveness. It can be a real handicap because it may prevent you from taking advantage of what your school, your family, and your friends may have to offer you. It shouldn't do any of this, and if it does, you need to talk about it with someone you can trust.

Some of us are slaves to our scales and think we're overweight when we're not. Looking at the height and weight charts may lead to panic if we exceed the recommended weight printed on the chart. But the charts don't include all the facts about height, weight, body type, and activity levels. Do you want to be liberated from this fat fetish? You need to get your facts about overweight straight!

Fact 1. There's no such thing as a perfect weight for a certain height. Those numbers you read are statistical averages only.

Fact 2. Muscle weighs more than fat. If you're even moderately athletic, you'll weigh more than you think you should. A better test of whether or not you have gained weight is how your clothes fit, not what a scale says.

Fact 3. Whether you're male or female has an impact on how "fat" you will be. Boys and girls should have different percentages of fat in their bodies: a boy's decreases from 16 percent to 10 percent during adolescence, and a girl's increases from 16 percent to between 20 and 24 percent. A girl needs 20 percent body fat to start menstruating.

Actually, during adolescence there are so many changes in the distribution of body fat and where it ends up on your body that it's hard even for doctors to assess whether you're overweight when these changes are going on!

Fact 4. You should arrange for a physical exam if you think you're too heavy, because it's important to find out the extent to which your weight may be affecting your physical and emotional health.

Fact 5. Your weight is just one dimension of the many qualities that make you a unique person. It doesn't have to be the main focus. It's something you can control, not something that should control you.

When "Diet" Is a Four-Letter Word and When It's Not

Since we live in an antifatness culture, we are a diet-conscious culture. People diet for many reasons, and getting thin is just one part of the ritual.

What does dieting do for people? It gives them a focus for their lives, a structure, a goal. It gives them something definite to do each day, something to talk about or complain about, an activity — like a sport — to do with friends. People sometimes use dieting as an opportunity for social activity (think of all the Weight Watchers groups with people who get together to discuss the results of their dieting).

You should pay attention to how you use food, because that's likely to influence the kinds of diets you'll choose to try, and the style of dieting you'll fall into. Do you eat as entertainment? Do you use food as something to make you feel better when you're under stress? Do you eat when you aren't hungry? Do you use food and eating as the focus of your life to the exclusion of friends? Do you enjoy eating? Do you really taste what you eat? Does your family encourage overeating? Did you grow up with a "clean your plate" message? Are you the only overweight person in your family?

The answers to these questions will give you clues about why you're overweight. You may find that you're eating to cover up a problem you don't want to deal with. You may find that you're overweight because you are consuming too many calories and just need to exercise to balance the food intake. People's attitudes about eating are often reflected in their attitudes about dieting!

What dieting *doesn't* do for teenagers, more often than not, is help them lose weight and keep it off. How you use food, the kind of diet you choose to go on, and your style of dieting give clues as to why you're dieting — to lose weight, because you think it's the "in" thing to do, or you're looking for a "quick fix" — and the kind of effort you're willing to make to achieve your goal.

Let's first look at some facts about diets and dieting.

1. *Crash diets on which you plan to eat very little (less than 1200 calories a day) for a brief period of time (two weeks or less) don't work well.* You lose water weight rather than fat, and when you go off the diet you're likely to regain any lost weight quickly. Also, your body gets fooled into thinking it's starving because of the strictness of the diet. When this happens, some physical changes occur in your body to protect you from the effects of starvation, the most obvious of which is that your metabolism slows down. As a result, you can't lose weight quickly! Finally, these diets are hard to stick with since they keep you hungry most of the time, and don't account for your special nutritional needs. They may actually enhance any tendencies you have to binge-eat once you're off the diet.

Libraries are filled with crash diet books that were former best-sellers: Judy Mazel's *Beverly Hills Diet*, Audrey Eyton's *F-Plan Diet*, Harris and Dolphin's *No Choice Diet*, Isenberg and Elting's *Nine Day Wonder Diet*, Robert Atkins' *Super Energy Diet*, Tarnower and Baker's *Complete Scarsdale Medical Diet*, and so on. The reason they're no longer best-sellers is that they offer gimmicks in place of nutritional advice that you can stick with, and they offer hope of results that few of us are actually able to attain. If you try such crash diets and fail at them, you may feel worse about yourself than when you started. But the fault may be more with the diet plan than with how well you followed it. Crash diets are not advised for anyone.

2. *Drugs and diets don't mix. Diet plans that suggest you use nonprescription, over-the-counter pills to help you stick to a diet are very dangerous.* Most nonprescription diet pills contain something called PPA (phenylpropanolamine), a decongestant

also found in cold and sinus pills. PPA is a stimulant (the "poor man's speed") that can cause high blood pressure in people who never had symptoms before, anxiety, agitation, dizziness, stomach problems, even hallucinations. These pills don't increase your chances of succeeding on a diet enough to offset the potentially serious harm PPA can do to your body.

3. *A slow, almost boring rate of weight loss with a gradual increase in your physical activity level is the closest thing to a guarantee of success on a diet.* If you cut out 500 calories a day, you'll lose one pound a week (one pound equals 3,500 calories). If you combine this with a physical exercise program such as walking or jogging three times a week for thirty minutes per session, you'll find that your body will begin to burn fat and begin to build muscle in all the right places at the same time.

And that's weight that will stay lost. It's not just "water weight" that will come back as soon as you take a drink of water or juice or soda. It's not a rate of loss that will make you so weak that you'll be unable to concentrate at school or participate in sports. It's not a rate of loss that will rob your body of the vitamins and minerals you need to stay healthy and grow. It's not a kind of diet that will first reduce your body's fat stores and then attack your muscle fibers, possibly endangering your growth. It's not a way of losing weight that involves medication that can make you feel hyper when you're on it and let down when you're not.

The best way to diet? Slow, sensible weight loss plus an increase in physical activity level. It's not the quick way, it may not be chic, fun, or interesting, it's not an instant answer to all your problems, but it's a manageable way to go about making a positive change, if that's what you think you want to do. We're sure you've heard statements to the effect that you should never start a diet without first consulting a doctor or nutritionist. We know that most people would no more consider asking for permission or guidelines before starting a diet than they would ask for permission to go to school each morning. It's not realistic.

But use common sense. If you're considerably overweight and have more than twenty or twenty-five pounds to lose, please realize that you may need medical help or therapy from a counselor who specializes in helping people who have problems with their eating behavior. No matter what the reason, your eating behavior is a habit that may be hard to change without some outside advice and guidance. There may be some underlying medical problems that are causing the weight problem or making it hard to eliminate. If you ask for help it is a sign of strength, not of weakness.

Anorexia Anguish; Binges and Bulimia

A recent *Glamour* magazine "Body-Image Survey" found that the majority of the 33,000 readers who responded thought they were too fat when in fact more of them were underweight than overweight. Half of them said they took diet pills, and 15 percent of them said they used self-induced vomiting to control their weight.

The surprising thing about this survey is not the results but the fact that it may actually underestimate the number of people whose concern with weight control and body image are putting them at great risk for developing the eating disorders of anorexia nervosa and/or bulimia.

Anorexia and bulimia are like the flip sides of the same coin. They have been referred to as "Cinderella's stepsisters," and even though they may seem like totally different behaviors — anorexia being a disorder of self-starvation and bulimia being a disorder of bingeing and then purging the food from your system by vomiting, laxative abuse, or the ingestion of emetics such as ipecac — more often than not they will be found affecting the same person. That person may suffer from anorexia and then flip over to bulimic behavior, stay with that until the guilt and panic sets in and switch back to anorectic patterns. This kind of seesaw can go on for months or years and professional help is the best way to break the pattern.

All of us have habits that we develop over the course of a lifetime. Sometimes the habits are useful, sometimes they're annoying. They are part of our personality and help make each of us unique. Eating disorders can start when some of these habits and attitudes about food, eating, and self-image turn into obsessions. While a habit is something you may do without thinking twice about it, an obsession is something that overtakes you, that you spend endless amounts of time and energy on, that begins to control your life and blot out other interests or relationships. Like drugs or alcohol, food has the potential to be misused with consequences that can be life-threatening.

Anorexia Nervosa

How can you tell if someone has anorexia nervosa? Anorexia means "loss of appetite," but this is a misnomer because anorectics are constantly thinking about food. They just refuse to eat it, or refuse to eat it in usual amounts and in a typical way. Anorexia is behaviors that occur as a group, much as a constellation is a group of individual stars that appear in the sky together and gain their identity from the image they project. Anorexia is a constellation of behaviors, the sum of its parts. The parts are:

1. *An inability to eat what most of us eat to maintain adequate health, growth, and psychological well-being.*

2. *An obsession with the purchase and preparation of food and the feeding of other family members, but not oneself.*

3. *The need to have rituals in order to eat at all.* For example, some anorectics refuse to touch a fork to their lips, others must cut their food into a set number of pieces arranged in a certain way on a plate.

4. *An intense fear of food and what it may do to you.* Even the smallest amounts of food or liquid in an anorectic's stomach can make the person feel bloated and trigger real feelings of panic. So, many anorectics have "safe foods" that don't throw them into a panic, such as one lettuce leaf per meal or two peas or just carrots.

5. *Body-image changes.* As anorectics lose more and more weight, they actually begin to see fat where none exists on their bodies. To hide the imagined fat, they tend to dress in baggy clothes.

6. *The belief that you need to starve yourself in order to maintain some measure of control over your own life.*

7. *The need to be alone.* When anorexia is in advanced

stages, some anorectics cannot stand to be seen eating or to see others eat. This solitude gradually extends to all other areas of their lives, isolating them (and insulating them) from family and friends.

In addition to these things, some serious *physical changes* occur if the anorectic loses between 20 and 25 percent of existing body fat.

1. A concentration camp appearance replaces their normal look. You need only to observe some of the photographs of the starving Ethiopian people or of victims of the Holocaust to know what look we are referring to. Cheeks are sunken, eyes are vacant; it is as if the soul is draining from the face.

2. Loss of hair on the head, accompanied by growth of a baby-fine hair called lanugo on the rest of the body. Doctors think this may be the body's way of trying to stay warm as protective fat layers are used up, since no other nourishment is coming into the system.

3. Loss of muscle, as muscle fibers are used up for energy. Many anorectics carry cushions to sit on since they have no padding left on their buttocks or hips and they find it very painful to sit or lie down.

4. The person is cold all the time. As a result, many anorectics are constantly in motion and will do six hundred situps when fifty would do, or might swim four miles when all the coach asked for is two.

5. Girls who are premenstrual may not get their periods, and girls who had been menstruating before becoming anorectic may stop menstruating.

Why would anyone do this to herself or himself? The singer Pat Boone's eldest daughter did and later wrote a book about it to alert people to the dangers and devastating effects of anorexia. The singer Karen Carpenter did and died. Elizabeth Barrett Browning, the poet, was thought to be anorectic. As we said earlier, anorexia nervosa involves obsessive behavior and logic flies out the window when an obsession takes over. However, certain people are known to be at greater risk than others. Teenage girls are fifteen times more likely to become anorectic than boys, and it is estimated that one in 175 teenage girls is caught in the web of anorexia nervosa. Anorectics often come from families in which communication patterns aren't clear: there is a tendency to make assumptions about one another and second-guess each other, there is usually very little praise when a child does well, and people talk *at* one another if they talk at all. Kids who become anorectic are usually described by their families as "good," having rarely caused trouble or given anyone cause for concern. One therapist calls them "the best little girls in the world." Anorexia becomes a very effective way for such teenagers to assert control not only over their bodies, but over their parents and environment as well! Sadly, it's a devastating route to take.

Binges and Bulimia

A binge can be defined differently by different people, depending on whether they are in control of the binge or are controlled by the binge. If you're a person who knows when you're hungry and when you're full, and who can stop eating when you're full, then you may consider an elegant meal at a fancy restaurant with your favorite friend to be a binge. If you're returning home for the Christmas holidays after a semester of eating dorm food, a binge may be the opportunity to pig out on your mom's homemade cookies and pies as often as you want until you can no longer stand the sight of them. Once you've had your fill, you'll go back to a more normal eating pattern. For others, a binge is a splurge, like a spur-of-the-moment trip to Baskin Robbins for a banana split with Quarterback Crunch, Peanut Butter and Chocolate, and Peach ice creams. Binges like that are pure fun and guilt-free.

If a generalization can be made about eating habits, it can be said that many teenagers binge regularly. Sometimes binges are a social thing, a chance to let it all hang out as at all-night fraternity beer blasts. Binges can be self-indulgences, ways of dealing with tensions, frustrations, hurt feelings. You may binge one day, fast the next, and then eat normally for weeks until you binge and fast again. If the binge habit gets out of hand, though, you will gain weight. If you binge to deal with anxieties and aggravations, your added weight may give you more problems (of the sort overweight teenagers regularly face that we have just discussed) and your binges will turn out to be harmful in the long run.

For some people, to binge means to lose control. Food isn't something delightful, pleasurable, and life-sustaining. It becomes a narcotic, a drug, a poison. The thought, sight, and smell of food makes you an irrational pawn. You become obsessed. If and when your existence becomes dominated by food and your normal daily activities are interfered with as a result of the obsession, if you are overly concerned with your weight at the same time you are obsessed with food, and if you choose to control your weight by purging your system of the food by means of self-induced vomiting (finger or fist down the throat), emetic-induced vomiting (taking syrup of ipecac, for example), or abuse of laxatives (*mistakenly* thinking that if you get rid of the food you eat you'll also get rid of all the calories), then you are most likely a bulimic.

Bulimia literally means "ox hunger," or a voracious appetite, and is also known as the binge-purge syndrome. A bulimic has an uncontrollable urge to eat large amounts of food (usually high-calorie "junk food") over a short period of time (usually less than two hours). Preferred foods may include a loaf of bread, a gallon of ice cream, several candy bars, Twinkies or cupcakes, potato chips, and bags of cookies, consumed at one sitting. Bulimics don't often binge on health foods and vegetables. A binge stops only when the binger experiences physical pain from the extreme stretching of the stomach due to the enormous quantities of food consumed (sometimes as much as 20,000 calories a binge), a social interruption (phone call, doorbell rings, someone in the family walks in) occurs, or because the bulimic falls asleep. Bulimics know that their eating patterns are abnormal, and live in fear of being unable to stop a binge voluntarily. Bulimics get no real pleasure from the food they eat.

> When I was on a binge I couldn't taste the food. I never knew when I was full and I ate just because I had to. It was a real compulsion. I just didn't know how to get my brain to tell my mouth to stop. I felt disgusting and ashamed. I couldn't control it.
>
> *Jennie S., age eighteen*

Bulimics lose the ability to know when they're hungry and when they're full. What do food binges do for them? They guarantee two sure things: feelings of depression and self-loathing after each binge.

The incidence of bulimia is on the upswing among teenagers, yet no one seems to be able to establish an accurate count, or a male-to-female ratio. Today, at least, females predominate, but boys get caught up in the purging part of the pattern, especially if they are in sports like wrestling that require staying within weight classes.

We also don't yet know how to describe a "typical" bulimic the way we can describe a "typical" anorectic. We do know that Jane Fonda struggled with bulimia for some sixteen years and that the Olympic gymnast Cathy Rigby almost let it destroy her career. We know that people who participate in sports (wrestling, swimming, gymnastics) or in art forms such as classical ballet and modern dance, all of which demand close monitoring of weight, may be at greater risk for becoming bulimic than are teenagers who aren't so keyed into having to keep their weights at certain levels. Therapists who help bulimic teenagers get over their obsessions report that many of these teenagers have difficulty dealing with combined pressures of carrying off school, job, social and family responsibilities. Bulimia, then, is not just a problem with food. It can reflect family or interpersonal stresses. Like anorexia, bulimia does not occur in a vacuum.

Bulimics don't look sick or different the way anorectics do, so bulimia is really a "hidden" disorder. Bulimics must live a double life, maintaining an apparently normal routine that masks the secret, private rituals of bingeing and purging. Because of the invisibility of the obsession, most bulimics get little or no sympathy from family or friends, who may not recognize, much less understand, the teenager's struggle with the food obsession.

> When I was at my worst my parents still hadn't figured out what was going on. They thought I was pregnant at first since I was in the bathroom so much, and started calling me "slut" and all that. Then they found the laxatives and really freaked out. Neither of them even had a word for what I was doing. There was always so much screaming, it was horrible. And I couldn't tell them.
>
> *Angela D., age seventeen*

Families and friends often react with disgust or revulsion when they do find out about someone's bulimia, since the end products of the binges — high food bills, empty food cartons or wrappers in weird places where the food has been hoarded — and of the purging — reeking bathrooms, vomit, and diarrhea that need to be cleaned — are unpleasant and stress-producing. Living with a bulimic can trigger feelings of intense anger, but scolding and blame don't solve the problem.

What does bulimic behavior look like? It's very ritualistic (just as anorectic behavior is). Bulimics usually set aside a portion of each day to binge for a set period of time and plan all their other activities around the binge. As do anorectics, bulimics have preferred foods, only theirs are high-calorie, snack-type items that require little or no preparation. (There are exceptions: fifteen-year-old Jennie T. had eaten so many carrots she turned orange from the carotene in her system!) The intensity of a binge can be so strong that a bulimic may appear to be in a trance. If disturbed, a bulimic may become enraged.

Bulimia causes people to do things they wouldn't otherwise consider doing. Because it's very expensive to keep yourself stocked with enough food, laxatives, and even diet pills (when bulimics don't lose weight by purging they will turn to diet pills and overdo it with them too) to be able to satisfy an obsession, bulimic teenagers in the advanced stages of the disorder often resort to theft of food or money from family, roommates, or strangers. In fact, this form of theft is now a major problem in college dorms and adds yet another source of stress to a bulimic's already tense existence.

My father is a minister and I was arrested at school for stealing. It didn't matter that I was sick. My defense? Bulimia! They were hardly sympathetic. I was suspended from school for a semester, my roommates threw me out, and my parents are so furious they won't talk to me. Sure, I'm living at home, but I'm worse off than I was before. I'm too mad now to get help.

Karolyn P., age eighteen

Bulimics can really damage their health when they habitually binge and purge. The purging is what does most of the damage. Vomiting upsets the body's mineral balance, and causes potassium deficiency, and can eventually lead to heart failure and death. It causes the salivary glands to enlarge giving the face a puffy, "cheeky" appearance. The acid produced by vomiting erodes tooth enamel and can burn and permanently damage the esophagus. A less serious result of self-induced vomiting is that many bulimics develop scars or callouses on their knuckles from jamming their fingers and fists down their throats. Bulimics who make themselves vomit by taking emetics like ipecac risk poisoning themselves. Purging by overuse of laxatives (many bulimics take sixty to a hundred per day) can destroy normal bowel functions. In fact, the laxative habit is like cocaine or heroin abuse in that the more you take the more you need to take with each use to get an equivalent effect. Also, your hormone production can be thrown out of whack due to constant bingeing and purging, and some obstetricians suggest that female teenage bulimics may seriously impair their future ability to conceive and bear children.

Bulimics, like anorectics, are at risk where health is concerned. One major difference between the two eating disorders, though, is that bulimia seems to be transmittable! It is a *learned* behavior that seems to be spreading like wildfire within "closed communities" like college dorms where people are in close contact and pick up habits and behaviors from one another. In that sense, bulimia is now considered to be a potential public health hazard that kids need to be educated about just as they would be about drugs, alcohol, or sexually transmitted diseases.

It's important to remember that there's a fine line between normal and abnormal, between habit and obsession: what is normal for one person may be obsessive for someone else. We all binge from time to time, we all like to pig out on the good stuff. An occasional binge isn't the same as bulimia, and going on a diet doesn't mean you're anorectic. So don't panic if your friend says she's been living on Doritos and Chocodiles for days. Don't panic if you look at yourself in the mirror and think you're fat when everyone else says you're thin. Family relationships, friendship networks, how you communicate with others, how you feel about yourself are all part of the picture. Since eating disorders don't occur in a vacuum *if those things are OK, you're probably OK too.*

However, if you feel that more than a few of the things we've discussed apply to you, if a raw nerve has been exposed that you are now reacting to, if that imaginary mirror you're gazing into reflects back a broken image, take that as a signal that you should investigate the possibility of talking with someone about your feelings. It can be a parent, a sibling, a friend, a teacher, a counselor, clergyperson, doctor or therapist — anyone you already trust and can be open and honest with and who will be open and honest with you. Eating disorders can be very dangerous to your physical and mental health and can rip your families apart if left untreated.

The good thing is that they can be treated by a combination of professional therapy, willpower, and participation in self-help groups with other kids who have gone through similar experiences and survived. Many hospitals now have eating disorder units set up just to treat adolescents, and auxiliary staff people to help the teenager's family members and friends deal with the aspects of the disorders that affect them too. Local social service agencies usually have staff people trained to help you figure out what kind of treatment you and your family might need.

There's one rub. If you need help, you must be willing to ask for it or at least be willing to say "Okay, I'll give it a go," if help is offered. Problems with eating behavior can't be dealt with effectively if you aren't sure you want the help.

All of the issues we've discussed in this chapter have something to do with needing to feel in control and yet not being in control of your life. It's never easy to admit you're imperfect, to admit you have shortcomings, to admit you have a problem. In fact, it takes a major effort and a lot of courage to do it. To take a positive step and get help with a problem is a way of reasserting that self-control. Taking charge of your life is a way of telling the world, "I like myself enough to want to improve things for myself," and that's a decision everyone will think is cool.

Part 3.

Crisis Time

11.

A Ten-Point Plan
for Recognizing and Resolving
Major Crises

Major crises usually grow from smaller problems that aren't solved around the time when they begin. They can start out like minor volcanic rumblings and then get stronger and stronger until they erupt with a huge lava flow that destroys everything in its path. We don't all define and handle crises in the same ways. Some people can deal with major problems (death of a relative, serious illness, accidents, divorce, unplanned pregnancy, etc.) without falling apart, while others let the unexpected turn of events rip their lives apart. Some people are calm and capable when faced with a crisis, but many of us don't know what to do and where to turn first.

Coping is easier if you are prepared. Though you may feel that it's morbid or unnecessary to think ahead of time about things in life that could go wrong, planning may be a good idea. It's a way to improve the odds that if something bad happens you won't panic; instead, you'll know what you can do either to solve the crisis or control it rather than letting it control you, or help someone else accomplish these things. In this chapter, we'll take you step-by-step through a strategy that can make it easier for you to recognize and resolve the crises that you may someday face, while the chapters that follow will explore some of these difficult situations in much greater detail.

Point 1.
Learn about what you can do if a crisis requires
an IMMEDIATE reaction from you.

I was fooling around with two of my friends at a down-
town construction site when all of a sudden a huge
mound of sand we were climbing caved in. Tom was
half-buried, and Jeff disappeared from sight altogether. I
called 911 and they sent an ambulance and a fire engine
squad that managed to rescue everyone with only minor
injuries.

Brian O., age fourteen

My sister tried to commit suicide by drinking Lysol and
eating a deodorant stick. She stopped breathing. I used
CPR on her until the paramedics got here. They told me I
may have saved her life.

Josh H., age seventeen

Life-threatening crises such as medical emergencies, accidents, suicide attempts, or drug and alcohol overdoses require
a quick reaction. In order to improve the chances that you'll
react correctly, though, you should have some basic survival
skills. These include:

— Knowing that dialing the 911 emergency phone number is
   often the quickest way to get outside help.
— Taking and passing a Red Cross first aid course at school
   or at your local Red Cross chapter. (This course teaches
   you how and when to apply a tourniquet or splints, what
   to do when someone is choking, etc.)
— Taking and passing a CPR (cardio-pulmonary resuscita-
   tion) course at school or wherever else it's offered (the
   Red Cross, the police and fire departments in your area
   may all have CPR classes).
— Learning about basic self-defense that could protect you
   in case of a surprise physical attack. (This doesn't mean
   you've got to earn a black belt in karate. Something as
   simple as learning the places on a human body that are
   "pressure points" and could stun an attacker [the eyes,
   the groin, the carotid artery in the neck area] might mean

the difference between escaping an attacker and being a victim.)

— Knowing the location and phone numbers of the hospital emergency room, health clinic, doctor, or counselor that you could get help from if you had to.

— Knowing the address and phone number of an adult (not one of your parents) you can trust completely to call on in an emergency if your parents aren't available or if they're part of the problem.

Point 2.
Define the problem and break it down into its parts.

The first step in coming to grips with a major crisis that you have the time to think about is to define it. This is true whether you're talking about a situation that happens at home and involves your family members, or a situation away from home that involves friends or people at school or work. It's also true whether you're the one in crisis or if you're trying to help someone else deal with a crisis situation.

Once you've defined the problem, breaking down the problem into parts makes it a little easier to understand and may make you feel like you can have control over some parts of it, if not the whole thing. Try to answer the following questions.

What's the nature of the problem? Is it a health crisis? Is it a problem that revolves around family relationships like divorce? Is it an economic crisis, such as when your parents lose their jobs and your family may have to change its life-style? Maybe the crisis is more of a social situation, like when you feel you have no friends and get depressed, which leads to other problems for you and your family. Is it something you might have control over (you could choose to stop drinking and get help for your problem, you have options when deciding what to do about an unplanned pregnancy) or something over which you have no control (such as a parent's final decision to divorce, or the death of a relative)?

When and how did it begin?

How long has it been going on? Problems that have gone on for a long time may be harder to get rid of than problems that have had less time to get ingrained into the fabric of your family life.

Has the nature of the problem changed over time? If so, how?

Who's involved? The crisis may affect only you or it can affect your whole family. The crisis may really be a friend's problem, but you're involved because that friend turns to you for advice and support.

How serious is it? It may be something so awful that you can no longer stand to live with it (sexual abuse, for example), or it may be a crisis that is annoying but less severe in terms of its impact on your day-to-day life (such as a relative's health problem). The seriousness of a problem often determines how quickly action is required to solve it.

Where did you get your facts about the problem (personal experience? gossip? intuition?)? Analyzing a crisis this way is very important because issues of tremendous concern to you may not pack the same emotional punch for other people (notably, parents and friends), and the things that really bother others — building up into seething resentment leading to a crisis — may seem just short of inconsequential to you. For example, you may completely ignore your best friend's reactions to the times you flirt with her boyfriend. At first, she may be afraid to tell you what she *really* thinks you're trying to do: steal him. You may have no such intention. You just feel at ease with them, and your personality shines when you're together. When your friend finally gets into a major fight with you about her interpretation of your behavior, you really can't believe it! That's why it's important to be speaking about the same thing.

With luck, you'll be able to discuss your definition of the crisis with the people who are part of the problem. You may be worried that your parents will blame you for screwing up or give you an "I told you so" lecture, but you can often rely on them to give you their attention and support. Parents tend to freak out about minor problems that their kids either cause or suffer through, but they often rise to the occasion when they know it's a major crisis you're facing.

Point 3.
Outline the reasons why this crisis has reached a boiling point.

Basically, this means that you have to do some honest soul-searching.

1. Did you realize your problems were getting out of control?
2. Did you refuse to admit that there were problems?
3. Do you sometimes like being in conflict with other people?
4. Do you have trouble standing up for yourself or saying what you really mean?
5. Are you the sort of person who believes you have to take what comes to you, good or bad?

In some cases, it's actually easier for people to live with major problems than to confront them and try to eliminate them when they first start. Maybe you've been taught never to talk back to other people, or maybe you fear for your safety if you rock the boat, or maybe you just don't have the right words to describe what's bothering you. Whatever the reasons, they need to be thought about and talked about.

Point 4.
Find an outside source of help to get you through the crisis.

You wouldn't shoot the Colorado rapids on a raft without the proper safety equipment and a guide to help you get through the rough whitewaters. You wouldn't trek through the Himalayas without a companion who spoke the language and knew the terrain. The same holds true for solving crises. You may know exactly what you want to do, but you may not have the experience necessary to do it. That's where outside help fits in.

That help can come from many sources, as long as they're neutral — that is, people who aren't emotionally tied up in the problem that you're facing. Sometimes close friends can do this, but more often than not a professional (therapist, school counselor, family doctor, teacher, social worker, psychiatrist, clergyperson, police officer, lawyer, psychologist) is needed.

There are times when you *can't* confront the person who

is causing the problem for you. For example, a girl who is being sexually victimized by her father can't turn to him for a solution because he *is* the problem. That's the kind of situation when you must turn to a professional for help, without worrying about being judged, and without fear of shame or embarrassment. Not only can the professional help you mentally, but he or she can arrange to get protection for you so that you don't have to suffer from further physical or psychological abuse.

You can get help, whether or not your parents want to be part of the process, by calling your local social service agency or Family Service Agency (listed in the *Yellow Pages*, sometimes under the heading of "Mental Health"), asking a teacher, or getting a referral from a friend. There may be self-help groups that advertise in your local newspapers.

If you are in the midst of a crisis and can't find someone to talk to face-to-face, and need *immediate* feedback, there are a number of toll-free phone hotlines that you can call. Many are local and you will need to look them up in a *Yellow Pages* phone directory under the topic such as "Suicide" or "Mental Health Services — Suicide." Some of the better known national hotlines can give you sound advice and referrals to local professionals. For example, the Cocaine Hotline (for help with any drug-related crisis): 800-COCAINE, and the National Runaway Hotline: 800-972-6004.

Some words of caution. Don't try to be your own therapist. It rarely works. You need that outsider's point of view (and expertise) to clarify things in your own mind. It can help you build the self-confidence you need to weather the crisis, and will give you someone you can trust and have confidence in to smooth the way for you to succeed when you try to put your plan of action to the test. Remember that while this is probably the first time you're facing this particular sort of crisis, a well-trained professional has probably dealt with it dozens (if not hundreds) of times before.

Point 5.
Devise a plan of action that suits your needs.

Once you have defined your crisis and you have discussed it with an outside source to learn what other options exist, then you'll be in a better position to know what you want to do and how to go about doing it. Sometimes there are several alternative ways to handle a crisis that can each be effective; at other times, one approach is clearly preferable to the other choices you have. But in devising your plan of action, consider the following questions:

— What would be different in your life if the problems causing this crisis were solved?
— What are you willing to do to bring about the changes that are necessary to solve the crisis?
— What do you expect your parents and other family members to do to contribute to these changes?
— Are these changes realistically possible?

Point 6.
Make up a timetable.

Decide how long you're willing or able to give yourself to see the crisis solved. If it's a school problem, for example, can you turn it around in one semester? If it's a family problem in which your own safety is in question, how long will you be willing to continue living at home if things don't improve tremendously? Other crises, such as living with an alcoholic, require a day-by-day approach. Making up a timetable can do two things: give you goals to shoot for, and give you an endpoint beyond which you may decide you need to remove yourself from the situation if it remains intolerable.

Point 7.
Avoid jumping to conclusions. Avoid making hasty decisions or snap judgments.

I was totally strung out by my parents' divorce. It took me by surprise. One day my dad announced my mom had kicked him out and he was leaving. I took it personally, like that my mom didn't want me in her life anymore either since I was a guy like Dad. My mom started acting like a kid herself, she seemed so happy, and I hated her for it. About a month after the divorce actually got legal, we got into a big fight. In a burst of anger, I went after her

with a kitchen knife. Now I'm in a group home and I'll be
lucky to get out in two years.

Zack V., age fifteen

People in crisis have a habit of not communicating very
thoroughly. A lot can go by unsaid that should be discussed,
and often assumptions are made that are completely un-
true.

Zack's case illustrates the problem quite well. His parents' divorce seemed to be more of a crisis for Zack than for
his mom. He resented her happiness. He concluded that she
wanted him out of her life the way his dad was now out of her
life. The snap judgments about his mom's state of mind (he
never really bothered to ask her if she was happy) and his
conclusion about what she wanted weren't based on fact at all.
He was second-guessing her, assuming all kinds of things, and
she may not even have realized the depth of his anger.

If you are in the position of helping someone through a
crisis, it's equally important for you to avoid making this kind
of snap judgment. If you're a friend or a relative, you obviously will have a bias. You are clearly an ally of the person
in crisis; otherwise, you wouldn't be willing to get involved.
But remember, he or she is emotionally involved, and you're
not.

What if Zack's case had happened like this: he went after
his mom with a knife, she disarmed him, and he got seriously
cut in the process. The next day at school he told you that his
mom had become violent and abusive since the divorce, and
showed you the cut as proof. You had been acting as his
source of outside help. What would you have been tempted to
do? Get help for his mother? Call the police about her? You
would have been trying to solve the wrong crisis, because the
facts you have would have led you to incorrect conclusions.
You might have assumed it was a case of child abuse when it
really wasn't. In this case, as in any situation where the potential for violence exists, it would be extremely important to
make sure Zack was telling you the truth. To do so might
mean going to his school counselor or your own counselor,
explaining what you know and how you got involved, and
asking the school to make some inquiries. It could be that the

family needs professional counseling or even police involve-ment. You don't have the expertise to solve Zack's problems, but you can set the helping process in motion. Be aware, how-ever, that not all people with problems really want to be helped, and your opinion can be misinterpreted as threaten-ing.

Point 8.
Help the other people you are close to
to understand what has happened to you.

A major crisis is like a stone thrown into a pond: it pro-duces ripple effects on the people close to you. Any nonpro-fessional person that has had to help you deal with the crisis is bound to experience some leftover tensions once the worst part of the crisis is past history. Parents often react by getting into hassles with one another over things that they normally wouldn't argue about. Brothers or sisters who haven't had their share of the family limelight when the focus had been on you and your crisis may start acting up themselves just to grab some of that attention. Friends you've confided in and leaned on may start treating you like you're made of glass and could break easily, or they might start to back off now that you're OK because they're emotionally drained and they don't want to have to constantly think about your problems anymore.

The best thing to do at this stage is be completely honest about what's happened and what you're doing about it. If you're talking to a younger brother or sister you may have to omit some of the details but, generally, honesty is preferable to letting their imaginations run wild. You can tell them this is a private family matter, not something to be discussed at school or with friends. You may need to reassure your par-ents, friends, and even your teachers, that you're fine now and don't mind if they ask you once in a while how you're feeling and doing. You might say things like:

> "I've learned a lot about myself lately, and I know it may take a while for you to stop worrying about me, but I'm OK."
>
> "I'm not the same person I was before all this started."

"I'm willing to listen to your point of view now, as long as you'll listen to mine."

"I hope you won't blame me for every little thing that goes wrong from now on, but I'll understand it if you do. I won't like it, but I'll undertand. But if that happens, we'll need to talk about it."

By the time you've reached point 8, you're really into the crisis resolution stage. Crisis resolution is a continuous healing process rather than a single stroke of action. The trick is to recognize that time is a great healer, and you need to give yourself (and anyone else involved in your crisis) time to get over it gradually. You can't force people to believe you're making changes, nor can you force yourself to instantly accept things your parents or friends may say to you and suggest you do. But cluing them in on what's happened to you *and being straight about it* is a great way to set the timer going.

Point 9.
Try to learn something from the experience.

The only real benefits from a crisis are its lessons. One is that you may find you can count on parents and friends in ways you never dreamed possible. Another is that you discover many strengths in yourself. If you follow this ten-point plan, you'll develop a new set of skills: how to think about a crisis, what happened, why it happened that way, and what could have been done to prevent it from happening. This equals *insight*, into your own behavior and other people's behavior.

Your new insights will probably last, so that even if you repeat the same mistakes, you'll at least have a sense of what can be done to short-circuit them and avoid another major crisis.

Point 10.
Do some long-range planning.

Was the crisis you've been dealing with an isolated occurrence that's unlikely to happen again, or was it a tip-of-the-iceberg thing with other problems lurking just beneath the surface? The kind of planning you'll do will depend in part on the answer to this question. For example, if you're struggling with deep-seated problems like depression, drug dependency, or suicidal impulses, you may be more at risk for a repeat crisis than you might be if your crisis had been over romantic problems or a conflict in school.

In any case, long-range planning means *you* have to make decisions about what you're willing to do in the future. If you've been coping with a crisis due to criminal behavior, for example, will you really stick to the terms of your probation? If your crisis had been due to unplanned pregnancy, will you now be responsible about birth control or limit your sexual activities? If your crisis involved being depressed or suicidal, and you now have a therapist, will you allow yourself to call that therapist if the depressed feelings start closing in on you again?

Long-range planning also means being prepared now. Keep a list of people you can contact in case of emergency. A ready reference like this can be enormously helpful if another crisis strikes and you're less than calm at the time. It may mean finding someone outside your immediate family who will let you stay at his or her home if you should need to get away from your own family. It may mean having one person you can always call on — at any hour of the day or night — to be that objective person who might be able to help you think through an impending crisis and maybe avoid it.

No crisis has to leave you permanently scarred. Give yourself permission to be in need of help at times, and give yourself points for taking the steps to change things that have hurt you in the past.

Scars are inevitable, but they do fade with time.

12.

How to Keep Your Cool
if Your Parents
Are Getting Divorced

The worst thing about telling the kids was having to see their reactions. My eldest son, who was seventeen at the time, slammed his fist into the table and then walked out. My thirteen-year-old cried. I just stood there numb.

Mrs. L., age thirty-nine, married twenty years before her divorce

I saw the divorce coming but that didn't make it easy to accept. I was scared then, but I'm used to it now, and I'm more curious than afraid about what's going to be.

Carly C., age fourteen

It would be easier to be an orphan than to have to deal with parents who are divorced.

John L., age sixteen

Finding out that your parents are getting a divorce can hurt, even if things at home were pretty rocky before the decision was made. It can be hard to separate your feelings about how you'd want things to be from the way things really are, and it can be just as difficult to understand that the direction your parents' relationship has taken doesn't necessarily reflect a change in their feelings about you.

Divorces are very common in our society — about a million kids go through them with their families each year — but that fact doesn't make it any easier for you if it's your family

238

that's splitting up. Because your parents are likely to be preoccupied with their own personal problems as well as with the
practical and legal details of divorce, they may forget to keep
you informed about what's happening, or they may purposely
keep you uninformed to try and protect you from the emotional ups and downs they're dealing with. Well-meaning as
their motives may be, your parents don't exactly help you by
keeping you in the dark, because what you may imagine as the
causes and outcome of a divorce can be far worse than the
truth, and you may worry much more than you should about
your role in the whole situation.

It's important to ask the kinds of questions that will separate fact from fiction in a divorce situation. This can be difficult because you may not know where to start, what to say,
and when to say it. You may be afraid of prying into your parents' private life, which you know is already tense, and you
may also want to avoid putting more stress on your parents
with your questions. This chapter is designed to help you understand divorce, learn what to ask your parents about and
how to phrase the questions, and say what you feel so that you
can keep your cool and recognize that even though divorce
may cause quite a few tremors in your family, it doesn't have
to set off a major earthquake.

Living with Parents
Who Are Having Marital Problems

In every family there are bound to be times when people don't
get along. No two parents are so perfectly attuned that they
agree on everything or never have second thoughts about decisions they've made either together or separately. No two
people can like each other all the time, and if your parents
criticize each other or seem to have tense moments together it
doesn't necessarily mean they are headed for divorce court.
There's a difference, though, between the kinds of arguing and
tension that occur as a normal part of living together and what
happens in families where the parents are not only unhappy
with their marriage, but can't seem to iron things out.

During the time leading up to parents' decision to divorce, it may seem like things "feel" different at home. Some of the changes may be subtle and others can be dramatic.

> My mom's posture changed the minute Dad walked in the door each night. It was like she got real straight, and she looked all pinched. Her voice changed too — it got tight.
>
> *Valerie P., age fourteen*

> My parents used to fool around a lot when I was little. My dad could always make Mom giggle. Now they're like two store mannequins when they're together.
>
> *Paul R., age sixteen*

> My parents were high school debate champs. I remember so many debates in our house — never arguments, always debates. Now there's a wall of silence. Nothing. You could choke on the quiet.
>
> *Saralynn E., age seventeen*

Teenagers who have lived through this predivorce stage say that the overwhelming sensation was one of tension that never eased up.

Tension like that takes a toll on every family member, but as an older child you may react more strongly than a younger sibling, who may not be quite as aware of shifts in the way your family operates. If you have to live with that level of tension, you may find that you don't feel quite like yourself, and you may try to change your behavior either to match how you feel or to cover up how you feel.

> I tried to act real cool, like I didn't notice what was happening. I didn't want to have to ask questions and hear awful answers. My parents probably thought I was dense, but I figured it was better to not react at all than to blow up and make things worse than they already were.
>
> *Sarah B., age fifteen*

> When my parents stopped talking I felt excluded from everything. It was worse than being yelled at because I didn't know where I stood and what was going on with them. At least when they fought, I could guess. I stopped

talking to them. I had no choice. I wanted to give them a taste of their own medicine.

Clark P., age fourteen

It's hard to ignore your parents' marital problems because they do affect you and can take a toll on you in many ways. The most obvious way is that they can make you feel unhappy because you can remember back to better times when family life was fun and relaxed. They can make you feel helpless, because you don't really have the ability to change things for your parents and solve their problems for them, no matter how much you may love them and want them to stay together. If you can't accurately define what it is that is happening between your parents and undermining their marriage and the family as you have known it, you can feel very frustrated and angry. You may not understand how two people can fall out of love and you may wonder who's to blame for the divorce. You may even start to feel responsible for some of their difficulties (you're not, even if you're the subject of their arguments) because some logical explanation is better than feeling like you're in the dark.

If your parents are having marital problems, they may not have as much energy to devote to you as you're used to, and you may think they no longer want to pay attention to you, or, worse, that they don't love you anymore. That's rarely the case, but they're so preoccupied with themselves they may temporarily forget about your needs. On the other hand, your parents may take a lot of their own frustrations and hostilities out on you rather than confronting each other, and so you may feel you have been turned into a scapegoat, constantly being blamed or treated unfairly.

It's very difficult to live in the midst of these kinds of tensions and you may take steps to change things. You may think you know your parents so well that you have the insight and skills to act as a kind of marriage counselor with the power to smooth over the arguments and ease the tensions. The truth is, though, you can't solve their problems — relatives rarely have the objectivity that's needed to do this, no matter what age they are.

There are, however, some other constructive ways to

cope with the frustrations of living with parents who seem to be headed for divorce court.

1. Express your feelings to someone. Talk to a friend who has been through a similar experience, to either or both of your parents, to another adult that you trust, to your siblings. If there is no one you want to actually talk to, at least write a letter to yourself. Get those feelings out in the open so they aren't hanging over your head like an enormous bucket of water that's on the verge of tipping and inundating you!

2. Write out a list of "what ifs". What if my parents stay together as they are now? What if they separate? What if they divorce? What if I have to live with one parent and not get to see the other at all? What if I have to live with the parent I don't want to live with? What if I have to move? What if I have to go to another school? What if I am separated from my siblings? What if my parents don't ask me how I feel about their decision? What if they ask me and don't agree? The list can go on and on. The important thing is to get down on paper all the "what ifs" that are important to you and that you need answered. If these "what ifs" aren't discussed with someone, your anxiety may increase to an uncomfortable level, which doesn't really have to happen. Since your parents may not realize the things you're concerned about, they may not volunteer the answers to the kinds of questions that are on your mind. That's why it's so important that you be prepared and willing to ask them.

3. Give your parents the opportunity to tell you the truth about themselves. It's very hard for parents to admit that they need to dissolve their marriage. They may feel guilty. They may want to explain that the reason it happened was because they became different people from the ones they were when they first married, that they grew apart, or grew in different directions. They may want to say that they hope you don't think they failed you. A lot of the tension that is felt in predivorce situations occurs because no one is really willing to sit and listen without being judgmental, accusing, harsh, and hostile. Your parents may want more than anything to apologize to you or to explain that their divorce doesn't affect their love for you, but they may not realize you'd be willing to sit through such a discussion. You have a right to your feelings, but try to give them a chance to express theirs too. Let them know you're available.

4. Ask your parents what they expect from you now that a divorce is a possibility. Most of us know what it takes to keep a family running smoothly, and know the differences between a parent's "job description" and the roles of children in a family. Being concerned with having to assume adult roles and maybe even taking the place of the missing parent and doing his or her jobs at home, or worrying about having to quit school and go to work to help keep the family afloat are reasonable concerns. Though it is rarely the case that you will have to take over for the soon-to-be-absent parent, you have every right to discuss this with your mom and dad.

Prepared or Not, Divorce Can Be a Shock to You

The trouble with having to face the finality of your parents' divorce is that no matter how prepared you are it's never enough. Divorce is a shock. This is true whether you're thirteen or thirty, whether or not you've been tuned into their habits and moods.

> My mom and dad have always been real loud. They argue a lot — we all hear it. They make up — we all hear it. I thought I could read them like a book. I didn't figure they were on the outs. I just thought the fighting was normal.
>
> *Betty S., age fifteen*

and whether you were consulted before the decision was made or told about it after the fact.

> They didn't ask me my opinion about a divorce; they just announced it. I thought they cared about my ideas, but now I don't think they do.
>
> *Martin L., age seventeen*

Divorce changes the way your family operates, and even though you may push for the right to make voluntary changes

Crisis Time

in your own life as you grow up, you may not want to have to cope with changes that you weren't planning on and that are imposed on you. Divorce redefines relationships, it opens the door for new and different people to become intimately involved in your family, it alters the roles each one of you has to play, and it can even change the way other people think about you and make you wonder about yourself.

> All of a sudden I was a kid from a broken home. I didn't know what I was expected to do, or if I was expected to behave differently.
>
> *Meredith J., age thirteen*

> My mom was the one who was moving out and I didn't know how I was going to be able to still be her daughter if I couldn't see her every day.
>
> *Annalee K., age fifteen*

> When my dad left I knew he felt he had failed because we had talked a lot before the divorce was final. Now I wonder what I'll fail at — everyone always said we were so much alike.
>
> *Peter K., age fifteen*

The newness and shock will wear off eventually, to be replaced with healing and acceptance. Don't be too concerned about feeling unsure, angry, worried, even depressed about the future (unless these feelings overwhelm you and prevent you from going about your life normally — in that case, get help from a counselor or therapist). These are normal reactions, and they're actually part of a grief process that you need to work through before you can start to feel like yourself again.

Custody

When parents divorce, one of the most important and difficult decisions that must be made is who will have primary responsibility for the children. This is what the legal term *custody* refers to.

> When I heard them talk about custody I thought one of
> them was going to . . . well . . . own me.
>
> *Patrice M., age thirteen*

> My folks argued for weeks about custody. I got a kick out
> of it — someone actually fighting for the right to take care
> of me!
>
> *Jay M., age fifteen*

> Custody? My initial reaction? I thought about jail.
>
> *Senta T., age sixteen*

The adult who has custody of the children is responsible for
making sure that you continue to have everything you would
have had if there had been no divorce — love, support, shelter, food, education, and so on — everything a family is supposed to provide you with. Some parents are able to work out
custody arrangements themselves, and others need to have a
family-court judge decide for them if they can't agree on the
details. However the decision is made, it is supposed to be
made in your best interest — that is, so that you will be properly taken care of and happy.

Sometimes kids whose parents are trying to work out
custody plans feel like pawns in a chess game when they don't
have the opportunity or ability to speak up for themselves and
have some input and influence over the family's discussion
about custody. Believe it or not, your opinions can and do
count.

> I felt like a traitor when I said I'd rather live with Mom.
> But I hate Dad's girlfriend and he knows it.
>
> *Jean A., age fifteen*

> I told the lawyer I wanted to live with both parents. The
> judge worked it out!
>
> *Nancy M., age sixteen*

> I said I'd rather go to boarding school than be split be-
> tween them.
>
> *Paula D., age fourteen*

Even in divorce cases where a judge must decide about custody, that judge will try to take into account your preferences

about who you'd like to live with and how you'd like to live. There are no guarantees that your wishes will be granted — judges aren't fairy godparents — but the odds are more in your favor than they would be if you never expressed an opinion.

There are many different kinds of custody arrangements and you should know about the options, because knowing may help you to decide what you think might work out best for you.

Joint custody means that you'd live most of the year with one parent, but both of your parents would share responsibility for all aspects of your life — financial, emotional, social, and so on.

Coparenting is a form of joint custody, and it means your parents are willing to consult each other about the day-to-day events of your life, not just the big issues like when you'll see the parent who moved out, how much money will be available for you to use, where you'll go on vacation, or what school you'll attend. Coparenting can make it feel like you still have two parents who are very actively involved in your life, even though they're no longer involved in each other's lives.

Sole custody means one parent has the lion's share of responsibility for your shelter and upbringing, and the other parent has to provide some financial support and is given some visiting privileges to be able to see you. In sole custody, the parents have much less contact with each other than they would have in joint custody, and their relationship tends to be much more formal.

Divided custody means you'd live with one parent for a set period during the year and with the other parent for the other part. Sometimes this works out to living three days with one, four days with the other, on a weekly basis (provided the parents live near one another and you can continue going to the same school), sometimes it means weekdays with one, weekends with the other, and sometimes it means the school year with one, the summer with the other. There's even something called "the bird's nest plan," in which you stay in one home and your parents alternate living there! There are endless variations that can be agreed on.

Split custody is possible only when there are two or more

children, because in that arrangement the kids are divided between the parents. For example, the father might assume custody of the boys and the mother get custody of the girls.

Living through the custody part of the divorce process can be very stressful.

> I didn't know where my home would be. Now I know why people are scared of not having roots.
>
> *Alice M., age seventeen*

> I started to think of myself as a giant prize that they were each trying to grab, a lifesize trophy.
>
> *Andre W., age fifteen*

> All of a sudden my parents started to try and buy me off, to buy my loyalty with promises and things.
>
> *Sylvia R., age fourteen*

Because there is so much uncertainty at this stage of a divorce, it's important to let your parents know how you are feeling and what you are thinking about. This will help you stay in control at a time when your family may seem out of control; it is a way to keep your cool. Here is a list of concerns you might want to discuss:

1. Who will I be living with?
2. Will I have to change schools?
3. Will we have to move?
4. Will we have enough money to live? Will we have to budget differently?
5. What if we're not happy with the arrangements? Can things be changed ever? If so, how will we be able to do that?
6. How did you decide on the custody arrangement?
7. If I can't see Dad (Mom) very often, can we at least talk on the phone?
8. If you're divorced, can we still see our relatives from both sides of the family?
9. What happens if you can't take care of us anymore? Who gets custody then?

10. If you start dating, how do you want me to act around your dates?

It's better to be informed than afraid, and it's better to have some information than none. You might want to refer back to the sections "The Single Parent Family Pattern" and "Stepparents and Remarriages: The Blended Family Pattern" in Chapter 1 and have your parents read them too so you can discuss them together. Even if you feel awkward asking questions like those above, they will help you to get a sense of the direction your family will be going in the future, and knowing this can help you stay on track yourself.

After the Divorce Is Finalized

Is there such a thing as a friendly divorce? Yes and no. It is possible that your parents will remain on good terms (or resume being on good terms) once they're divorced and that your own daily life won't be too different from what it was before. It is possible that your feelings about both parents won't change much, either. But there are bound to be scars that show up from time to time, even under the best of circumstances, and you need to be prepared for them to surface.

"I feel like each parent wants me to spy on the other and report back." Try to understand that for whatever reasons, your parents are still going to be interested in each other's lives even if they can't admit that openly. Since you are the link that still exists between the two of them, they are bound to ask questions like "How is Mom doing these days?" "Is your dad dating a lot?" The questions may have no ulterior motives at all, but you may feel like you're being asked to betray a trust or to reveal confidential information. If you're uncomfortable having to answer such things, tell your parents, "I'd really appreciate it if you didn't quiz me every time I come home from seeing Mom (Dad)," or "Could you please ask Mom (Dad) that directly?" Stating your preference up-front is better than letting feelings of entrapment and resentment build up and

possibly boil over, when your parents probably meant no harm to begin with.

"I'll never get married. I don't want to have to live through this again." After you've been through a divorce with your parents, no matter how brave a front you all put up, and no matter how easily everything was decided and implemented, you're bound to feel an aftershock when the reality of all that's happened hits. Many kids react by blaming the state of marriage itself and swear they'll never try it. It's understandable that you may reject marriage as an option at this point in your life, but also give yourself permission to change your mind. Pain does have a way of easing with the passage of time, and as you get older you may begin to see things about your family from several different angles and actually learn from your parents' mistakes.

"Since the divorce, my parents are trying to buy my love and approval." After a divorce, it may seem like your parents are in a contest to get you to prefer one over the other. It may seem like they are each going about it by bribing you with things, so that if one of them offers to buy you some new clothes, for example, you may suspect the motive and be unable simply to enjoy the possibility of getting a new outfit. In fact, your parents may not realize what they are doing. Parents who seem overly generous after a divorce may simply be trying to make things up to you, and, knowing what you have liked in the past, may choose material things as a way to show you they're sorry. "Let's go shopping" may be a way of saying "Let's spend some time together," no more, no less. You can ask your parent, "Mom (Dad), do you realize how much money you've been spending on me lately? What have I done to deserve this?" or you could say, "Could we please talk about why you're suddenly so generous? Do you think I need all this stuff? It's making me feel a little uncomfortable because I'm not used to it." Statements like these won't make you seem ungrateful, and will make it clear that you feel something unspoken is going on that needs to be discussed.

"My mom is so critical of Dad that I just have to defend him." You may have a better sense of fair play at this point in

your life than either of your parents does. Right after a divorce there can be a lot of anger that bubbles up and over after weeks or months of legal actions. Your parent's anger may trigger a protective response in you — the urge to stand up for the parent who is under attack. There doesn't have to be logic in this, it's just a natural reaction. Some teenagers have to straddle a fence in order to get along — they side with the angry parent but secretly sympathize with the attacked parent. Others cope by leaving home altogether.

> My mom had custody but I couldn't handle the tirades about Dad. I knew I wasn't supposed to live with him, so I ran. I figured neither parent would get in trouble with the judge that way and at least I'd be free.
>
> *Celine O., age sixteen*

Sometimes you may feel like your parent is becoming mentally unglued when he or she spends so much time and energy badmouthing the other parent. You may begin to question his or her judgments in all things, and this can make you believe you have to start being your own parent and rely only on your own instincts. In situations such as these, it's important to get professional help. Local social service agencies can refer you to therapists and counselors who specialize in helping kids cope with divorce. Self-help groups of kids who are experiencing similar divorce situations can be very helpful. Parents Without Partners runs a program called the International Youth Council, for teenagers who live in single-parent families. You can get information about their activities by writing:

Parents Without Partners
   International Headquarters
7910 Woodmont Avenue
Suite 1000
Bethesda, MD 20814

They have a toll-free phone number, 800-638-8078, that operates from 8:30 A.M. to 5:30 P.M. (E.S.T.) Monday through Friday. In Alaska, Hawaii, Maryland, and Washington, D.C., you can't call toll-free but have to call 301-654-8850.

Family therapy is very desirable, but it requires that your parent attends too, and that may be a problem. Don't try to go it alone, though. You need someplace to vent your own frustrations and emotions. It's not selfish to want to do that; it's sensible.

Family tensions and the insecurities after a divorce are difficult to face. As a teenager, you are in a particularly tough position because you ordinarily establish your own independence and identity using your family as a frame of reference. When the family unit is shattered by divorce, it's like breaking your only compass when you're trying to find your way out of the woods. It's scary, it's confusing, and it's frustrating. But if you've been trained to get along without a compass, to rely on yourself and know what to do to get yourself out of the woods, you can emerge with only a few scratches and no major trauma. Think of this chapter as your Outward Bound guide to divorce — it should make the going a little smoother.

13.

"I Think I'm Pregnant"

Having a baby has taught me one thing: the meaning of exhaustion. I have no energy left to have fun at the end of a day, and I'm losing all my friends.

Sasha P., age sixteen

Getting pregnant wasn't all that much fun because I didn't love the guy. Being pregnant isn't all that great either — my friends pretend that everything is normal but I know they're talking about me behind my back.

Celeste H., age sixteen

First I was happy when I thought I was pregnant, then I got angry. My boyfriend acted like it was no big deal and I thought I could count on him. He didn't pick up on my emotions. When I got my period we broke up.

Amy N., age fifteen

It is very possible that you'll choose to be sexually active when you're still a teenager. If you're sexually active, it's then also possible that you'll be faced with the prospect of an unintended, unwanted pregnancy. There are now so many options regarding the possible outcome of a pregnancy that it can be confusing to know which one would be right for you. This chapter is designed to help you learn how to make those difficult choices should you ever need to.

Some Eye-Opening Facts about Teenage Pregnancy in the Eighties

If you become pregnant during your adolescence (or if you are a teenage boy who gets a girl pregnant) you have plenty of company. Approximately one million teenage pregnancies occur each year in the United States: 2,740 conceptions a day, 114 pregnancies each hour, one teenage pregnancy every 35 seconds around the clock! Thirty thousand girls under the age of fifteen get pregnant every year, and many of these twelve-to-fourteen-year-olds have their babies and raise them without getting married rather than releasing them for adoption. The odds are that 6 out of 10 teenagers who give birth before they are seventeen will be pregnant a second time before they are nineteen. That gives the United States the highest rate of teenage motherhood among all the nations in the Western Hemisphere. In fact, in 1985 the United States was the only developed nation in the world in which the number of teenage pregnancies was increasing.

Unplanned teenage pregnancies happen to every imaginable type of person, from the junior high school dropout to the college student — rich, poor, and in between, all races, colors, creeds. It may surprise you to know that large numbers of kids you'd consider sexually inexperienced — who have had sexual intercourse only once or twice — are often the ones who get pregnant. Half of all pregnancies occur within six months after the first time of having sexual intercourse. Many girls don't marry their babies' fathers and some don't even know who the fathers are. Most of the kids who become pregnant didn't plan to, don't really want to be, and don't really know what the long-range impact of having a child may be.

Many of the girls who get pregnant and the guys who father the babies have a basic knowledge of contraception but don't use any birth control. Among the reasons given to explain this pattern are:

— "I didn't plan to have intercourse and didn't think I'd need to be prepared. So I wasn't."
— "If I went to a drugstore and bought foam or one of those

new contraceptive sponges, or worse, if I got fitted for a diaphragm, everyone would think I was cheap because it'd look like I was out to get laid. I couldn't handle that kind of reputation. It's better for me to take my chances."
— "Sex is supposed to be spontaneous. Putting on a condom or using a diaphragm isn't spontaneous."
— "The easiest thing in the world is to know when in your monthly cycle you're fertile and when you're not. All you have to do to be completely safe is keep track of your calendar. That's all the preparation I need."
— "If you go with someone who's experienced, you don't have to worry since those kinds of people are always prepared and protected."

If you are sexually active but operate under incorrect assumptions and inaccurate information such as these above, you're practically guaranteeing yourself a trip down the path to unplanned pregnancy.

Why Teenage Pregnancy Is a Downer

It's not easy being pregnant when you're still a teenager, and it's even harder to be a parent. It's not simply a matter of letting nature take its course. Raising a child demands an enormous amount of time, energy, and money. If you come from a large family and have had responsibility for younger brothers or sisters, or if you have baby-sat a lot, you probably know what we mean. The difference is that siblings or the kids you sit for are still someone else's responsibility, even if you act as their caretaker from time to time.

When you're a parent and choose to raise the child yourself, you can't walk away from the responsibility. Contrary to what you may think about life with a baby, there's actually not much glamour in it. It's not like a job you can quit if things don't go right or if it doesn't meet your hopes and expectations. Being a parent is a permanent job that affects every aspect of your own life.

Numerous studies show that the impact of pregnancy and

parenthood on teenagers and their children is more often negative than positive. For that reason, we believe that before you choose to have intercourse you should understand how the odds are stacked against you should you have to deal with an unplanned pregnancy and parenthood while you're still in your teens.

Health Risks for a Pregnant Teenager and Her Baby

Teenage pregnancies can cause major health problems for the mothers. One reason is that a teenage girl's body is not really meant to bear children. It's not physically ready. When you're pregnant, the developing baby (fetus) uses up a lot of the nutrients that you need for your own growth. If you don't make sure that you are eating enough so that both you and your baby are properly fed, it's possible that your own growth will be stunted or stopped completely.

If you are pregnant before you've grown to your full adult size you may have a difficult delivery. Your pelvis may not yet be wide enough for the baby to pass through and be born naturally. In this case, you may need an operation called a cesarean section, in which the baby is delivered through an incision in the abdomen and uterus.

Babies born to teenage mothers often have low birth weights (under five pounds), which can threaten their odds of surviving. Many of these infants need to spend their first weeks of life in intensive care in hospitals' neonatal (newborn) units. The sad fact is that *babies born to teenagers are more than twice as likely to die in infancy than babies born to women in their twenties.*

Many teenagers who decide to let their pregancies continue (as opposed to choosing abortion) don't ever have their babies because they suffer miscarriages. This means that something goes wrong during the development of the fetus that causes the mother's body to go into a kind of premature labor and expel that fetus before it's ready to be born, and before it can survive on its own. Why this happens and when this happens varies from person to person. Some girls miscarry very early in a pregnancy and don't even realize what has occurred or know that they actually were pregnant: they may think they had an extra heavy period after skipping a cycle or two. But sometimes, when a miscarriage happens later in a pregnancy, the girl may have labor pains, lots of bleeding, and will actually deliver an incompletely developed fetus. This kind of miscarriage is a serious matter and requires immediate medical attention. Sometimes hospitalization is needed so that an operation called a "D and C" (dilatation and curettage) can be done to prevent excessive blood loss, eliminate the risk of infection, and make sure there is no damage to the mother's reproductive organs.

Some other serious health problems associated with teenage pregnancy are hemorrhage (excessive blood loss), anemia (low red blood cell count), and toxemia (a combination of symptoms: high blood pressure, too much protein in the urine, swelling of parts of the body like fingers, ankles, and feet, and sometimes even convulsions).

The most extreme complication of pregnancy during adolescence is death as a result of the pregnancy. *Maternal death risks are 60 percent higher for pregnant girls under the age of fifteen* than for older women. Even in the sixteen-to-nineteen-year-old group, the risk of maternal death is 13 percent higher than among women in their twenties.

How Teenage Parenthood Can Affect Other Aspects of Your Life

If you become a teenage parent, your life may turn into a combination juggling and balancing act. In the space of each day you'll have to make time for taking care of a child's needs and interests in addition to (and sometimes instead of) your own. If you haven't ever thought about what this means, here's what a seventeen-year-old mother of a five-month-old son told us:

> I really thought I knew what I was getting into when my boyfriend and I decided to have a baby. I always had been

an organized person and had been able to do a lot —
school, sports, and a job. That job was almost full-time:
every evening baby-sitting my neighbor's two kids until
she got home from work at around 10 P.M. I couldn't
imagine a baby would make a difference, since I was
going to be allowed to live at home *and* keep my job because my neighbor said I could bring the baby with me.
What can I say? I was dead wrong. I couldn't do it all. The
more I did for my baby and the more stuff I did with him,
the more it seemed I had to do. I couldn't concentrate on
school, and I'm not earning enough to even pay for half of
his clothes, much less his food and diapers and medical
care. I dropped out of school at the end of my junior year.
My boyfriend's pressured too — he's got two after-school
jobs now and we want to get married but can't afford to. I
want at least one of us to graduate and it looks like he's
the one. Right now I feel like a sacrificial lamb.

This is a common experience. One of the major problems unmarried teenage mothers face is having to drop out of school.
That, in turn, can really limit your future earning capacity (as
we explained in our discussion of dropouts in Chapter 6).

It's extremely expensive to bring up a child today. It's estimated that it now costs around $232,000 to raise a child from
birth to the age of seventeen, and people without a high school
education may have trouble getting jobs that pay enough to
cover that kind of expense. The link between teenage parenthood and poverty has been clearly demonstrated: *three out of
four children born to unmarried women are poor, and the poverty rate
is more than 90 percent for kids in families headed by single women
under the age of thirty who didn't complete high school.* Many teenage
mothers and their children rely on government services and
support ("welfare," "AFDC" — Aid to Families with Dependent Children) to help with the basics like food and shelter.

Unemployment, poverty, and short-circuited opportunities to live life the way you really want to can combine to
make you feel powerless. Feeling that way can be frustrating
and may cause you to lash out at your kids, even if you don't
really mean it. That's one of the reasons why children of teenagers are more than twice as likely to be physically abused by
their parents than kids whose parents are married and older.

Teenage fathers can be negatively affected by unplanned pregnancies in ways that may not be immediately obvious. A boy may get lost in the shuffle in terms of decision-making about the pregnancy, and his feelings tend to be forgotten. He may be the focus of much anger from the girl and her family, especially if he refuses to assume full responsibility for his part in the pregnancy.

Sometimes, though, a boy who wants to be a part of the process has little or no say about what should happen to the child he has fathered. Many boys actually go through a process of mourning and intense grief when their girlfriends choose to have abortions rather than letting the pregnancies continue. Some boys want to participate in their children's lives, but the parents of the teenage mothers won't allow it, or the girl herself won't because she has a new love interest or is too filled with anger to allow visitation privileges. Many teenage fathers are caught between a rock and a hard place for other reasons too:

> When I saw my son for the first time I felt like I was in a dream. I wanted to hold him and kiss him, but my buddies were watching and I couldn't. I was afraid they'd laugh at me — I'm Mr. Macho in my gang — and it felt so bad. My girl was furious and told me I had no emotions. She wasn't right. We got into a huge fight. The kid is six weeks old now and I haven't seen him since that day in the hospital. She won't let me in the door, and won't take my calls.
>
> *Carlos S., age seventeen*

The emotional baggage that results can be a pretty heavy burden to carry around, may make it impossible for a boy to feel that there is hope for his relationship with the mother of his child, and may cut off any possibility for family ties to develop when the baby is born.

Luckily, there are exceptions to these general patterns. Some teenagers are excellent mothers and fathers. The ones who do the best almost always have support from their families. Even younger teenage parents can handle things better if their own mothers are willing to help out with child care so the teenagers can continue attending school. An interesting benefit of such arrangements is that the babies' mental and physical development is enhanced because the babies get lots of mothering.

Teenage parents need a total package of support systems: health care, psychological counseling (to help sort out your own needs and the needs of your child), family encouragement and help with child care, a school system that either has a special program for you and your child or that can assist you in finding day care so you can return to school, a community that doesn't look down on an unwed mother, and the willingness of employers in the community to hire you and make some allowances for your unique needs. But these "support packages" are few and far between, and in our society the odds are heavily stacked against unwed teenage parents. You should try to keep all these facts in mind when you enter into a sexual relationship.

Practical Pointers for Coping with Unplanned Pregnancy and Parenthood
Make Sure There Really Is a Pregnancy

The prospect of having to admit, "I'm pregnant," or "I got a girl pregnant" can be devastating. Sometimes it throws you into a state of shock to such an extent that you may panic and do things that aren't logical. You may react and make decisions based on the belief that there really is a pregnancy without first checking to see if that's actually true.

> I spent the last two months of my junior year thinking I was pregnant. I walked around like a zombie. I cried at the drop of a hat. My boyfriend and I made plans to run away. I was sure I felt nauseous in the mornings. I lost my appetite and then it came back like I was a starving person. I was tired all the time. It never dawned on me that something else might be wrong with me and I was too

scared to go to a doctor. I wasn't pregnant and I ruined two whole months of my life.

Karen K., age sixteen

A much more extreme example of this is illustrated by the case of Cathleen Crowley Webb, who accused Gary Dotson of raping her in July, 1977. He was tried, convicted, and sentenced to twenty-five to fifty years in prison and had served six years when, in March 1985, Mrs. Webb came forward and admitted she lied about the rape (thus gaining Dotson's release).

I concoted the whole story . . . because I had sex with my boyfriend, and I thought I might be pregnant and didn't want to get into trouble with my foster parents.

Cathleen Crowley Webb
(People Magazine, April 28, 1985, p. 36)

To an outside observer these two situations seem unbelievable. They're not. Panic reactions happen when they don't need to. There are a few easy steps to follow to determine accurately whether you're dealing with a pregnancy or something else (like an irregular menstrual cycle).

1. *Buy an in-home pregnancy test kit and use it.* These tests are marketed under a variety of brand names such as E.P.T. and Daisy II. Depending on where you buy them (drugstore, discount store) they cost between five and ten dollars. They are sold without a prescription and the only expertise you need to use them is the ability to read and follow directions.

Here's how they work. By mixing a small amount of your urine with a chemical in the test kit, waiting about forty-five minutes, and checking your results against a picture (included in the kit) of what a positive (pregnant) or negative (not pregnant) result looks like, you'll have an almost instant answer to your question. These tests are quite reliable if you follow instructions and use them at the proper time (a certain number of days after your first missed period: for example, Daisy II says it can be used as early as three days after that missed period). It's hard to misread the results. Some of the kits give you two tests in case you make a mistake the first time around (spill the contents, contaminate the urine or the chemicals) or want to double-check at a later date. Some tests include a toll-free telephone number to call if you have any questions. But as with any test, it is possible that you'll get a negative reading when you really are pregnant, or that you'll misinterpret the results, so don't rely exclusively on this result.

An in-home pregnancy test is not a substitute for a medical check-up. It's an acceptable first step in dealing with a problem. It's an especially good choice if privacy is an issue for you, if you have a poor relationship with your parents or guardians, or if you fear (as Cathleen Crowley Webb did) what they might do to you if they found out.

2. See an obstetrician/gynecologist or a health care professional who specializes in caring for pregnant women (nurse-midwives, doctors and nurses who work at women's health centers). Making an appointment for a check-up is easy; keeping the appointment may be harder, especially if you are scared. You may be worried that the doctor or nurse will notify your parents and you may not want your parents to find out just yet. If that is what's preventing you from getting health care, you have the right to request that any information you tell the health care professional is to remain *confidential* — a private matter between you and the person examining you. Most doctors will respect such a request. If you think you want to see a doctor but can't afford to pay the fees, you can go to a public hospital and ask about their clinic services. Many pregnant women, not just teenagers, get all their prenatal care this way, so don't be surprised if you find women of all ages waiting to be examined by the health care professionals. Clinics also have social workers available to discuss the emotional impact of your situation, and if you don't have family support, social workers can really fill in the gaps and help you through a scary time. In addition to hospitals, there are women's health centers run by organizations such as Planned Parenthood, Pro-Choice, and various religious groups that will examine you at little or no cost. Look in the *Yellow Pages* phone directory for their locations, or call your local social service agency for help in contacting one.

To make sure you get the best care possible, you should have the following information to give to the person examining you: the date of your last menstrual period, the age at which you began menstruating, the average number of days your periods last, the average number of days between periods, whether you are regular or irregular, how often you have intercourse, when you had intercourse during the past few months, the kind of contraception you use, any other health problems you have. Also, to make sure you get your own questions answered, write them down before you go for the check-up and bring them with you. If you have them on paper, you won't forget them in your nervousness.

You can expect to be given an *internal exam* so that the doctor or nurse will be able to examine the condition of your reproductive organs (cervix, uterus, ovaries, fallopian tubes). You lie down on your back on a special kind of examining table and put your legs into *stirrups* so that they will be raised. A bright lamp will be shined on your pubic (crotch) area (the rest of your body will be draped to help you feel less exposed) and the examiner will insert a *speculum* into your vagina to make your internal organs visible. This isn't painful, but since the speculum is made of metal it may feel cold, and you will feel pressure as the examiner inserts his or her gloved fingers into your vagina to do the internal exam. You may feel embarrassed, and this is natural. Usually, if a male doctor is examining you a female nurse will also be present. If this is your first internal exam, tell the doctor or nurse and ask them to explain what is happening at each stage of the check-up. In addition to the internal exam you will probably also have your urine checked, your blood tested, your blood pressure will be taken, and your breasts will be examined.

3. *Confide in your parents or guardian.* Ideally, if you think you're pregnant you'll be able to tell your parents and ask for their advice and help — financial and emotional. But if you can't, don't let that stop you from assuming responsibility for getting medical attention for yourself.

In this day and age, there is absolutely no reason why anyone should go around guessing about a pregnancy. The earlier you can find out whether or not you are pregnant, the better the outcome either way. If you're not, you'll save yourself lots of turmoil and anxiety. If you are, you'll be in a position to know how to protect your health and decide what to do next.

Learning the News

Reactions to the news of an unplanned pregnancy tend to be predictable for parents and teenagers alike, and occur in a series of stages. The first stage is usually denial. On the parent side, this takes the form of the "It can't be" syndrome. You may hear, "It can't be because . . ."

> "... I taught my son to be respectful where girls are concerned."
>
> "... my son would *never* take advantage of a girl that way."
>
> "... I gave my son a box of condoms for his fifteenth birthday along with a book about sex."
>
> "... my daughter is an assistant teacher at Sunday school."
>
> "... my daughter has plans to go to college next fall. She would never do this to herself."
>
> "... my daughter is too smart to let that happen to her."
>
> "... my daughter told me none of the kids in her group approved of premarital sex."

There are endless variations of "It can't be" and parents say them in an attempt to establish logical, believable reasons why their sons or daughters would never get into a situation like that.

The denial on your side works slightly differently. Girls tend to acknowledge the obvious physical signs but attribute them to some other factor (which the guys are more than willing to believe at first).

> "I'm never regular with my periods anyway so I'm not worried."
>
> "I've been exercising a lot lately and I've read that women who are very athletic miss their periods."

"I'm under a lot of stress lately and my system is screwed up."

"I've had a long bout with the flu."

"I'm *finally* developing a bigger bust. It's about time."

The stage of denial can be a time of great creativity and story-telling.

The next stage for parents can be shock and anger (with a large dose of guilt). It was this kind of reaction Cathleen Crowley Webb was herself afraid of when she made up the rape story. Parents may say things like,

> "I'm going to kill you and (her, him)."
>
> "Look what you've done to our family." ("How could you do this to me?" is a variation.) "What will the neighbors say?"
>
> "Get out of my sight. I'm not going to support someone who sleeps around."
>
> "You'll pay for this. You've lost every privilege you've ever had."

If these are their reactions, try to understand that your parents are being so emotional that they're temporarily incapable of dealing reasonably with the stress of the situation. Unplanned pregnancies throw parents into a state of shock too, and their early reactions may show they're just as scared as you may be.

> When I found out that Marina was pregnant, all I could think of was that she let me down. Those years of teaching her moral values just flew out the window — it was like a slap in the face. Honestly, for days I couldn't consider her side of it. I felt as if she did it to hurt me personally. I told her I'd arrange for an abortion, I'd pay for it, and we'd never mention it to anyone. I didn't ask her if she wanted one. I worried what her uncle would say (her father's dead). I tried to take control. Finally, she ran away. It was only for two days but it woke me up. We could talk after that.
>
> *Mrs. S., age fifty-two*

Anger often masks parents' underlying feelings of pain and confusion. It can also make it seem like they won't be there to help you, and it can drive a wedge between them and you just at the moment you need them most.

> I tried to tell my mom it had nothing to do with her. I really loved the guy I was dating and was hoping to marry him. He usually used condoms but the night I got pregnant he was out of them and I thought I was too close to getting my period to be able to get pregnant. We usually were responsible and careful about having sex. My mom called me a whore. I told her I was sorry, and she kept getting angrier and angrier. That's why I left. I thought she'd physically hurt me she was so mad.
>
> *Marina S., age sixteen (Mrs. S.'s daughter)*

If you're pregnant and caught up in this web of miscommunication with your parents, you might tell them, "I'm sorry," "I didn't mean to hurt you," or "I didn't mean to do it," but those answers don't really help solve the question of what to do next.

The third stage is accepting the pregnancy as a fact of life, abandoning the arguments, blame, and guilt, and turning the feeling of "this can't be happening to me" into one of "this *is* happening to me and I can deal with it."

Think About What You Want to Do

When we say "you" we mean *you*. Early in a pregnancy you must decide what you think is best for you. We don't mean what you think your parents think is best, or your boyfriend, or anyone else. First, examine the situation only from a selfish perspective. Assume responsibility for what has happened and begin to rely on yourself for solutions.

How should you begin? Approach the problem the way you would deal with a school assignment about which you have absolutely no information. Clear your mind of any pre-existing ideas and start from scratch. Be an investigative reporter. Do some library research: read some books or articles about pregnancy, childbirth, abortion, and child care. If you're reading this chapter now, you've got a head start. Do some in-person interviewing. Try to locate some unmarried kids who've gotten pregnant while still in school and talk to them about their choices. See if you can talk with someone who's had an abortion as well as someone who's had the child and released it for adoption. Try to talk with someone who is raising a baby and has stayed in school herself. If you can't easily do these things, call a health center that advertises abortion and family planning services and see what they have to say. You might also try calling a pro-life center that suggests alternatives other than abortion. Take notes as you talk. Later on, reread your notes but with the understanding that each position comes with a particular bias.

Once you've done these things, you can begin to think about everyone else. What will your parents want? Do you think they'll let you stay at home, or is it likely they'll kick you out, or send you to live with a relative in another area? Will they help support you? What about the father of the baby? What is your relationship with him? Was the pregnancy the result of a fling, of a long-standing commitment, or the tragic result of a forcible rape or even incest? Can you count on the father of the child to help out with financial support? Do you have the skills necessary to get a job that can support you? Is marriage an option or is it out of the question? How will your religious beliefs affect a decision? Next, you can start thinking about other circumstances. What point are you at in your schooling? Does your school have a program for pregnant teenagers and teenage parents, or will you have to attend school somewhere else, even in another community? Are you so young that your health may be seriously jeopardized by a pregnancy? Do you have any other health problems (like diabetes or heart problems) that might make it dangerous for you to be pregnant now? Are you early enough in the pregnancy to consider abortion? It all boils down to weighing the pros and cons of continuing the pregnancy or opting for abortion.

When I found out I was pregnant I forgot that my instincts counted. I felt like I had to make everyone else feel better about this — my mother, my boyfriend, even my priest. I was more worried about what they'd want for me and how they'd feel than anything else. My girlfriend saw how upset I was and talked me through all this. She made me list what a pregnancy would do *for* me and what it would do *to* me. Then she asked me to list all the good things about it and all the bad. She made me focus on me. It really helped me decide to rely on my own gut feelings.

Felicia C., age fifteen

Whatever you choose to do, it must be an informed choice and it must reflect your own needs. You don't need to isolate yourself or hide in shame. This isn't Puritan America and you're not Hester Prynne walking around with a scarlet letter on your dress. Making a mistake doesn't brand you forever, and there are many people out there who will help you without judging you or pressuring you to do something you don't want to do.

Decision Time: What Are the Options?

There are many options. For some of you the decision will be simple, for others it may require many hours of negotiation with your family and possibly with the father's family.

1. "I'm going to marry the baby's father and have the child."

I bought into the whole ideal of love and marriage. I didn't think it made a difference that we were both seventeen. I was so happy I was pregnant with his child. I couldn't wait to have an apartment, be a wife, cook meals, be romantic — openly and legally. You know what I got? I got a guy who prefers his baseball buddies to spending evenings at home with me. I got a guy who suddenly has a roving eye. He's okay with the baby, but she's mainly my responsibility. Equality doesn't exist in my house right now. I've been reading a lot about women in history lately and I feel like I'm in a time-warp, trapped in the 1940s.

Elissa T., age eighteen

Before you make the leap into marriage and parenthood, answer these questions. Do you love each other? Do you like each other? How well do you know each other? Are your values and goals similar? Do you realize the odds against teenage marriages lasting? Can you list the ups and downs you think your marriage might encounter in the next few years? What are the chances you'll be able to complete your education? What are the chances you'll be self-supporting? How will you care for the baby? What emergency resources do you have to rely on? What are your individual strengths and weaknesses? What do you think your strengths and weaknesses are as a couple? How do you each define "parenting"? Do you know what it means to be flexible?

It takes a lot of work to maintain a marriage on a happy, even keel. If you go into a relationship with fantasies of "happily ever after" you'll find the going tough, and with a baby added to the picture the marriage may feel more like a trap than a triumph. If you know the answers to the above questions before you decide to marry, then your chances of success are much greater.

2. "I'm going to remain unmarried but will keep my baby."

> Now that I've been a mother for six months I wonder why I did what I did. I think it was because of my friend Carla. She kept telling me that the baby was a gift, and I'd be such a good parent. I feel like I was seduced into believing something when I was very vulnerable. I feel almost as if I was tricked. I gave up the chance for a scholarship at a good school to have this baby. I don't know if I'll ever get that kind of offer again. Being smart academically sure didn't stand me in good stead. Not this time, anyway. I love the baby, but I really feel like I've made the biggest mistake of my life.
>
> *Doreen P., age eighteen*

Before deciding to have a baby, do some really hard soul-searching. Are you doing this because of parental pressure? Are you doing this because you think a baby will give you someone to love and will love you back completely and adoringly? Are you reacting to peer pressure ("My best friend is doing it, so I will too")? Are you doing it because of religious conviction but not personal conviction? Do you have any idea of what raising a child alone involves? Do you know what it means to discipline a child? What would you do if your child became difficult to handle or emotionally disturbed and in need of special care? What would you do if your child were born retarded or physically impaired? What would you do if your pregnancy left you physically ill or permanently impaired? Can you see yourself and your baby ten years from now? Can you realistically project your responsibilities far into the future?

3. "I'm going to have the baby and release it for adoption."

> This was the hardest decision of my life. But I know I can't care for a baby. I'm not ready for that kind of responsibility. I know who the people are who have him, and they seem nice. I have a paper that says when he's ten years old I'll be allowed to contact him if I want. That makes it a little easier for me.
>
> *Tina W., age fourteen*

> I just had my first "legal" baby. My husband doesn't know that when I was fifteen I had a daughter and gave her up for adoption. He thought the tears I was crying on the delivery table were tears of joy that we had just had a boy. They were tears for the baby I never got to hold, never got to nurse. I will live with that hell forever unless I can track her down someday. I don't know how I'll ever be able to make amends. No one should have to carry around this much guilt.
>
> *Pamela D., age twenty-seven*

Releasing a baby for adoption involves many decisions. Why are you doing this? Have you examined all the alternatives to giving up the baby? Is the decision yours, or was it made for you by a parent, guardian, or other adult authority figure? Today a mother has more options than she had in the past. Will you work with an adoption agency? Do you want to work with a lawyer, physician, or clergyperson who arranges private adoptions and will take care of the cost of your prenatal care and the delivery of the baby? (You must investigate the legality of doing this, because in some states it is prohibited.) Do you want the birth records sealed, preventing the child from ever knowing your identity, or do you want them open so that you might be able to have contact with the child at a later date? Do you want to meet the adoptive parents ahead of time? Do you want to have a legal agreement that will allow you to visit the child in his or her adoptive home from time to time?

Can you imagine yourself married and a mother again? Will you want to tell your family later in life about this part of your past? Are you prepared to cope with occasional feelings of sadness and guilt?

4. "I'll have the baby and arrange for foster care until some later date when I'll be able to assume full responsibility."

> When I was growing up I lived with foster parents for a few years. They were wonderful people. My own mother was from Germany and came over here with me when I was an infant. She worked as a maid to earn enough money so we could live as a family. It took her three years and she got me. My foster parents taught me my letters and numbers, they taught me to knit, they included me in everything, and still do, fourteen years later. I hoped that would be the case with my baby. It wasn't. His foster parents didn't want him after a year, and since I still couldn't keep him, they sent him somewhere else. He's been in five homes in three years. I'm taking him back now, but I'm not sure what shape he's in.
>
> *Jeannie T., age seventeen*

Foster care is not just extended baby-sitting. Do you fully understand what this can mean for the quality of your child's life? Do you know what the odds are of your assuming full care? When might this happen? Are you thinking in terms of months or years? Do you know the drawbacks of extended foster care? Can you make sure the child will be in only one home and not shuttled between many homes? Is there a possibility you will change your mind and release the child for adoption later on?

5. "I'm going to have an abortion."

> My boyfriend and I discussed this at length. I thought I was prepared and happy with the decision. We couldn't afford a child, and Gary was going into the army in the

spring and wouldn't be there for the birth of the baby if we had it. Neither of us was particularly religious, so we didn't have to hassle with what the Church would say. And we both had read a lot about the safety of the procedure. My doctor was terrific and he didn't lecture me. He answered all my questions. He only left one thing out. He didn't tell me how empty I'd feel even now, and it's ten weeks after I had it done.

Theresa R., age sixteen

The best thing I ever did was have the abortion. I was so scared to have a baby, and I couldn't think straight until I found out that there was a safe place I could go to have it done. My mom helped a lot. She didn't think I should have to do something I didn't want to do, and she convinced my dad to let me have the abortion. I learned that I could count on my family when things were lousy, and after the abortion I got information about birth control and how not to let this happen again. I don't think I would have paid much attention to that sort of thing before, but I've really grown up.

Krista B., age fourteen

Having an abortion is an intensely personal event and can mean having to make some tough decisions. There may be a lot of pressure from parents and other adults (such as the parents of the baby's father), or from the father himself, or from friends, either to have an abortion or, conversely, to have the baby. There may be pressure from your religious group or even from your own doctor to make your decision in a certain way.

If you're young, unmarried, and pregnant you're very vulnerable to these outside influences and may abandon your own initial instincts in favor of the majority rule. Because deciding to have an abortion means deciding to end a pregnancy, it is a decision that is final and can't be reversed if you change your mind afterwards. So it is very important — *critical* — that you have all the facts straight about abortion before you take that final step. You owe it to yourself to take the time to get the information and think about the options for your situation or you may experience regret and guilt rather than relief as a result of your choice.

There are two categories of abortions: *spontaneous* and *induced.* Spontaneous abortions are also called miscarriages (which we've discussed earlier in this chapter) and usually occur because there was something wrong with the fetus to begin with. There has been no controversy about spontaneous abortions because in our society we're taught that these are "accidents of nature" and there is no choice involved in these cases. Induced abortions are a matter of choice. They are made to happen by medical procedures that range from relatively simple techniques that can be done in a doctor's office, to complicated operations that require hospitalization.

A successful abortion removes the contents of the pregnant uterus: the fetus (or embryo, as it is called before the end of the second month of pregnancy), the placenta (which nourishes the baby as it grows), and the built-up lining of the uterus. The kind of abortion that will be safest and most successful depends on how big the embryo or fetus has become.

When you go to a clinic, hospital, or doctor's office to arrange for an abortion, you will be asked how many weeks pregnant you are. You may have to fill out a form on which you see the letters, "L.M.P." These stand for "last menstrual period," and it is necessary that you know the date when it occurred (or *about* when it occurred) because the length of a pregnancy is usually figured from the first day of your last menstrual period, not from the date your child was conceived (when a sperm fertilized the egg). Pregnancies are divided into *trimesters:* the first is one to thirteen weeks after the L.M.P., the second is fourteen to twenty-four weeks after the L.M.P., and the third is twenty-five weeks after the L.M.P. and beyond.

The most common, and actually the safest, method of abortion is a *vacuum aspiration* or *suction* (also called E.U.E. — early uterine evacuation). It can only be done during the first trimester. The girl's cervix is numbed with Novocaine (the same medicine a dentist would use when drilling a tooth), and dilated (widened) so that a plastic tube can be inserted through the cervix into the uterus. At the other end of the tube is a kind of suction pump that breaks up and removes the developing fetus and the tissue that surrounds and nourishes it. It is a technique that can be done in a doctor's office, clinic, or hospital; it has a low risk of infection, and there is little chance for tearing of the uterus if it is done properly.

A *D and C* (dilatation and curettage) is sometimes used to abort pregnancies from eight to sixteen weeks L.M.P. It requires general anesthesia (you are put to sleep), because after the cervix is dilated, the lining of the uterus is scraped with a sharp spoon-shaped metal instrument called a curette. It is riskier than vacuum aspiration because of the general anesthesia, and the chances of infection and bleeding are greater.

A *D and E* (dilatation and evacuation) combines aspects of both vacuum aspiration and the D and C, and is used for abortions during the second trimester. It is usually done between the thirteenth and sixteenth weeks of pregnancy. Greater dilation (stretching) of the cervix is needed so the girl goes into the hospital a day ahead of the abortion, and the procedure itself is done under general anesthesia like a D and C.

Abortions done late in pregnancy (between the sixteenth and twenty-fourth weeks) usually involve injecting solutions of salt (*saline*) or hormones (*prostaglandins*) into the amniotic sac that surrounds the fetus. The injections cause contractions, which make the mouth of the cervix open, after which the fetus is expelled. Sometimes the placenta doesn't come out, and the doctor has to perform a D and C. This is an expensive procedure because it requires a twenty-four-to-forty-eight-hour hospital stay, and it's emotionally traumatic too, because it's a lot like going through labor and delivery.

A *hysterotomy* is surgery, like a mini cesarean section, because it involves making a small cut in the abdomen and uterus to remove the fetus. It is used when the induction methods we just talked about don't work or can't be used for health reasons.

Most doctors don't like to do abortions late in a pregnancy because they are riskier for the mother and there is a chance that the fetus will be born alive and may survive (with an increased chance of brain damage or other problems that affect very premature babies). Current research indicates that one abortion, as long as it is performed by a trained medical practitioner under sterile conditions, will not impair your ability to bear children in future years. However, there is evidence that having more than one abortion increases the risk of later fertility problems. You must discuss the odds for or against your continued reproductive health when you are trying to decide whether or not to have an abortion.

One cautionary note about induced abortions is in order. No matter what anyone else tells you, trying a do-it-yourself abortion by any means at all is extremely dangerous. Pregnant women who try to cause a miscarriage by self-inflicted injuries or taking drugs run the risk of serious illness or even death. Be smart — the only safe abortion is one done under medical supervision.

Discussing options and making decisions shouldn't turn into a battle for control over the outcome of a pregnancy. Think of the discussion as similar to buying an insurance policy — you need to look at lots of programs before finding the one that suits you best, even if the process is tedious, confusing, and sometimes scary. That insurance policy is designed to protect you and make your life more secure. Finding the correct option you and your family can live with comfortably will do the same.

An unplanned pregnancy does not have to signal the end of your world or doom you to a life-style you don't want to live. It can actually become a catalyst for positive change — the event that gets you and your family talking or helps you develop a more realistic view of life, something that pushes you to acknowledge your strengths and use them in solving your problem. It is also an event that forces you to come to terms with the power of your sexuality and what can happen if you are careless with it. The bottom line is that you are in charge of your sexuality; the choices are yours. Try to make them informed choices based on accurate facts.

14.

Loneliness, Depression, and Suicide

My brother was smart, popular, and great looking. He had a partial scholarship to college. He had money in the bank, a girlfriend, and my parents made a down payment on a car for him for high school graduation. He had a big party last weekend when my parents were out of town. He went up to his bedroom at around eleven and blasted his brains out with a shotgun. He was splattered all over the room. I threw up when I saw it. He had such an easy life. He was never alone, never without friends. He was almost perfect in school. I don't understand it.

Dane S., age fifteen

There are a lot of teenagers who seem to have it all — brains, popularity, physical attractiveness, money — and yet these very same people can be unhappy, lonely, depressed, or, like Dane's brother, suicidal. The pressures that come from having to figure out who you are, whether what you feel about yourself matches what other people think about you, and whether what you hope to do with your life matches what other people have in mind for you, can be very stressful. It's difficult to discuss these self-doubts — you may worry that if you do you'll seem incapable, or childish — but admitting them, defining them, and discussing them are the best ways to conquer them. At the same time, you need to be willing to recognize the good things about yourself.

This chapter will help you define and deal with feelings of loneliness and depression, will alert you to the signs of suicide, and provide guidelines for how to get out of your rut. Even if you're not usually lonely or depressed and haven't felt suicidal, by familiarizing yourself with these topics and being alert to these problems in your friends, you could potentially save a life.

Loneliness

> When I walk down the hall between classes it's like the Red Sea parting in that old movie *The Ten Commandments*. Kids are all over the place, hacking around, looking good, being tight, and there I am — alone in the middle of hundreds of people.
>
> *Todd N., age fourteen*

Every person knows what it feels like to be lonely. There are many kinds of loneliness that we experience in different ways and to different degrees. It can be a sense of emptiness and longing, a blend of sadness and anxiety because you don't feel connected to the people you're with, or because you want to be attached to someone but aren't. You can feel loneliness in a physical way — in the pit of your stomach like you haven't eaten for days, or as a headache that builds and builds until you notice it. Loneliness can creep into your awareness and then leave almost as quickly as it came, or it can be much longer-lasting, like an aura that surrounds you and follows you wherever you go. Sometimes it's the most reasonable, logical way to feel. No one would question your explanation if you said "I'm lonely because . . ."

". . . my best friend just moved away."
". . . I just moved and I'm in a new neighborhood and a new school."
". . . my parents divorced and I miss my mom (dad)."
". . . I'm the only one left on the team from last year and I don't know any of these new guys."
". . . my pet was stolen and I miss it."

You don't even have to be alone to feel lonely. "Lonely in a crowd," or "alone in a crowd," aren't clichés; they're accurate descriptions of what can happen when you spend time in group situations — at school, at work, at parties or on dates, even on vacations.

Loneliness and being alone are not the same things. Some people are loners by nature and actually choose solitary lives. Others may not exactly be loners, but may like their moments alone because they're comfortable with themselves and don't need to be with other people constantly.

> My friend Katie does everything in a group. I swear, they're connected by some invisible cord. If I say something to Katie I know it's going to be repeated like that telephone game little kids play. It drives me nuts. I like my privacy, and I like to be alone at times. We've talked about this but Katie still gets insulted when I refuse to go to their hangout every afternoon.
>
> *Bessie P., age fourteen*

Loneliness is not the same as the need for privacy. We all need to hole up in our rooms and shut out the rest of the world once in a while. We all need time to think, and time to day-dream, and time to wonder about all the "what ifs" in our lives. That process is like a "time out" at a game — a chance to develop new strategies and mull over the old ones, so that you're ready to go back into the game with renewed confidence and a slightly different perspective.

Temporary loneliness is bearable. If it bothers you enough, you can usually do something about it: call a friend, join a group or a club that has regular meetings so you'll know for sure that at certain times you'll be with people you like, take the dog for a walk. That's assuming that loneliness isn't a major problem for you.

But what if it is? How can you tell? According to the authors of *In Search of Intimacy* (Random House, 1982), if you're dominated by loneliness you tend to do things that won't overcome the loneliness. Sure, you'll react to it, but in ways like crying, watching a lot of TV, sleeping excessively, or even drinking or using drugs. You'll blame yourself for the loneliness by thinking you're unattractive or have a lousy personality. You may not know how to reach out to other people because you're shy or self-conscious and come across as self-centered even though you really aren't. You may not be realistic in what you expect from a relationship with someone else, so you may not know how to begin a friendship and make it last. It may actually turn out that it's easier to be lonely than to have to change, and so loneliness can become a habit!

A good technique for breaking that habit is to rehearse how to change. Ask your parents to help you by role playing. Set up a situation that has made you feel lonely or isolated in the past. Let's say it's having to ask someone out on a date, and you're afraid because you don't know what to say and you're sure you'll be rejected. You play the role of the girl or guy you want to ask out. Have your parent play you. Then switch roles. Explore all the possibilities in rehearsal, so when you actually do it, it will seem like the most natural thing in the world!

Many people are lonely whom you wouldn't expect to be. Kids who seem so "perfect" that you assume they're unapproachable — like beauty queens, super jocks, or teenagers who are in the public eye because they're on TV or model, and so on — are often lonelier than you'd imagine.

> When I won the modeling search and started working, at first everyone was real supportive. Then I got the reputation of being snobby and it wasn't that at all — I was real tired and couldn't hang out with people after school because if I didn't get everything for school done, I couldn't model, and if I didn't eat right and get enough sleep, I'd lose bookings. Very few kids stayed my friends and I'm the one who has to call them. They assume I'm too good for them now. I've become suspicious of the people who do stick around. Do they want something from me or do they like me? It was easier before this publicity.
>
> *Annette M., age sixteen*

Sometimes you assume that being lonely is your fate because you're "different" in some way, such as having a physical disability or a chronic illness that restricts your ability to get around and do the things other kids your age do. Often, other people want to get to know you but may not know what to say or how to approach you without offending you. That's when you need to take the first step, be a little aggressive, and help the other person get comfortable with your situation. "Could you help me push this wheelchair?" "Would you like to try my crutches?" "This is a designer back-brace!" or "Want to see what my mechanical hand can do?" can really loosen the tension. If you're homebound and are attending classes by telephone hookup, inviting someone over to work on a project can be an icebreaker and erase your sense of loneliness and isolation.

There's no rule book that says the only way teenagers can overcome loneliness is by hanging out with people their own age. You can develop some wonderful, long-lasting relationships with adults.

> Doc B. was as important to me as anyone during my adolescence. He was a volunteer track coach and really got me through the rough times. I could always count on him to listen. He never judged me, and never lied to me. I still see him, and my kids like him as much as I did!
>
> *Robert K., age forty*

You don't have to count on the people at school to ease you through lonely times, either. You can have phone friendships with people you don't get to see in person often. You can have intimate and important friendships with pen pals who you may never actually meet face-to-face. Volunteering is another great way to overcome loneliness, and it often leads to friendships with other volunteers, the staff, or the people you're working with. Church or temple activities and youth groups associated with them are also good ways to break the isolation barrier.

If loneliness consistently interferes with the quality of your life, ask yourself the following questions:

1. When and where am I most likely to feel lonely?
2. What is my typical reaction when I feel lonely?
3. Do I blame other people or something else for my loneliness, or do I think I might have something to do with it?
4. What are the main differences for me between feeling lonely and feeling terrific?

5. If I had the best life going, what would it be like? What can I do now to make some of those things happen?
6. What's good about me?

If you can't seem to get the upper hand over your loneliness by yourself, ask for some professional counseling. Your guidance counselor at school can help you and your parents find the right person. Often, conquering loneliness is as simple as having someone who is a good listener be available to hear you out when the lonely mood hits. Sometimes, it may require more intense therapy from a psychiatrist, psychologist, or social worker. Admitting that loneliness is a bummer for you is the first step, the hardest step, and the most important.

Depression

"Depressed" is a term we tend to use rather loosely. "I'm depressed" is a catchall phrase to describe how you feel when you don't get a date with that special person, when you come home with a rotten report card, when you don't have enough money saved up to buy something you *really* want, or when your mom asks you to baby-sit and you had plans to go out with your friends. It's a way of saying you're annoyed, upset, feeling down, frustrated, angry, or exhausted. But *depression* is actually an illness, a psychological disturbance that is common among teenagers and is one of the earliest signals of potential suicidal behavior. Unfortunately, even severe cases of depression may be written off as "just a passing phase" or "typical teenage moodiness."

There is no sure-fire way of recognizing depression, but there are some symptoms that occur often enough (in varying combinations and to different degrees) to suggest strongly that the person who has them is suffering from depression. We'll consider the case of seventeen-year-old Roger K. for some clues.

> I used to love doing sports at school. I was Mr. Extracurricular. At the end of my sophomore year, it all began to seem stupid to me, and I didn't know why. I had agreed to coach the following summer at a soccer camp, and I hated

it. By the middle of my junior year I couldn't do anything. I quit the teams. I couldn't concentrate on play books. It all felt like a big waste of time. I started cutting school because I didn't want to have to keep answering, "Why, Roger?" I really became a bum. I began to have trouble sleeping at night, so I was always tired and then I started staying home and sleeping during the days. My parents kept making excuses for me. When I stopped eating meals, my parents thought I'd become anorectic — can you believe it! — and then they sent me to a therapist.

Sign 1. Mood Disturbances. Roger lost his enthusiasm for the things he used to love to do — namely, sports — and found no more pleasure in them. His personality changed ("I really became a bum") and he became listless ("I couldn't do anything") — all signs of mood disturbances. (Sadness, dejection, and hopelessness can also be signs of mood disturbances.)

Sign 2. Changes in Biological Functions. Roger's appetite changed. He had trouble sleeping normally. These signs fall into the category of changes in biological functions: that is, changes in how your body actually works. In addition to appetite and sleep disturbances, being tired out of proportion to the kinds of physical activity you do is a sign of depression.

Sign 3. Drastic Behavioral Changes. In depressed people, behavior sometimes changes drastically. In Roger's case, he isolated himself by cutting classes and staying home to sleep during the day. Other kinds of behavioral changes that might be signs of depression include rebelliousness, constant fidgeting (hyperactivity), and drastic changes in study habits, telephone use patterns, social life.

Sign 4. School Problems. Roger became a truant and that is clearly a school problem. Any abrupt change in how you behave at school — frequent problems with your teachers, cutting, and truancy — may be a warning sign of depression.

Sign 5. Suicidal Talk, Suicide Attempts. A symptom Roger didn't have but that is common in depressed people is talk of suicide, fascination with death and dying, and suicide attempts.

What makes any of these symptoms an actual danger

sign of depression rather than just a way to cope with one or more of the stresses of adolescence? Three factors:

— Duration (How long does it last?)
— Intensity (How drastic? How severe? How extreme?)
— Seriousness (How does it affect your ability to function normally?)

There are also "trigger situations" that you may experience that can tip a symptom from being a normal reaction into the depressed range of behavior. Some of these trigger situations are not being able to communicate clearly and honestly with people in your family, family conflicts, and parents' marital problems. Separation from loved ones, illness or death of a family member, or your own illness or injury can be triggers. Major changes in how you and your family are able to live (if there are money problems, for example, or you must move, or your parent loses a job) can trigger depression. In fact, if your parents suffer from depression, you may also become depressed.

Being severely depressed is more than being in a blue funk. It's like being in a black hole that you can't seem to find your way out of. If you or someone you know has symptoms from three or more of the categories we listed as "signs" in discussing Roger's case, and they last for more than a few weeks, or if there's talk of suicide (even if it seems like it's said jokingly) in combination with any of the signs, professional help is needed.

Depression can be treated and it usually involves a combination of "talking therapy" (actually talking things over with a medical doctor who is a psychiatrist, or with a psycholgist, or psychiatric social worker) plus *prescribed medicine* that a doctor will give you to help ease some of your down feelings and help you to get back in control of your life.

Suicide

I turned my light on and saw Justin hanging from a tree. That's the thing that still keeps me awake in the middle of the night, that vivid image. . . . His eyes and mouth were open, and his tongue was swollen and protruding. I shined the light across his eyes. . . . I knew because his eyes were fully dilated and by his color that that was it.

Mrs. Anne Spoonhour, talking about the suicide
of her fourteen-year-old son, Justin.
(*People*, February 18, 1985, p. 78)

SUICIDE. The word leaps off the page and challenges you to take notice. The people who attempt suicide or actually commit suicide are also challenging you to take notice. Logic says that suicide is an act of violence directed at oneself, but people who are suicidal may see things differently. For some, it's the ultimate act of rebellion, a way of confronting the people or institutions that may have misunderstood or ignored them in the past. For others, it's a solution to what feels like an insurmountable problem or series of problems, a way of saying, "Look, I'm finally taking control of my destiny." For still others, suicide seems to be almost a romantic, exotic thing to do, as in the case of troubled lovers who make suicide pacts and kill themselves together to prove to everyone that they were really in love.

Unfortunately, many people commit suicide without really comprehending the finality of death. Odd as it may sound, they do it without actually believing that they won't be back tomorrow and won't be there to see how others will react to what they've done.

It's not easy or pleasant to think about or talk about suicide, but it's important to do both, because today teenage suicide is an epidemic: *500,000 young people attempt suicide each year and 5,000 actually kill themselves.* The best way to combat an epidemic is to find out what's causing it so we can learn how to treat and prevent it. In order to find out what's causing it, we need to talk about it, get it out in the open, and reveal it for what it is — a very poor way of trying to come to grips with the problems in one's life.

There are two categories of kids who are involved in suicidal behavior, according to the president of the American Association of Suicidology, the *attempters* and *the committers.* They are very different.

— Ninety percent of the attempters are female, many have very close relationships with their mothers and poor relationships with their fathers, and these kids tend to feel responsible for their parents' marital problems in situations of divorce. They usually use overdoses of drugs such as sleeping pills in their suicide attempts.

— Three out of four committers (the kids who actually kill themselves) are boys. Most don't let their emotions show and keep things bottled up inside. Many are loners, under a lot of pressure to achieve, who don't know how to ask for help and don't feel they are appreciated. Their methods of self-destruction are usually hanging or shooting themselves.

The warning signs of suicide, like the warning signs of depression, are often ignored because they look so much like what our society has come to define as "typical" teenage moodiness and rebellion. That's one of the reasons, if you notice these signs in your friend's behavior (or if you are seeing yourself in these descriptions), it's so important to talk about them *so that you can know that they aren't a joke, they aren't "typical" of anything normal, and they must be confronted quickly and properly.* The warning signs are:

Sign 1. Symptoms of Depression. The risk of a depressed person's committing suicide is fifty times higher than for a person who isn't depressed.

Sign 2. Self-Mutilation. Some suicidal teenagers have a thing about cutting themselves or abusing their bodies in other ways. This does not mean that all teenagers who like the punk style of wearing safety pins through their cheeks are suicidal, but in combination with other warning signs self-mutilation is not to be ignored.

Sign 3. Preoccupation with the Subject of Death in Art, Music, Poetry, Other Literature, or in Your Own Writings. There's a difference between being preoccupied with these things because you have to write a paper in an art history, music appreciation, or literature class about some artist who has committed suicide, and being preoccupied for reasons that come from deep inside you.

Sign 4. Giving Away Treasured Possessions. When we say "giving away treasured possessions" we don't mean giving your little brother the fire engine you no longer play with and that has outlived its usefulness to you. We're not talking about giving your boyfriend or girlfriend your favorite ring as a token of love. We're not talking about trading clothes with your friends. We mean a housecleaning of things that were so meaningful to you in the past that no one was allowed to get near them.

Sign 5. Writing a Will.

Sign 6. Expressing Feelings of Worthlessness, Saying That Your Family Would Be Better Off without You. This is one of the most often ignored warning signs because such statements come across as exaggeration of how you're feeling on a given day. Because your moods tend to fluctuate anyway, your parents and other people may completely miss the seriousness of what you're expressing.

Sign 7. Visible Cues. You wear a strand of wire for a belt. You begin to carry knives of different shapes and sizes around with you. You make earrings out of bullets. These cues can be missed if other people think this is just "style," but if they start up abruptly, are a complete switch from what is your norm, if they're coupled with statements like "I'm wearing this belt so I can strangle myself," they're serious signs of possible suicide.

Sign 8. Previous Suicide Attempts.

Sign 9. The Apparent Lifting or Disappearance of a Person's Previous Depression. This is very peculiar. There are two theories that try to make sense of this. One holds that only when a teenager is no longer depressed can he or she have the psychological strength to plan and go through with a suicide. The other suggests that a decision to commit suicide is a decision to exert control over your life. Since the lack of control is an issue for suicidal teenagers, the decision to commit suicide is reason for optimism precisely because it's a decision to do something, and so depression lifts.

There are "trigger situations" for suicide just as there are "trigger situations" for depression. The ones we discussed in the section on depression also apply to suicide, but there are some others that are specifically linked to suicide. Something like the hostage crisis in Iran in 1980, the taking of the T.W.A. plane and its passengers as hostages by the Shiite Moslem extremists in 1985, or the threat of nuclear war — that is, any event that threatens your own happiness and security because it threatens the actual future of the country — can be suicide triggers. A sense of powerlessness is another, and it's one of the reasons that teenagers from wealthy suburban areas seem to be a high-risk group for suicide. According to the American Association of Suicidology, the message kids from these environments get is "If you go to school, it doesn't mean you'll get a job; if you get a job, it may not be meaningful; if you get married, it may not last." Sometimes, the suicide of a friend or relative can trigger a suicide attempt. Suicides seem to occur in clusters: nineteen teenagers took their own lives within an eighteen-month period between 1983 and 1985 in Westchester, Putnam, and Jefferson counties in New York, and all you need to do is look through back copies of newspapers to see that similar patterns are being repeated all over the country.

If being depressed feels like you're stuck in a black hole, being suicidal is like suffering from tunnel vision. You can't see the light at the end of the tunnel, and you can't locate yourself in the tunnel either. It's worse than Alice in Wonderland falling down the rabbit hole, because there's no place to land. You don't have to label yourself a loser if you're feeling suicidal. Consider this: the rock star Billy Joel contemplated suicide as a teenager and is now donating royalties from his song "You're Only Human (Second Wind)" to the National Committee for Youth Suicide Prevention.

If you are contemplating suicide, you need immediate help to enable you to see that there are other alternatives. You may not want it, but you need it. (If you don't know where to turn for help, check the *Yellow Pages* to find a listing for your local suicide hotline.) Therapy is similar to treatment for depression: there is talking therapy for you as an individual and family therapy that includes other people in your family along with you; antidepressant medication that is prescribed by your doctor to help get you through a crisis; and an emergency plan for what will be done for you should you ever become suicidal again. In the talking therapy part of your program, you will probably explore these topics:

1. What have you been doing in your life that you really didn't want to be doing?
2. What are your goals, and what obstacles have made it hard for you to achieve your goals?
3. What seems to trigger your feelings of depression?
4. What are your strengths and talents?
5. How can you use these strengths and talents to cope more productively with your problems?

If you attempt suicide and don't actually kill yourself, it is possible that you will be hospitalized. The purpose of this is to give you time out in a controlled environment where you can get through the worst of your self-destructive feelings, and start to pull together the threads of your unraveling life into a stronger fabric with the help of professional therapists. If you are hospitalized, it's because people care about you and not because they want to put you away, or put you out of their lives.

If you get therapy, with or without hospitalization, there is one important concept we hope you'll learn: the concept of *positive failure*. Whatever you do to try to make things better for yourself, or whatever you do in life at all, recognize that the effort you make is positive regardless of the outcome.

What happens if you're a friend or relative of someone who has actually committed suicide? You'll need some help too, because your own emotions will be in turmoil.

You may feel rage and resentment:

"How could he (she) do this to me?"
"How could he (she) leave me like this?"
"He (she) had so much to live for!"

You may feel guilt:

"I should have been able to prevent it."

"Did I do something to cause it?"

"I thought I knew all the signs to look for."

"Sometimes I actually wished he (she) was dead and now he (she) is."

If it's your brother or sister who has committed suicide, you may feel torn between loyalties to that dead sibling and the desire to make things easier somehow for your parents by being a super kid yourself and being better than that dead sibling.

If suicide has touched your life, you need to give yourself permission to feel the whole range of emotions — rage, fear, misery, relief (yes, even relief). You must *feel* before you can *heal*. It's okay to ask "Why?" or "What if. . . ?" but don't let the questions dominate your life. Talking about the suicide is very important, but you may not want to for a while. Self-help groups made up of people like yourself can be the key that unlocks the door to your emotions, and individual psychotherapy is also very useful.

You must constantly remind yourself, though, that you weren't responsible for that person's death and you shouldn't allow that suicide to be something that plagues you for the rest of your life. What counts is that you'll be able to turn the suicide, the grief, and the guilt into something positive for yourself, for others, and for the memory of your friend or sibling. Perhaps you could start a group in your school for the prevention of suicide patterned after S.A.D.D. (Students Against Drunk Driving). Silver linings can be found in even the darkest of clouds.

15.

Dealing with Tough Topics — When a Parent or Friend Dies, Sexual Victimization, Breaking the Law

There are times when life seems to deal out bad luck or tragedy from which no one is completely immune. In this chapter, we will discuss several such situations that are unpleasant or even frightening — but nevertheless very real. Reading about these topics can help prepare you for dealing with them if they ever strike close to home.

When a Parent or Friend Dies

There's never a good time to have to cope with death, and even if you think you're prepared, you can never be prepared enough. When someone you love dies, whether the death happened unexpectedly and quickly (the result of an accident, sudden illness, physical violence) or after a long period of illness and physical suffering, whether it happened by natural causes or was self-inflicted (drug overdose, suicide), you can expect to feel a whole range of emotions. Some of them may surprise you. That's because grief takes many forms: shock, sadness, anger, disbelief, rage, even relief if the person who died had a terminal (incurable) illness and was in a great deal of pain.

The finality of death is overwhelming at first, and it takes

289

quite a while to get used to it. People go through several stages of mourning that help them make sense out of something over which they have no control, and something that can seem incredibly unfair. Whether it's a parent or friend whose death you must deal with, you can expect to start looking for answers to dilemmas and questions that may be unanswerable.

> My friend never even had a chance to live a full life. He was too young to die. It doesn't seem to me that there are payoffs for being a good person if this is what can happen.
>
> *Arlene H., age fifteen*

> My dad was the best one in his family. Everyone said so; it's not just that I'm his daughter. His brother and sister are so nasty, and they're all alive and he's dead. I'm having trouble trying to figure this one out.
>
> *Phoebe L., age sixteen*

It's not at all selfish if your first reactions upon learning that someone you're very close to has died are like these:

> I'm so angry at my mom for dying. She knew she shouldn't smoke after her heart attack but she kept doing it. She should have taken care of herself. How could she have done this to me?
>
> *Dale V., age fourteen*

> You know the first worry I had when my dad died? Who'd take me to the "Father-Son-and-Daughter Dinner" at our church. The thought that I wouldn't get to go upset me so much, it's incredible.
>
> *Nancy S., age fourteen*

You may wonder, "What will happen to me?" "How will I be able to live without him/her?" "Why me?" Angry, self-centered reactions are normal parts of grieving. They're a way for you to express some of your anxieties. However, you may not find that anyone has immediate answers to your questions or answers that will satisfy you.

If one of your parents has died, you may want to discuss your concerns with your surviving parent and other relatives.

You should be prepared to see your parent very upset, crying, confused, unable to decide what to do first, even dwelling on the past and refusing to discuss the present — in short, not at all the person you're used to being around. This is a temporary stage that will ease with time. Having already lost one parent, you may be terribly worried that the other will die too. Don't confuse his or her state of grief and lack of energy or other personality changes with illness or impending death. For your own well-being, don't let remembrances of the past get too strong a hold on the present. Let your friends and the adults you trust — your support system — ease you through these early stages of mourning. Allowing them to be part of your grieving process by accepting their offers of help — letting them take you out places, or cook meals for you, or do your errands — is a way of making everyone feel useful. Offering help during a time of mourning is how many people assert that they are in control of life, having just experienced a death over which they had *no* control.

If you lose a parent you may find it extremely hard to accept help from friends. All of a sudden you're different from the others who have both parents and that feels terrible.

> I got the call about my dad's death at school. My friends found out and met me outside the counselor's office. I was crying and looked awful and they were trying to comfort me and I couldn't accept it. I was embarrassed. I got real flip. I actually said, "That's OK. I'm only half an orphan." But they stuck by me even though I was super nasty. Later on I was so happy to have them around me.
>
> *Roseanne T., age fifteen*

The pain of losing a parent may be so intense that your reaction may be to want to take off and not let anyone know where you're going. This isn't a good way to deal with your feelings because it just adds another layer of grief to the existing ones for your surviving parent and other relatives, and it doesn't help you come to grips with your feelings. It's a way of avoiding them.

If it's a friend who has died, your reactions may be a bit more detached, maybe even subdued. Some kids who've gone through this say at first it felt like they were watching a home video of someone else's life. Others say they felt guilty that they were alive and their friends weren't and that even though they knew there was nothing they could have done to change things, they searched for days for some clue as to what they could have done differently to possibly change the course of events.

Embarrassment is a common feeling that creeps in along with sadness and disbelief: you may be afraid to talk to your dead friend's family because you're uncomfortable showing your own feelings in public among strangers, especially if you're going to be at the funeral or paying a condolence call. You should only do what seems right to you. Sometimes a sympathy note will convey your message better than an in-person visit, and going to a funeral is a matter of choice.

If you've never been to a funeral before, you may wonder, "What will the funeral be like? Will I be able to handle it? How am I expected to behave?" Ask an adult who's been to a funeral to prepare you for what you might encounter. Funerals differ according to religion and personal family preferences. You may be concerned about "What does a dead person look like? What if I'm afraid?" If the casket is closed, you won't have to look. If it's open you can expect to see a person who looks mannequinlike, but not all that different from the person you knew in life. Being afraid is a normal reaction, and you can always leave before the ceremony begins. People will understand and appreciate that you've made an effort to come. Sometimes there is no casket because, for example, the dead person has willed his or her body to a medical school or hospital. A memorial service is held to let people pay last respects and talk about the deceased. There is no burial following the ceremony, since there is no corpse to bury. "What if I break down and cry? What if I can't cry?" People mourn in all sorts of ways at funerals and memorial services, and nobody will notice if you cry or don't. Be yourself.

If you're dealing with the death of a parent, it may be that helping to arrange the funeral will alleviate your fears. It's a way of continuing the bond between you and your dead parent and it's also a way to take the mystery out of what's happening and help you to frame it in reality. Writing a eulogy — a personal recollection — that you may want to read is something to think about and discuss with your surviving parent. You shouldn't consider yourself morbid if you're interested in the funeral preparations, nor should you consider yourself unfeeling if you're not. These are very individual preferences, and there's no right way or wrong way. You may find that if you want to take an active role in the funeral, your remaining parent may resist in an effort to protect you from further sorrow. If it means a lot to you, you'll need to be prepared to be assertive about your decision. It really is a "now or never" situation.

If you're planning on attending the funeral of a friend and you're afraid, going with classmates and teachers can ease the tension. It helps to have a group of friends and trusted adults to discuss things with and be with. A funeral is a ceremony designed not only to pay last respects to the dead, but it's a way for you to say good-bye. A funeral or memorial service can actually create some good feelings. This is true whether you are coping with the loss of a loved one or someone you didn't even know, as was true of the feeling of comfort the people of the United States got from collectively mourning the deaths of the six astronauts and one civilian teacher that occurred when the Challenger space shuttle exploded on January 28, 1986. The need to be together with other people who are bereaved and can understand the intensity of your emotions, and the support people can give each other, are very positive aspects of such ceremonies. Some people find the experience to be intensely personal and spiritual and are glad to have had the opportunity to participate in the conclusion of that person's life.

You may wonder how life can go on normally after the death of a parent. It does, but there may be some subtle changes along the way. Here are some of the more common ones:

1. A son is often compared to his deceased father, a daughter to her deceased mother.
2. A widowed mother may refuse to approve her son's dates; a widowed father may refuse to approve his daughter's dates. This is because you may be replacing

that dead husband or wife in the surviving parent's mind.

3. At least for a while, you may be put in the role of having to care for or discipline your siblings.

4. Your parent may turn you into the "man" or "woman" of the house and lean on you for emotional support almost like you were a substitute husband or wife.

If these kinds of burdens are placed on you, we strongly suggest you discuss them with your parent. If your mom or dad denies this is what is happening, ask for professional help. (Your minister, priest, or rabbi may be a good resource person to turn to for help.) If your parent refuses, speak to your school counselor and get help that way. You may be like your dead parent in many ways, but you are yourself and shouldn't be forced or expected to play a role that wasn't yours to begin with.

When a friend dies, especially if he or she was a close friend or your best friend, there's a void in your life and in your social group. Sometimes your other friends may expect you to fill in for the person who has died. It's not unlike what happens when a parent dies and you're expected to take that parent's place in the family. Sometimes your friends behave as if the dead friend was still alive and make decisions taking his or her preferences into account. If you're the one to disagree, you may be made to feel disloyal to that friend's memory. You may decide to go along with the group for a while, but at some point you'll have to put on the brakes and say, "Enough." The fact is that your group of friends will never be *exactly* the same as it was before that death and you'll all need to do some serious thinking about how you want to reorganize. Perhaps the dead friend provided the glue that held you all together, and without that person there isn't a real basis for continuing friendships. You may need to try out new friendship patterns till you find the ones that work best.

You may think you've handled the death of a parent or friend quite well. But if you notice yourself starting to have problems in school, if you feel depressed or withdrawn or, conversely, you start getting very aggressive, if you turn to alcohol or drugs and you'd never indulged in these things before, if you start stealing things or get into any kind of criminal behavior, you may not be handling it so well. You probably have left a lot of things unsaid, and they're coming out in these kinds of behaviors. It's really better to say them and get your life back to normal. You may need counseling to help you do this. Getting it is a sign of strength and maturity on your part.

Perhaps you feel the need to visit a friend's or a parent's grave weeks or months after the funeral. You may want to maintain close contact with your dead friend's parents, especially if you had a comfortable relationship with them in the past. Don't be put off if people say you're weird to do any of these things. You need to rely on your gut feelings and come to terms with the death in whatever ways work for you.

What Everyone Needs to Know about Rape and Other Forms of Sexual Victimization

Rape is not a pleasant topic to think about, so many of you may be tempted to skip this part of the chapter. *Don't.* While there's no way of knowing in advance if you will ever be the victim of an attempted sexual assault — even if you're male — there are definitely some things you need to know about preventing rape, what to do if you (or a friend or a relative) has been raped, and common myths about rape and rapists. Thinking about these topics is not meant to frighten you but to alert you to some straightforward facts that it's important for all of us to know.

Let's begin with a simple definition: rape is a form of sexual assault in which the penis enters the vagina without the consent of both partners. (While this legal definition doesn't work in cases of males "raped" by other males, common usage applies the term to these situations, too.) Partly because it is an emotion-laden subject, it has been surrounded by many myths and misunderstandings, and has been mistakenly seen as principally a sexual act. Today, however, new research has proven that rape is primarily an act of aggression, an expression of violence, anger, or power — in short, a crime that violates the victim's personal sense of safety and control over her life.* Despite these findings, one of the most troubling aspects of the myths about rape is the idea that the victim actually provoked the rapist's act in one of the following ways.

Females dress and act provocatively in order to "turn men on"; they are really "asking" to be raped. This is a bit like arguing that people who wear nice clothes are really asking to be mugged. It misplaces responsibility from the criminal to the victim.

Women secretly "want" to be raped and really enjoy the experience. Although some women may fantasize about rape, this doesn't mean that they want the actual, real-life experience of a violent, frightening assault any more than a man who fantasizes about being a war hero wants actually to go to war.

Women find overpowering men sexually irresistible. This misconception is based on the old (incorrect) stereotype that females are passive, wishy-washy creatures, while men are strong, decisive leaders who "really" know what women want. Scores of psychological studies have proven that this isn't so. (Actually, females are more apt to be attracted to men who show tenderness and consideration than to men who use the "Me Tarzan, you Jane" approach.)

Despite increasing awareness of these sorts of myths about rape, females are still frequently "blamed" for being raped because of the mistaken notion that a female who resists *cannot* be raped. This bit of folklore is completely inaccurate for a variety of reasons. For one thing, many rapists either carry a weapon or threaten their victims with violence or death if the victims resist. To give in under these circumstances, especially if there's little chance of escaping without physical injury, is the smart thing to do — but not a sign of wanting to be raped. Second, many rape victims are so frightened at the suddenness and surprise of the assault that they are physically and psychologically immobilized — in effect, unable to fight back or resist out of fear.

* Because the overwhelming majority of victims of sexual assault past childhood are female, our discussion will use feminine pronouns describing rape victims and male pronouns when talking about those who rape. Readers should realize that the roles can be different — in fact, there are documented cases where males have been raped by females.

While you might suppose that most rapes are carried out by strangers in dark alleys or side streets late at night, the truth is that in many instances the rapist is a friend, relative, neighbor or acquaintance of the victim and many attacks occur in or near home. Furthermore, while you might think that it's easy to spot a rapist because he must somehow look deranged or ferocious, this isn't usually the case — many rapists are perfectly normal in appearance and couldn't be singled out from a crowd.

One form of rape that teenagers need to be particularly aware of is *date rape* — being forced by a date into having sexual intercourse. Several experts believe that this is a far more common occurrence than had been thought, with as many as one out of every twenty women being victimized by this form of sexual assault by the time they reach their mid-twenties. Because the victims are often reluctant to report this type of rape to the authorities (in part, because it's difficult to prove unless witnesses were present), its true frequency has been widely underestimated in the past. The following comments underscore the fact that such rapes are far from rare:

> When I was seventeen, in my junior year of high school, I went to a party with a guy I really liked a lot. We had been out together twice before, and although we had gotten into some heavy necking and petting, there was nothing about his behavior that led me to think he wouldn't respect my saying "no." At the party he had four or five drinks and then we went out to his car, where we were making out. All of a sudden he was climbing on top of me and pushing my legs apart, and while I was struggling to try to make him stop, he did it. Afterwards I was really upset and confused. I knew that he had raped me, but then I was thinking that I had led him on at least a little, so maybe he couldn't be blamed for it. The hardest part was facing him at school after that. I hated him, but I hated myself too.
>
> *A nineteen-year-old girl*

> I know that this sounds corny and all, but I was out on a date with a boy I didn't know too well, and we drove out to a deserted beach so we could walk around and talk. When I said, "It's late, we better go," and started to get

back in the car, he said, "I'm not taking you anywhere until you put out for me." I couldn't believe it — at first, I thought he was just kidding. But then I saw he wasn't, and I got scared because the beach was about twelve miles from town and there wasn't even a telephone around. I tried to talk him out of it, but finally I just gave in. I cried through the whole thing and all the while he drove me home. When he got to my house, he said, "See you," just like we'd had a lot of fun together.

A seventeen-year-old girl

This is really embarrassing for me to talk about, but when I was fifteen I went out with a senior who took me to a party at his friend's house. I could see he was trying to get me drunk, but what I wasn't prepared for was that he took me down to his friend's basement to show me some exercise equipment he had and he just attacked me. I screamed, but no one heard me because of all the music and noise going on, and even though I tried to fight him off, I lost my virginity to this ape. I was afraid to tell my parents because I thought they'd get mad at *me*, so I just kept quiet about the whole thing. Later on, I heard that he was bragging that he scored with me.

An eighteen-year-old girl

As you can see from these remarks, date rapes can occur in a variety of situations. Commonly, the male tries to seduce his date by getting her drunk or high on drugs, thinking this will lower her resistance to his sexual advances. What may happen instead is that the effects of alcohol or drugs on *him* distort his sense of right and wrong, preventing him from seeing that forcing someone into having sex is a criminal act. In addition, some researchers think that males who commit date rape are relatively unable to admit to themselves that a girl would reject them sexually — they think they're so "macho" and irresistible that they simply don't believe it when a date says "no."

There's no sure-fire way of avoiding date rape, but the following practical pointers will help keep the chances of being raped by a date at a minimum:

1. Avoid the use of drugs, including alcohol, on dates or at parties, and don't go out with boys who are drinking or using drugs.
2. Do not go off to remote, secluded spots on a date.
3. Until you know a date really well, try to stay with a group of friends or in public places (like the movies) for your dating activities.
4. Always have some money with you when you're on a date so you can use a pay phone or get a cab to get home by yourself if necessary.

Finally, if you are raped or otherwise sexually assaulted by a date (or by anyone else), *don't* keep it a secret. If you feel that you can't tell your parents, most communities have a rape crisis hotline that you can call for help (you can find this phone number in the *Yellow Pages*), or you can go to a hospital emergency room or call your family doctor. Talking with a knowledgeable person will help you deal with your own feelings about this very personal matter, which is important because if your feelings are bottled up inside, they can leave permanent emotional scars. In addition, you should be examined medically for any injuries, for possible sexually transmitted infections, and for the possibility of pregnancy. Going to the hospital emergency room or seeing your physician doesn't mean you have to report the rape to the police, although doing so can help you feel more in control and also may protect others from being victimized by the rapist.

It's quite common for rape victims to have complicated emotional reactions in the weeks and months after the assault, so if you've been raped (or if a friend of yours has been) getting counseling to help deal with these feelings is very important. Initially, rape victims usually react with a sense of shame, shock, disbelief, fear, anger, and sometimes even guilt. In some cases, though, the rape victim seems to be very cool and composed, which is usually just a sign that she's blocked out her awareness of the inner turmoil she's experiencing, as though she's denying the reality of the experience she's gone through. This can be a sign of more serious emotional problems ahead, when these bottled-up feelings come spilling out all at once. In the longer range, it is often helpful for the rape victim to join a support group or get continuing counseling at a rape crisis center in order to deal with recurring anxieties, fears, and self-doubts.

Another form of sexual victimization that all teenagers should know about is *incest* — sexual activity with a relative. Although the most common form of incest is between brothers and sisters, the most serious form involves an adult relative's forcing a child or teenager into having sex with them. While this may sound shocking or even unbelievable, it is estimated that 100,000 children are sexually victimized by adult relatives each year, with a majority of these cases involving the sexual molestation of a daughter by a father or stepfather. Unfortunately, there are also cases where uncles, cousins, or even grandparents sexually abuse their children and teenage relatives.

Although incest is against the law in every state in America, one of the problems an incest victim may have is getting someone to believe her (or him). Often a parent who is told about the sexual abuse may refuse to believe it and may accuse the teenage or child victim of "having a vivid imagination" or of "exaggerating" or "misinterpreting" the other parent's affectionateness.

If you are ever approached sexually by a family member, the sensible thing to do is to say "no" in no uncertain terms. But since there are times when this may not work — when physical force is used, for example, or where you've been threatened or blackmailed into having sex with a relative against your will — you must be prepared to tell someone you can trust what has happened. This accomplishes two things: first, it can put an end to the sexual abuse, and second, it can give you a chance to get help. This is important because many people who were incest victims and never told anyone about it wind up carrying around tremendous burdens of guilt, resentment, anger, and poor self-esteem; in addition, they have an increased chance of having sexual problems when they reach adulthood. Today there is increasing public awareness of incest as a problem and many opportunities for incest victims to get helpful counseling so they can deal effectively with the situation and their feelings. So if you or someone you know has been involved in incest, don't keep quiet about it. *Get help!*

The final form of sexual victimization that we will mention is sexual harassment, which can occur either at school or at work. While females are most often the targets of sexual harassment, males can be victimized too. Typically, sexual harassment involves a person in a position of power or authority (for example, a teacher, an employer) attempting to obtain sexual favors as a form of "payment" for giving you special treatment. The following examples show two of the many different forms that sexual harassment can take:

I had a job working evenings and weekends as a waitress at a restaurant in town. My boss kept coming on to me, but I didn't think too much of it because he was so much older than me and he flirted with all the waitresses. One night he called me into his office in back and asked me if I liked my job. I did, because I was making pretty good money, and I said so. Then he said, "Well, if you like your job, you're going to have to put out for me — otherwise you can go work someplace else." At first I thought he was kidding, but before I knew it he was grabbing for me and trying to paw me all over. I got out of there as fast as I could and never went back again.

A seventeen-year-old girl

In my junior year of high school I was doing really badly in a trigonometry course I had. My teacher asked me to come in for a conference after school to discuss my problems. He started talking about how a bad grade in math would hurt my college admission chances, which I realized all too well. Then he said that he thought that he could help me get an A in trig if I really wanted it badly enough. I said that of course I wanted an "A," but I didn't see how I could do that level of work. He put his hand on my knee, and started rubbing up my thigh, and said, "You don't need to do any work at all if you know how to be nice to me." I didn't know how to react, I was so surprised and scared. He took my silence to mean I agreed, and he pushed his hand under my sweater and started playing with my breasts. Then he told me he would give me two private lessons after school each week, which would guarantee me getting an A. I was so confused that I said OK. It was only after another girl told me he had tried the same bit with her that we got up our courage and told the principal what was happening.

An eighteen-year-old girl

Sexual harassment at work is a violation of federal law. It is defined very specifically in the Equal Employment Opportunity Commission Rules and Regulations (1980). Sexual harassment at school is also illegal, but no one is certain yet of the scope of this problem. In 1983, an official of the Association of American Colleges estimated that one out of five college coeds is subjected to one form or another of sexual harassment. The extent of this problem in high schools across the country is less clear; often, when cases come to the attention of school authorities they are hushed up. Despite the lack of solid information on the frequency of sexual harassment, what *is* clear is that the person who is victimized usually feels degradation, humiliation, and helplessness — feelings that are very similar to those voiced by rape victims. In either case, it's important to consult with an attorney to get advice about the options available to you if you feel that you are the victim of sexual harassment.

Breaking the Law

I wanted to be tight with a certain bunch of guys, so I went with them one night to spray graffiti on some subway cars in the trainyards. It was real dark and looked deserted, and then we got caught. Now I've got a police record.

Carlos V., age seventeen

I was doing my brother a favor. He was sick, so I passed some pills and joints along to his friend at school and took the money for it. The principal passed by as the deal was going down. I was suspended and sent to a juvenile court. I got a bum rap. They weren't *my* drugs.

Alica N., age thirteen

There's a big difference between doing things that are risky and legal and doing things that break the laws in your community and might subject you to arrest and punishment. You probably know someone who'll admit to doing something illegal — using a fake I.D. to buy a drink, making prank phone calls, sneaking into a movie without paying, smoking some pot. Trying to get away with something you know isn't right but that doesn't intentionally harm someone else or someone else's property is a form of risk-taking. Most parents understand that you're bound to do such things (though they don't necessarily approve) once in a while. It's a little like testing the water in a lake before plunging in for a swim — it allows you to see what something feels like before deciding if you enjoy it, and to check out the consequences of that activity. If you're fourteen and get drunk one night and end up sick to your stomach, you might decide the consequences aren't worth a repeat performance. If you choose to experiment with drugs because your friends are doing them, but your fear of being caught offsets any social or physical highs, then that activity's not for you.

Lawbreaking that is done on purpose with some understanding of the possible consequences is another thing entirely. Consider the difference between riding a motorcycle without a helmet (illegal in most states) and stealing someone else's cycle and taking it for a joyride. Breaking the law is risky not only to you, but it involves danger or harm to someone else, which magnifies the impact of the activity. There are so many teenagers who break laws today (we're talking about vandalism against school property, petty theft, auto theft, drug and alcohol abuse, muggings, murders, and sexual assault) that it costs tens of *billions* of dollars each year to repair acts of vandalism, run the juvenile court system designed to apprehend and convict these kids, and to run the programs designed to help them once they're in court custody.

Look around you. Your friends may be breaking the law on a regular basis, or maybe you are. Does that mean any of you are "bad," "hopeless," "misfits"? Does it mean any of you are doomed to a life of crime? Not necessarily. People who turn to lawbreaking activities often have problems that they can't come to grips with. They may not feel good about themselves. They may think nobody cares about them anyway, so why follow the rules? They may have problems in school and may have problems communicating with people in nonviolent ways.

You need to do some serious thinking about why law-breaking happens. Answer these questions for yourself (or if it's a friend you're trying to help break the habit, discuss these things with him or her):

1. What are the payoffs for breaking the law? Maybe you see that kids who rip off lockers or break into cars are loaded with money all the time. You work after school and can barely make ends meet. You think the risks of getting fingered aren't as bad as having to be poor all the time.

Maybe school is a rotten experience for you. You don't understand your subjects too well and can't seem to get ahead. You don't know where to go for help or don't want to, so your frustration mounts and mounts. You rationalize that it's better to get rid of the anger in any way than walking around ready to explode. You figure the school deserves to be vandalized because it has caused you so much heartache. You don't think about getting caught or having to pay for your acts.

Maybe you're not getting attention at home. Maybe you don't have many friends. Being a lawbreaker gets you noticed and gives you a reputation. You're willing to go for that kind of reputation rather than being a zero. It gets you associated with a group of people and that's preferable to having nobody to hang out with.

2. What are the consequences of lawbreaking? You may have only a vague notion of what it means to break the law and think of it as a lark. You don't think beyond the moment. You don't consider the other people whose lives will be badly hurt by your actions. Kids who think there won't be consequences are fooling themselves, because lawbreaking is the sort of thing that catches up with you. If you were caught, you might

— be arrested,
— be sent to a juvenile correction facility or even to an adult jail,

— be put on probation and remain in court custody for months or years,

— be sent to a juvenile rehabilitation program.

3. Do the payoffs outweigh the risks?

4. What alternatives exist to lawbreaking? The number one alternative is to say "no" to friends who entice you to join them in criminal actions, and "no" to yourself when your thoughts turn to any kind of preplanned violence. If you think that's easy, think again. It takes more guts and self-control to do that than it does to rip someone off.

Try to get yourself out of your routine. Explore the possibility of switching to another school where your reputation won't make you feel obligated to keep breaking the law over and over. See if you can get into a work-study program so you'll have a legitimate excuse of "I can't, I have to work" when your old friends ask you to do something illegal.

Find one law-abiding adult you like and can trust who could become your mentor and advisor (a priest, pastor, or rabbi, someone else's parent who isn't emotionally tied into you, a teacher or counselor at school, your probation officer). Lay things on the line to that person. Pick his or her brains for ideas about things you could be doing that are legitimate and that you'd enjoy. Call him or her when you're under stress and feel tempted to slip back into your old routine.

Become a volunteer at a place where people really need you. Old age homes and V.A. hospitals give you access to adults with varieties of life experiences that they'd be willing to share with you as you do your job, and you might learn about careers they had that you'd never heard of or thought about before. Also, volunteering and being appreciated may give you a new sense of your own worth. When you start feeling good about yourself, lawbreaking may seem less enticing. The contacts you make as a volunteer may lead to paying jobs and sources of references later on.

If you've really been locked into the lawbreaking course, but you don't yet have a criminal record, see if your parents would consider letting you move in with relatives in another location. Sometimes a physical break with your environment is necessary.

Set reasonable goals for yourself that you'll be able to accomplish, and you'll probably succeed in kicking the habit.

What if you have a friend whose illegal activities are so intense that you feel you should report him or her to the police? Consider the following:

1. What is the nature of the offense?
2. Is anyone or anything else endangered by your friend's actions?
3. Are you prepared to see your friend arrested?
4. Would you be in any danger by reporting your friend?
5. Are you willing to risk losing the friendship?
6. Are you willing to tell the police everything you know?
7. Why are you doing this?

You may be labeled a stool pigeon, you may be harassed, you may even put your own existence in danger. On the other hand, you may save a friend's life by making such a report, or at least be the catalyst that forces your friend to get some help. Make sure you've done your homework and can prove what you suspect before contacting the police, and make sure the benefits outweigh the potential risks to you.

Part 4.

Reaching
for Independence

16.

College Admissions

College may not be for everyone, but if it's what you want, then getting into the college of your choice is a quest that will preoccupy you during your junior and senior years in high school and maybe even earlier.

What Are Colleges Looking for?

Because there are so many types of colleges and universities to choose from, there should be one or two at the very least that will suit your needs. The trick is to know how to find the school that will be a good match for you, and that will want you to become part of its academic community. The truth is that there is no such thing as the "perfect candidate" because the qualities that are very desirable and might guarantee acceptance at one school may be less desirable at another and might actually jeopardize your chances of acceptance there. In general, though, there are some things that any college would want to see in a prospective student: *maturity*, as shown by an eagerness to learn and a willingness to work at it; the ability to make a *commitment* and stick to it; and a sense of *direction* — setting goals and trying to achieve them.

You don't necessarily have to be a well-rounded student to get into the school of your choice. It may come as a shock to you to hear this, but many schools are more interested in accepting a mix of students so that the incoming freshman class is well rounded than accepting a majority of students who are

themselves well rounded! Many teenagers mistakenly believe
that their best hopes for acceptance will hinge on how many
extracurricular activities they can list on their applications.
They assume that even if they don't have straight A's and high
600's on their College Boards, an admissions officer will recognize their multiple interests and give them points for trying so
many different things.

In fact, many colleges today prefer students who seem to
be committed to achieving excellence and have a sense of direction, as shown by "stick-to-it-iveness." That means they
look for teenagers who are outstanding in one or two areas,
rather than for people who flit from interest to interest. How
do you become that student with a clear sense of direction?

1. Join a few organizations at school, but try to become an
   officer, or at least someone who has a say in decision
   making.
2. Play a sport and try to excel rather than being a member
   of several varsity teams and only managing third-string
   positions.
3. Play a musical instrument and try to gain some recognition. Aim for first or second chair. Try out for recitals.
   Volunteer to play solos. Offer to teach younger players.
   Ask to learn how to conduct.
4. Find a "cause" and work for it in such a way that you
   really accomplish something.

Organize a fund-raiser for muscular dystrophy; become a
tutor in a literacy-volunteer program; work for a political candidate during a campaign. Having some experience as a volunteer for "adult" causes sets you apart from the students whose
activities are all focused around school activities. It can also
give you contacts who may be able to help select and get you
into a college or university.

Colleges want some proof that you'll be capable of making a constructive and creative contribution to *both* classroom
and campus life. If you show them evidence that you've been

able to do this in high school, you already have one of the keys to open the door to the college of your choice.

Choosing a College

Trying to choose a college can make you feel like you're looking for a needle in a haystack. It's hard to know where you want to go if you have no points of reference. It's hard to know where you'll be happy based on vague notions of what you want to be in the future and the kinds of courses you'll want to take. In many ways, finding a college is a gamble because you never quite know what the outcome will be, even when you get there. So it's important to do some legwork before you send out that first application.

Write for college catalogues or go to the library and look through their books on colleges. Usually, public libraries carry up-to-date information on colleges and universities, as well as having copies of guides like *Barron's*, which are useful but which you may not want to actually buy. Talk to your guidance counselor at school. There may be some colleges that take more students from your particular geographical area than from others, there may be some colleges that have had very good luck with students from your high school and might be happy to admit you on that basis, and so on. You wouldn't necessarily learn about these kinds of things unless you spoke to a counselor who had access to this information.

Talk to your parents ahead of time. Ask them to be straight with you about the money picture in your family. Their financial status might determine whether you'd be limited to applying to lower-tuition state schools as opposed to private colleges, whether you'd be expected to foot part of the tuition bill yourself or if they will take care of that for you. If scholarship money is needed, you can then do some research about sources of tuition monies. Here again, your guidance counselor can help, and you may discover that you fulfill all the requirements for some obscure grant that you'd never heard of before. The company your parent works for may have scholarships available at certain schools for children of employees. Some schools offer merit grants based not on financial need but on how well you've done academically up to now. Some schools offer work-study plans in which tuition is offset by work you agree to do on campus. Don't automatically assume that a door will be shut to you just because you and your family don't have tuition money immediately available.

Here are some questions to think about before filling out your college applications. They represent some of the most common problems teenagers face in trying to choose a college.

1. *Should you apply to the college your parents both went to, just because they want you to go there and in spite of the fact that you're interested in fine arts and they both majored in engineering?* Your parents may hope that you'll attend a college they went to. There *is* such a thing as preference given to children of alumni/alumnae and you might consider this as a key to unlock an academic door that might otherwise be shut to you. There might be tremendous pressure on you to become a second- or third-generation student at that school, and it might be an easy solution for you. But to apply to a college just because a parent or other relative went there might not be the best reason to do so. Even though you might not be certain of what career choices you're prepared to make, you probably have some idea of where your interests lie. If those interests have little or no chance of being served at that school, discuss this with your parents and explore other options.

2. *Should you apply to a school that is known for its rigorous academic standards, just to satisfy your parents (who want you to be pre-med or pre-law and are paying for your tuition), when you really would like to go to a school known to have a good fraternity system and where students can have an active social life?* While it's possible that your parents might be right in seeing the seeds of a serious student and potential professional in you, there is no reason why those goals can't be obtained at a school that will suit your current needs for social life as well. If your family feels that paying tuition gives them the right to dictate your choice of schools, and you are unhappy with their choices, you may want to negotiate with them. What if you pay part of your own tuition? Will they allow you to change schools if you attend their choice and you find yourself un-

happy or unable to handle the academic pressures? Conversely, will you entertain the possibility of going to a school of your choice and if you do well, transferring to one of your parents' choices after your freshman or sophomore year? There *are* options, and your best bet will be to examine them with your parents before taking the plunge.

3. *Should you apply only to preppy, East Coast schools because they represent your "dream," even though you're from the East Coast, your grades haven't gone above the C+ range, and your combined College Board scores are less than 900?* No matter how badly you want to spend four years in a particular college or university, limiting yourself this way seems self-defeating. For example, in a *New York Times* article (December 9, 1985), "Admissions Is Anxiety for College and Student," the Dean of Admissions and Financial Aid at Wesleyan University in Connecticut pointed out that it's possible for him to know what the makeup of the class of 1990 will be like, based on "years past and from the school's priorities" — in spite of the fact that there are "no official quotas." But there are student profiles, and at Wesleyan that means certain things — average SAT scores of 625 in English and 651 in math; 70 percent admitted on their academic strengths, 5 percent the sons and daughters of alumni, and so on. The point is that you can find out about the student profile at the school you apply to and see how and if you match it. You don't want to have your dream turn into a nightmare.

4. *Should you apply to only three colleges: one you know you can get into and would feel comfortable at (your safety school), one you may be able to get into because a relative went there, and one that's a long shot but your first choice and that might accept you because you have a unique talent that you think they could make use of?* This approach to college admissions is probably the most logical, because it lets you cover your bases and it shows you have thought about your strengths and interests and made your selections accordingly. There's also nothing wrong with applying to a few more schools if they have something unique to offer and you think you may have a chance at getting in.

But try to be realistic. If you're a 5'8", 147-pound second-string wide receiver at your high school, you might not make the big time in the football program at the University of

Alabama no matter how much athletic potential your friends, parents, and coaches at home say that you have. If you don't have the academic skills to be accepted at a very competitive college, it's a little silly to apply there right out of high school. Even if you were to get in on probation, you might have a really tough freshman year that could sour your taste for college life. If you've messed up in high school, you can apply to a less competitive school, go there for a year or two and do really well, and then transfer to that other school once you've proven that you can do the work that college demands.

If you think that you have something really unique and terrific to offer, then try to maximize that asset. If you have your heart set on a school and don't quite fit the student profile that they're looking for, making personal contacts ahead of time and tooting your own horn may actually tip the scales in your favor. There are exceptions to every rule, and if you want to be that exception you'll need to take the initiative to get the process rolling. The great part about choosing a college and going to school in this day and age is the number of options that are available to you: you don't have to stay at the same school all four years if you should find you've made a mistake, and you don't even have to take all four years in a row if you want to stay but the pressure gets tough. Lots of kids choose to work for a year or two, or go overseas, and many schools are more than willing to accommodate these students. You can personalize your education in ways not possible in the past.

There are some other important factors to consider when choosing a college.

Geographical Location

If you're a surfer, you might not enjoy spending nine months out of the year going to a school in a ski resort area; if you love active city life, don't choose a school that's isolated or in the middle of farm country.

Size of the School

Don't choose a large state university if you're anxious about being lost in a crowd; a small independent college might be better for you. Similarly, don't automatically discount a school that's much smaller or larger than what you've been used to. Go to the campus if you can, and see what impact the actual size has on the daily lives of the students. A large university may be broken down into smaller colleges and might have the atmosphere you're seeking. A small school might have a big school feel because of the way the student body hangs together.

Style and Reputation of the School

All schools are not created equal. There are some that have a reputation for being artsy, or superintellectual, or party schools, or jock schools. Some are very conservative and others are very liberal. Some allow students to create their own academic programs and others have rigid requirements and offer few choices to their students.

Specific Strategies to Improve Your Chances for Acceptance

1. Consider attending a summer program that accepts high school students at the college you'd like to go to, or at a comparable school if the college of your preference doesn't offer one. Select academic courses that interest you enough that you'll be likely to work hard and do well. If you can get an "A" or "B" in a college-level class, it will look very good on your transcript and it may give you a competitive edge at the college when you apply. It also gives you a teacher in that system who can write a positive recommendation for you. If the teacher happens to be a full professor, so much the better, and if two courses interest you equally but one is taught by a graduate student and the other by a tenured faculty member, you might choose the latter with the idea that his or her recommendation may be more useful to you in the long run.

2. Get all your application materials in as early as possible once you've decided where you want to go. You might consider applying under an Early Decision plan because that signals the college that you've made it your first choice. But since acceptance under Early Decisions is a binding agreement, you should apply this way only if you're positive it's where you want to go.

In any event, don't wait until the deadline to send in your application. There's a very practical reason for this bit of advice. Admissions personnel usually aren't too busy during the months of September or October because few students apply that early. If *you* do, though, you may reap the benefits of having an admissions officer really spend time reading through your materials, more than would be possible if he or she were overwhelmed by having to process many other applications.

3. *Schedule an on-campus interview.* You need to make an appointment for an interview, and since there may be more requests than time slots, the earlier in the semester you do it the better. Contacting the office of admissions as early as the July or August before your senior year in high school can get you the date that best suits your schedule. It's wise to write directly to the person who booked the appointment to confirm the time and date. Keep a copy of the letter for your own records.

Speaking to a representative of the admissions staff isn't just a formality; it does more for you than answer questions that weren't addressed in the college catalogue. When the decision whether or not to admit you has to be made, your file goes before a committee. It's definitely to your advantage if an admissions counselor can say, "I remember X. I was impressed by his achievements but also by his self-confidence and by his ability to articulate his goals. I think he'll be an asset to the class."

Come to the interview neatly dressed and well groomed. First impressions may be the only impressions in such a situation. Don't be afraid to ask questions yourself. That's what you're there for. But that leads us to the next pointer.

4. *Do your homework.* Study the college catalogue before the in-person interview. Talk to some current students, recent graduates, or older alumni/alumnae before meeting the interviewer. Treat the interview as though it was a tryout for a play.

One of the biggest turnoffs for an admissions counselor is to discover that you haven't read the college catalogue, which contains information about the college, its philosophy of education, its strengths, and the requirements for all the courses of study.

Try to relax during an interview. Listen carefully to what the counselor says. If you're asked a question that you don't understand, ask the person to repeat it so that you don't answer a question that wasn't actually asked and come across as scatterbrained or inattentive, or, worse, uninterested. Make sure to explain to the counselor why you want to attend this college. If you're familiar with the catalogue, you could say something like, "I'm applying here because I'd eventually like to be able to study with Professors X and Y. I've already read some of their books and am intrigued with the idea of becoming a . . ." This shows you've done some advance thinking.

A catalogue always has information about grading. You might want their system explained to you, and that could also lead into a discussion of your current grade-point average. If you're not a good student currently, you might ask the admissions counselor what you could do to improve your chances for acceptance. You might inquire about the possibility of being admitted on probation, and whether going to summer school and getting a certain average there would tip the scales in your favor.

If you've spoken with current students or recent graduates, you could tell the interviewer some of the things they've said to make the school sound interesting to you. You can use this as a way to bring up the question of whether their perceptions are accurate, and if the counselor thinks you're basing your decisions to apply on correct information.

All of these things give you something to talk about. Admissions personnel will probably be impressed that you've done your homework. And, speaking of homework, you might also consider the following suggestion.

Before you've gotten a few college interviews under your belt, it may be helpful to rehearse them with someone who can play the role of the college admissions officer. While you might think this sounds hokey, it can help give you self-confidence and a sense of what to expect from the actual encounter.

By rehearsing — and getting feedback from your helper — you can spot potential problems that can mar the impression you make. Among the most common are (1) giving long, rambling answers; (2) starting all your sentences with the word "Well"; (3) sounding uncertain about why you're interested in a particular college; (4) fidgeting and avoiding eye contact with the interviewer.

5. *Try to spend a day on campus after your interview.* This is helpful if you want to get a taste of campus life. Take a tour. Visit the dorms, the library, the student center, even the bookstore. Try to audit one or two freshman classes. Observe how students spend their free time. Visit the dining hall and eat a meal there. Find out about off-campus housing, who lives in it, and what it's like. If you think you might be a commuter student at a school that is mainly residential, talk to some commuters and ask if this poses any problems for them in terms of fully participating in campus life. See if you can stay on campus long enough to attend a social function. If there are sororities and fraternities, try to visit some of the houses and talk to the kids who belong. Find out how important such organizations are on campus.

While one day (or even one weekend) on campus won't tell you everything you want to know, it can give you some of the flavor of the place and the people who are part of it. Don't be embarrassed to ask questions. Remember, you're not on trial — the school is on trial, and you're the judge and jury, at least for now.

6. *Try to get recommendations from people whose opinions count at that particular college, or whose opinions will be taken seriously.* Influential people connected with any college include trustees, prominent graduates, and people who donate large sums of money to the school. If you know someone like this personally and that person is willing to write on your behalf, it's to your advantage. If push comes to shove, and your record makes it seem iffy that you'll get in, such a person can use his or her influence to improve your chances. On the other hand, if such an individual writes something like this, "I'm a friend of X's family and I recommend X be accepted," that letter isn't generally worth the paper on which it's written.

You'll need at least two letters of recommendation written by high school personnel. Teachers and administrators who know you well enough that you think there's a chance they'll spend some time writing a positive recommendation are the people you should ask. Anyone who writes, "Sally is a good student who tries hard," isn't doing you a favor. In fact, such letters are like a code that signals the admissions committee to reject you. It would be better for a teacher to write a candid letter containing a realistic assessment of your strengths and weaknesses. Remember that unless the writer can convince the admissions committee of his or her own credibility, that letter may not have much influence.

Good teachers who have reputations for writing strong letters of recommendation are often flooded with requests to write them. Once you've decided who you'll ask to write the recommendations, you can do a few things to help make their job much easier and that may pay enormous dividends for you.

Ask them early.

It's not too early to ask them when you're a junior. You can tell them that you'd be honored if they'd do this, and that you're alerting them before summer vacation so they can do it at their lesiure. This shows you appreciate their time and effort. Also, teachers suffer burnout from having to write so many letters of recommendation, so it's often to your advantage to ask them when they're still fresh.

Make a copy of your entire application and give the writers of your recommendations a complete set.

This way they know what you have written, and they can confirm or clarify what you've said in your application.

Give them stamped, addressed envelopes to the specific college so they don't have to spend their own money on mailing expenses.

This is a mark of consideration and respect from you to them.

7. *Take time to prepare the best application you can.* A college application is a personal statement, and it's regarded as such by the college. It's not a form of medieval torture. Admissions people read thousands of applications, so the more interesting, well-planned, and clearly written yours is, the better.

It's okay to be a little creative in your writing style, but a word of caution about humor — what you think is funny may not seem so funny to a total stranger. While *you* may think it's terribly creative to write your admissions essay on the inside covers of matchbooks from all the restaurants you've eaten in, the admissions office may see this as a signal that you're weird.

It's okay to be thorough, but don't let your essays run on forever. It pays to have a few adults who aren't relatives read your application. They can be objective whereas most parents can't. They may offer constructive criticism about how to say the same things more concisely, or how to make your points more clearly.

Your application must be neat. Typing (or using a word processing program) to produce the final product is a good choice, and you should use a clear, dark ribbon. If you write in longhand, make sure you use your best handwriting and use white-out rather than an eraser, which might make holes in the paper, to correct mistakes. Erasable ball-point pens can be used as a last resort.

8. *Send your application by certified mail, return receipt requested.* This is worth the extra money and time it takes to go to the post office. Since admissions offices get so much mail, it's possible that some might be lost or misplaced. A crucial recommendation could even be misfiled in someone else's folder. Two applicants may have the same names. If you send your application by certified mail, return receipt requested, you have a record that it was received. If you don't get the return receipt back within a few weeks, you'll need to put a tracer on the packet and call the college.

9. *Call the college and make sure your application is complete.* It makes sense to contact the college and find out if your application file is complete, even if you know the materials have arrived. If for some reason the application is incomplete, the college may assume you weren't interested in following through with the entire admissions procedure and might send you the standard letter of rejection, and once that happens, it's literally impossible for the decision to be reversed.

These nine suggestions are designed to make the process of college admissions more manageable. Unfortunately, there's really no substitute for demonstrated excellence and proven leadership. Competitive colleges receive many more applications than there are openings, and sometimes even the best qualified students don't make it into their first choices. You have nothing to lose by following these steps, and potentially everything to gain.

17.

On Your Own

As you approach that point in your life when you can taste and feel the lure of being on your own, you are really like a track runner who is suspended in time between the starter's commands of "Get Set" and "Go!" You know what you're supposed to do, you've practiced the moves and you have the skills, but you don't have total confidence that you'll be able to put them all together when you get the signal.

To be on your own means to leave the security of family behind and substitute dependency on yourself for your previous dependency on parents. This is an exciting moment in a person's life, but it can be stressful if he or she doesn't take time to consider all the options. This chapter will explore some of the situations you may face on your own — going to college, joining the military, finding a job, getting housing — and it will examine the reasons why being on your own does *not* mean being alone. Interestingly, you can start to make many of your decisions while you're still at home and consider your family's opinions about them if you want, if that will make the process of actually going out on your own more comfortable for you.

Going to College

For many teens, going to college is *the* event that marks the transition from childhood to adulthood more clearly than any other. It accomplishes that for several reasons: your eighteenth birthday usually occurs around that time, and in our society eighteen is the magic age when you are no longer considered a "minor." Right or wrong, many adults begin to treat you differently when you're that old. Many adults assume that if you're going to college it means you'll be "serious" about life, and they may begin to react to your ideas and actions accordingly. They may listen to you more carefully, worry less about you, and many are willing to accept you as peers rather than as children in need of guidance or kids in a grownup world.

> I swear my dad started to confide in me right around the time I was going off to college. I don't mean father-son talks either. He told me some family stuff that was real personal, and he even showed me financial papers that I had no idea about. It blew me away! I wasn't any different but he sure was.
>
> *Faron L., age eighteen*

Going to college is the first time many of you have extensive choices to make about what direction your education will take. Not only must you decide what school(s) you will apply to, if you are accepted at more than one you must decide which is best for you, and then you must choose which classes will prepare you to achieve your goals. That, of course, means that you must have begun the process of deciding what you want to be or do when you are an adult, and rather than just fantasizing about it, you must find the path to get you there!

However, going to college is not completely idyllic, and if you live away from home the adjustment may be more painful than you might have anticipated, even if you're going to be living in a dorm — a relatively secure and self-contained youth community. Believe it or not, the overwhelming majority of incoming college freshmen report feelings of depression and loneliness when they arrive on campus.

> It was just like my first week at camp when I was ten. I knew who my counselor was, I knew where my bunk was, but everything else felt so unlike home. No friends, a different routine. I didn't think I could make it, and I cried for two days solid — both times.
>
> *Claudette R., age eighteen*

My brother went here and so did my dad. I'd been coming to homecoming football games since I was five. If anyone knew about this campus it was me. But for my first
two months as a freshman I was in a fog. I wanted out so
badly, and couldn't tell my folks — they would have been
too disappointed in me.

Merritt F., age eighteen

You may feel like you're sailing in uncharted waters, but
you have the power to control that sail. Here are some practical suggestions for your first semester at college.

Don't panic. It's OK to be scared and the feeling's not
going to last forever.

Try to get your routine set from the start. In practical terms
this means to get a study regimen going so you don't fall behind in your work, to set limits for yourself so that you don't
get into the habit of staying up all night or partying in place of
studying. Pace yourself so that you're not overwhelmed by
either the social *or* intellectual demands of college.

Learn to use the college library. College libraries can be
confusing places until you learn what the unique organization
is of the one you will be using. The *stacks* are where the books
are shelved, and before attempting to find a book you should
get a map of the library showing where books on particular
topics are located. The *reserve desk* is where books or journals
that are reserved by certain professors for the use of their students can be found. Usually, these materials must be read in
the library or can be checked out only for overnight. The *reference room* is where journals (periodicals), encyclopedias, dic-
tionaries, and other sorts of reference tools are found. There is
usually a computerized listing of the periodicals the library
subscribes to, what years are available, and where they can be
found. *Interlibrary loan* is a service most schools offer free or at
low cost to get a book or article you need from another school
if your library doesn't have it. Learning to use the library right
off the bat can pay enormous dividends over the course of
your college career.

Plan a budget. There are many hidden expenses that pop
up in college that make it necessary for you to have a realistic
budget for yourself. Even though your parents may have paid

for your room and board in advance, and even though you may have a certain amount of money set aside as a book allowance, what about the extra paperbacks you need? How about money to pay off overdue-book fines to the library? What about money for the dinners off campus when you just can't face another cafeteria meal? How about paying for the tickets to the fraternity carnival or the rock group that's coming to campus? You'll feel much more independent and on your own, and also "in control" if you come to college with a specific budget in mind that you're willing to stick to.

Develop your own support system. As soon as possible, try to meet and talk with older students who not only have been through the same experiences, but also have survived them and are presumably a little wiser. Older students can give you excellent advice about the "best" and "worst" professors and courses, they can tell you about whether or not it makes sense on that particular campus to join a sorority or fraternity, and they might even become your good friends. Another kind of support system usually develops from within your group of roommates, classmates, and students who you're thrown together with because you have similar schedules. Don't assume that because you're not taking the same courses that you can't be friends. If you're willing to be a little bit vulnerable and open at first, you'll find you have lots to say to people with whom you may initially have thought you had nothing in common.

Familiarize yourself with the student counseling center and student health center on campus. There may be times when you are really feeling down and when your support system of friends isn't helping you. That's when the campus counseling center or health center can help you out. The people who staff these places are trained to work with college students and are almost always tuned in to the problems that are cropping up on campus. Sometimes, there are peer counselors you can talk to — students like yourself who have been through similar stresses and strains. There are also psychologists, social workers, doctors, and nurses you can request appointments with. It is in no way a sign of failure if you go into one of these centers to talk with the personnel there. It is a sign of maturity and strength on your part.

Get to know your faculty advisor and try to establish a comfortable working relationship. A faculty advisor is similar to your high school guidance counselor. In college, though, you may have many more occasions to consult your advisor, and that individual can be a key person able to help you in many ways. An advisor may have the power to help you get into a course that would otherwise be closed to you. An advisor can sometimes help you find better housing accommodations. An advisor can write persuasive letters on your behalf to graduate schools and potential employers.

However, all advisors are not created equal and there are some who are almost like double agents: since they are employed and paid by the college, their allegiance may be primarily to the college rather than to you. Some take their jobs seriously and others, less seriously. Some are very skilled at what they do and others are not particularly effective. You may be assigned to an advisor who isn't even expert in the field of study you plan to focus on.

> I assumed too much when I first met my advisor. I thought she'd know all about me. She hadn't even read my file, since her student assignments had just been reshuffled that day. She was a physical ed teacher and I was pre-med. I was so angry and I know I showed it; I think we really got off on the wrong foot.
>
> *Marlon Z., age eighteen*

When you first meet with your advisor it is probably to your advantage to be a little cautious. Once you have met, you can make some inquiries. Consult with other advisees and compare experiences. Find out whether your advisor is the kind of person who follows through or tends to let your requests slide by for weeks at a time. Be sensitive to whether your advisor is quite formal and distant with you or whether he or she is someone who seems to be willing to be a confidant. Adjust your posture accordingly so that you can maximize the possibility for a working relationship based on trust and respect for one another. An advisor can be a powerful advocate who, as a member of the college establishment, can do some important downfield blocking to make it easier for you to score a touchdown.

If you need to, don't be afraid to ask your parents for advice.
Many teenagers incorrectly assume that if they're on their
own, asking their parents for advice about anything would
prove that they aren't yet ready to be independent. Nothing
could be farther from the truth. A bank president we know
checks in with his seventy-year-old mother before he makes a
final decision about any major deal, and we're sure that if you
asked your parents whether they ever had that kind of relationship with your grandparents, you'd find similar examples.

More often than not, parent-child bonds grow stronger as
you get older, partly because your parents don't have the day-
to-day hassles with you that they used to, and partly because
they are changing their view of you, from child to adult. So,
you may be surprised to find that if you call them or write
them with a problem they may be able to give you excellent,
realistic, and objective advice!

By the end of your first semester, you'll have a much
more realistic idea of what being on your own at college
means for you. With any luck, you'll be able to make adjustments as necessary and without too much stress because you'll
have friends you like, trust, and can rely on, your study patterns will suit your work load, you'll have enough leisure time
to relax and enjoy yourself and a support system to help you
weather any storms.

Joining the Military

The military is an excellent option if you either want to make
it a career or utilize military training and experience as preparation for one. Being on your own in the military is a lot different from being on your own on a college campus. Both require
major decisions, but once you join the armed services you
must stay for a certain length of time. Whereas you usually
pay to go to college (unless you are on scholarship), you are
paid to be in the armed services, and you sign a legally binding
contract when you enlist. The rules and regulations of the military are strict, and should you decide you no longer want to
abide by these rules and regulations, you could end up in jail
or with a dishonorable discharge (which could affect you ad-
versely for the rest of your life). The life-style in the military

is more structured than what you may have been used to; in fact, you don't need to worry too much about what you will do, when you'll eat, where you'll live, because you're basically told by the military *exactly* what's expected of you. The positive side of this is that it really helps you to develop discipline and an "esprit de corps" — a sense of belonging to a group of people with similar goals, responsibilities, and lifestyles.

There are some wrong reasons for joining the military. If you do it on impulse, or because you like the way the uniform looks, or because you're trying to impress a boyfriend or girlfriend, or even because you think it's going to be your travel ticket to exotic places in the world, don't sign on the dotted line just yet. The military isn't as glamorous or exciting as the ads and recruiters would like you to believe. Actually, military recruiters and used car salesmen have a lot in common. Both try to entice you to want their product. They will each use personal charm to gain your trust and make you think they're being absolutely straight with you. (Sometimes they are, sometimes they aren't.) Recruiters rely on the assumption that because they're in uniform, represent the United States government, and have a U.S. flag and picture of the President in their office, you will be more apt to accept their sales pitch. You may not know this but recruiters have quotas — they're expected to sign up a certain number of people per month. This is especially important for the military today, since there is no longer a mandatory draft. So it's to their advantage to have you sign a contract immediately and close the deal.

You wouldn't buy a used car without doing some comparison shopping or without examining the vehicle and making requests to improve the deal for yourself. You shouldn't automatically join the military without trying to negotiate the best contract for yourself.

Don't be in a hurry to sign any contract. Take your time. Talk to others. Tell the recruiter you're planning to consult with other branches of the military to see what they have to offer you. If you are successful and lucky, you might get the recruiters into some sort of bidding war to see who will offer you the best deal. Let them compete against each other and then you can evaluate their final offers.

Take all the aptitude tests before you sign any document that states you want to join the service. Do this because testing might help you discover a hidden aptitude for which the military has specialized training. Once you see you have scored high in a given area, you can request that the military help you develop this asset. Discuss all the options with the recruiter. If you are unsatisfied, there is no reason why you cannot talk to someone else.

Resist being manipulated by the recruiter. This is no different from being a cautious consumer when you go out to make a major purchase. The recruiter might try to make you believe you need to sign up today or risk not getting what you want or what has been promised. If the recruiter says that registration for the perfect training program for you will end tomorrow, just reply that you are willing to be patient and would appreciate being notified when the program reopens. You are free to negotiate and make requests before you sign the contract. You might even get what you request if it isn't too outrageous. You can certainly ask for a specific kind of training or geographical placement; if the military wants you badly enough, they will make every attempt to accommodate you. You can also state when you want to be inducted. If you have major commitments coming up, clearly it would be to your advantage to wait awhile.

Get everything in writing. Request that the recruiter's superior sign the document, and even get the document notarized before you sign anything. This is to protect you, and even though the recruiter may resist, and may say that his or her word is good, stick to your guns.

If you play your cards right, the military can be a wonderful way to start being on your own. It can give you valuable training and experience that will make you more employable when and if you return to civilian status. While you are in the military you can start taking college courses or earning college credits by taking tests. The military might even agree to put you through college or graduate school before you go on active duty, which would mean that you could build up some seniority in the National Guard or the army reserves. The military has many fringe benefits if you are smart enough to ask for them.

Getting Your First
Full-Time Job

Most teenagers have had some experiences as employees: baby-sitting, working newspaper routes, restaurant work, even part-time office jobs. Some teenagers participate in work-study programs through their schools, and some serve internship programs, which may or may not pay them for the work they do. Some of the most sought-after internship programs are summer internships at the offices of congressmen or senators and the Senate Page program in Washington, D.C. Any employment experience you may have had can pave the way for you to find full-time employment.

When you get your first full-time job it means that you are finally in a position to declare your financial independence from your family. In return, you're expected to be a responsible, trustworthy person who works hard to earn your pay.

How do you land that first full-time job? The initial step is to prepare a résumé, a document that is designed to convince an employer that it is worth his or her time to interview you and then hire you. A résumé must be concise and well organized so that it quickly grabs the attention of the person reading it. It includes your name, address, and phone number at the top of the first page. Then comes a section that lists all your education and training so the potential employer knows immediately whether or not you are a high school graduate. The next section should include all the part-time jobs you have had either as a paid employee or as a volunteer. It is helpful to give a one- or two-sentence description of what you did and why you left. If you have no prior job experience, you might want to list some of the activities that have prepared you to work, such as caring for your brothers and sisters while your parents work, doing the grocery shopping for your family and keeping within the budget your parents set for you, helping your parents do maintenance work around the house or on the car, obedience-training the family dog — in short, any activity that shows you can set a goal and meet it to other people's satisfaction. It is appropriate to list any honors or leadership positions you've had. The final section of a résumé contains the names of people who can give you some sort of reference or recommendation. You can divide this section into two parts: personal and professional references. You can mention in what capacity each person knows you and then list each one's professional title (if applicable), address, and phone number. Before you list any person as a reference you should ask his or her permission. If the person agrees, say that you are sending a copy of your résumé so the person will know exactly what your potential employer knows. Here is what a résumé might look like.

Résumé

Name: Amy Anybody

Address: 38 Main Street, Apt. 7G
City, State, Zip code

Phone: 000 000-0000

Date of Birth: Month, day, year

Education:

XYZ Elementary School (Address) Graduated: (Month, year)

ABC Junior High School (Address) Graduated: (Month, year)

GHI High School (Address) Graduated: (Month, year)

Employment Experience:

Volunteer at X Hospital   (Address)   (Dates: From _____ to _____)

I have worked as a candy striper on the obstetrics floor since the summer of 1982. I now supervise incoming candy stripers. I am committed to working five hours each Wednesday and will continue to do so until I graduate from high school in June, 1986.

French Fry Cook at McBurgers (Address) (Dates: From _____ to _____)

I now work the night shift on Fridays and the day shift on Saturdays.

Word Processor at NOP Corporation (Address) (Dates: From _____ to _____)

This was my summer job after my junior year in

high school. I used an IBM PC and did BASIC programming, which the company trained me to do.

Honors:

Outstanding _____ of 1985, awarded by _____

National Merit Semifinalist, 1985.

Teenage Volunteer of the Month, April, 1983, awarded
   by _____

References:

Name   Address   Position (or relationship to you)

Name   Address   Position (or relationship to you)

Only apply for a job for which you're realistically qualified. If you're just a high school graduate, you shouldn't apply for a job as a college instructor — you'd just be wasting everyone's time since you wouldn't have the credentials to be considered even if you were the most talented, creative, brilliant person in the world. Similarly, an English major who has never sewn a stitch shouldn't apply for a job as a pattern

"My ambition is to be a talk-show host. I myself don't have much to say, but I'd like to offer encouragement to those who do."

maker in a design house. We mention this because many people do apply for jobs they're unqualified for, and the end result is frustration. However, there are some jobs that give you training as you work. If you love working with animals but have little or no science background, it's possible that you could be hired by a veterinarian who'd train you to be his assistant. People who have no background running heavy equipment can be hired as apprentices and end up as skilled workers in a field they never would have considered open to them. Check out the options before you make any hasty decisions about what you can or can't try for. If you aren't sure what you want, sign up with an agency that will send you on varied temporary job assignments, or see a career counselor.

If you're asked to come in for an interview, you should try to be prepared to answer any questions clearly and confidently. A good way to do this is role-play an interview with one of your parents or a friend. Try to anticipate the kinds of questions that might be asked (Why do you want this job? Why do you think you'd be good for this job? What are your career goals? How does our company fit in with these goals? What do you expect to gain from a job? What do you think we want from you? How long do you expect to stay with us if we hire you? How did you find out about us? What do you know about our product? Would you be willing to be trained for a different job from the one you're applying for? and so on). Keep in mind the fact that an interview is designed to give you a chance to impress the employer. You act as your own best booster, and your goal at this point is to convince the interviewer that you should be hired.

Since first impressions are very important, and the way you look makes the very first impression, dress neatly and appropriately at the actual interview. If you're applying for a job as a gardener you don't have to wear a three-piece suit, but if you're applying for an office job, conservative clothes are best. Try not to be too nervous when you walk into the interviewer's office; maintaining good eye contact and having a firm handshake are always advisable. Try to answer all questions honestly and briefly, and don't be afraid to ask questions yourself. If you have done some homework and found out as much as you can about the place of work you are applying to, your questions will reflect this and your interviewer will probably be impressed with your initiative and interest. You may want to ask about working conditions, starting salaries and raises, opportunities for advancement within the company, educational benefits, insurance benefits, whether employees tend to socialize (are there company picnics, parties?), and how long the average worker remains on the job.

After a job interview it is a good idea to write a brief thank-you note to the interviewer. This can do two things: it shows you are a courteous, thoughtful person and it can give you the chance to reaffirm your interest in working at that company. It in no way commits you to accepting a job offer, but it might be the thing that tips the scales in your favor if it is a question of two or more equally qualified people vying for the same job.

There are several key issues which you should consider before accepting your first full-time job.

Recognize that in all probability your first employer will not be your last. The overwhelming majority of workers have several employers. In fact, it is often to your advantage to switch employers because your job skills change, and you should be able to move up the job ladder as your abilities and experience incease.

Consider whether it is more important for you to get a relatively big salary at first, or to acquire training and experience. Some jobs are dead-ended with no chance for advancement, yet they may pay more initially. Getting more training and a lower salary might translate into your ability to get a much better job a few years down the line. You should consider your long-range goals as well as your short-term needs in deciding what job to accept.

Remember that it is always easier to find a job once you're currently employed. No, this isn't double-talk; it's the way the job world works. It may make sense to settle for a job that is less than you'd hoped for because it could be that you will remain there only a short time and you need that opening into the work world to gain credibility as an employee. At the least, it will give you contacts who might prove useful in the future. The fact is that in the beginning, you might not be able to afford to be too selective. The personnel departments might not be knocking down your door to entice you with fabulous job offers. While it might be a disappointing experience to accept employment that doesn't reflect either your intelligence or training, in the long run it can pay dividends because you need to start somewhere, and a résumé is more likely to be given priority if it shows you have some job experience.

On the other hand, you might want to be more selective and keep job hunting until you find your niche. Your decision may be affected by the prevailing employment condition in your area at the time. If the country is experiencing a financial recession or a depression, any job is better than none. But if the country is experiencing prosperity, you might want to risk waiting for the perfect job to come along.

Accept the fact that every employee makes mistakes at some point in his or her career, and you will too! You may feel somewhat insecure in your first job (or even your first few jobs), and this discomfort may increase the chances of your making some mistakes. They're not likely to be costly ones, either to you or your employer, but errors are a fairly common part of the process of gaining experience.

Ultimately, experience is what you need to move ahead in the work world. If you are confident and determined to work and are willing to learn from each job you have, eventually you'll be in a position to get the perfect job for you.

Finding Housing

Affordable, decent housing is becoming increasingly hard to find under the best of circumstances, and when you are first starting out on your own it can be even more difficult to obtain. You don't have much money. You don't have a long work history or many character references. You may not have an established line of credit. In spite of the fact that state and national fair housing laws guarantee that no person will be discriminated against, any landlord is certainly entitled to use discretion when renting. No court will force a landlord to rent to someone who might be a disruptive or questionable tenant.

Unfortunately, the odds are against you when you're young and starting out. Landlords tend to assume the worst when they see how youthful you are: they may think you'll be messy, noisy, unable to pay your rent on time or at all, and that you'll be a troublemaker. Landlords detest loud music, loud parties, and people who let their friends crash at their apartments and possibly destroy property. Some forbid pets.

"But this isn't me!" you say? You have the burden of proof. You must convince the landlord that none of these things will occur. Think of yourself as a competitor in a talent contest. You need to outshine the other contestants and show that you are the best, perhaps the only, choice for that landlord. Whenever you look for a place to rent, dress conservatively just like you would when going on a job interview. If your parents are available, take them with you (even if this makes you feel like a child). Have at hand information about your savings, your credit history, and employment, along with some character references. If you have spoken to the landlord on the phone ahead of time and think you might want to rent that day, find out if a security deposit is required and make sure you have enough money in your savings or checking account to pay it. You may even want to ask your parents to guarantee your payments so you can use their financial record to help you get your first place.

If you are considering renting a room in a private house and you sense the landlord is resisting because of your age, see if you can negotiate. Convince the landlord that it is in his or her best interest to rent to you because you have something besides rent money to offer. If you have talents in home improvement such as yard work or outside painting, perhaps you can offer your services as part of your rental agreement. If there are elderly people living in the house, you might agree to do errands once a week for them, or more simply, to help them with heavy lifting or emptying the garbage. If the landlord has small children, you might offer to baby-sit. See what works in your situation. But don't give up until you've exhausted every avenue of negotiation.

Landlords aren't necessarily dying to rent to you, and the

truth of the matter is that the landlord is in the catbird seat. Try to put yourself in his or her place and ask yourself, "Why would anyone want to rent something to me?" Here are some things you might do to improve your chances of obtaining the kind of housing you want.

Make yourself look "establishment" when you appear at the landlord's doorstep. This may mean getting a haircut and shave or toning down the makeup and wearing boring clothes, but it's a small price to pay if it means getting a chance to rent the place you really like.

Work with a real estate agent. This may end up costing you a hefty fee, but a real estate agent can get you in to see places that you might not be aware of otherwise. Also, the real estate agent can do a lot of legwork for you and eliminate places that are obviously wrong for you so you won't have to waste time seeing them.

Use contacts. There's almost always someone you know who might have a lead. Church or temple members, friends, even relatives can be enormously helpful in locating a place. Be prepared, however, to have to listen to their ideas about where and how you should live.

One last bit of practical advice. No matter how badly you want to rent that apartment, never (repeat, *never*) sign a lease or contract without reading it through carefully. A lease or contract is a legal document that obligates you to pay hundreds, or thousands of dollars even, if you decide to move away, leave town, drop out of school, et cetera. Ask an adult (parent, advisor, teacher, relative) to help you make sense of the "legalese" in the contract or lease. Ideally, you should have a lawyer look it over before you sign it. If you don't know or can't afford a private lawyer, consult the local phone directory to find your nearest Legal Aid Society and make an appointment to have one of their staff look it over with you. Legal Aid lawyers are very well qualified, but you may have to wait awhile to get an appointment with one. Also, make sure you know in advance if there are up-front finder's fees or security deposits that will have to be paid before the first month's rent is even out of your pocket. You don't want to be in debt before you get to move in!

Being on Your Own

Being on your own can be a mixed bag. On the one hand, it's probably what you've been dreaming about and striving for for a long time. On the other hand, it may not be working out precisely as you had imagined.

When you're on your own, you're accountable to yourself first and foremost, not to your parents, and it means you must assume total responsibility for your behavior and the choices you make. You may find that these are difficult things to do, and you may wish, at times, that you were back at your parents' so you could blame them when things aren't going exactly right. When you're on your own, at first, you may find yourself arguing an awful lot with your family, and, believe it or not, this is normal. In fact, some psychologists have given a name to this process: they call it the "battered nest." The idea is that teenagers who are on the verge of becoming adults need to get into really big hassles with their families in order to make "home" seem less attractive and to make the actual break from it easier to take. If you talk to older teenagers or people in their early twenties who've been away from home and on their own for a while, you'll find that things smooth out relatively quickly and family relationships get better as everyone gets accustomed to the new roles they have to play.

Being on your own doesn't mean being alone. It isn't meant to be taken literally. No matter how old you are, you can still turn to parents and other family members (or anyone else you have ever confided in) for advice and encouragement. The nice thing about getting to this stage of life is that they are just as likely to turn to you for advice and encouragement. When parents and siblings perceive you as an adult, a balance usually enters into your relationship that *does* make it possible for friendships to develop where before there may have been conflict or dislike.

There can be other surprises involved in being on your own. One is finding out just how capable and resourceful you really are. When you have to rely on yourself, you may be amazed to discover talents you didn't know you had, interests you hadn't been able or willing to explore before, strengths that may have been overshadowed by others when you were living in your family group. And that's one of the greatest things about maturing and hitting your stride: surprising yourself and all your relatives and friends with your new-found abilities. A common example of this phenomenon is the college student who makes the dean's list when away at school after being a mediocre, indifferent student in high school and living at home.

Being on your own is a tremendous challenge, but it's an exciting, exhilarating one because now you really have the chance to show the stuff you're made of. Go for it!

Suggested Readings

Family Dynamics and Other Sticky Matters

Understanding How Your Family Operates

Ainsworth, Catherine H. *Family Life of Young Americans*. Buffalo: The Clyde Press, 1985.

Bell, James B. *Family History Record Book*. Minneapolis: University of Minnesota Press, 1980.

Colwell, Stella. *Family History Book*. Salem, NH: Merrimack Publishers Circle, 1985.

Colwin, Laurie. *Family Happiness*. New York: Fawcett, 1983.

Gilbert, Sara. *Trouble at Home*. New York: Lothrop, Lee & Shepard, 1981.

Games Parents Play

Klein, Norma. *Family Secrets*. New York: Dial, 1985.

The Art and Science of Communicating with Parents

Branden, Nathaniel. *"If You Could Hear What I Cannot Say": Learning to Communicate With the Ones You Love*. New York: Bantam, 1983.

Freed, Alvyn M. *T.A. for Teens and Other Important People*. Rolling Hills Estate, CA: Jalmar Press, 1976.

Johnson, Rex. *Communication: Key to Your Parents*. Eugene: Harvest House, 1978.

Slagle, Robert. *Family Meeting Handbook: Achieving Family Harmony Happily*. Sebastopol, CA: Family Relations, 1985.

Dealing with Everyday Realities — Facts and Feelings

School Days, School Days

Armstrong, William H. *Study Tips: How to Study Effectively and Get Better Grades*, 2nd ed. Woodbury, NY: Barrons Educational Series, 1983.

341

Barr, Margaret J., ed. *Student Affairs and the Law.* San Francisco: Jossey-Bass, 1983.

Carman, Robert A., and Adams, Royce W., Jr. *Study Skills: A Student's Guide for Survival,* 2nd ed. New York: Wiley, 1985.

Duda, Phyllis, and Sebranek, Patrick. *Study Skills and Writing Process Workbook.* Burlington, WI: Basic English Revisited, 1983.

Fischer, Louis, and Schimmel, David. *The Rights of Students and Teachers: Resolving Conflicts in the School Community.* New York: Harper & Row, 1982.

Guggenheim, Martin, and Sussman, Alan. *Rights of Young People (American Civil Liberties Union Series).* New York: Bantam, 1985.

Kesselman-Turkel, Judi, and Peterson, Franklynn. *Study Smarts: How to Learn Mor in Less Time.* Chicago: Contemporary Books, 1981.

Rubin, David. *The Rights of Teachers.* New York: New American Library, 1983.

Dating, Romance, and Love

Booher, Diana D. *Love.* New York: Julian Messner, 1985.

Cahn, Julie. *The Dating Book.* New York: Julian Messner, 1983.

Ephron, Delia. *Teenage Romance: Or How to Die of Embarrassment.* New York: Viking-Penguin, 1981.

McCoy, Kathy. *The Teenage Body Book Guide to Dating.* New York: Simon and Schuster, 1983.

Schneider, Meg. *Romance! Can You Survive It? A Guide to Sticky Dating Situations.* New York: Dell, 1984.

————. *Two in a Crowd: How to Find Romance Without Losing Your Friends.* New York: The Putnam Publishing Group (Pacer Books), 1985.

Straight Talk About Sex

Bell, Ruth, et al. *Changing Bodies, Changing Lives: A Book for Teens on Sex and Relationships.* New York: Random House, 1981.

Carrera, Michael. *Sex: The Facts, the Acts, and Your Feelings.* New York: Crown, 1981.

Gordon, Sol. *You Would if You Loved Me.* New York: Bantam, 1978.

Kaplan, Helen S. *Making Sense of Sex: The New Facts about Sex and Love for Young People.* New York: Simon and Schuster, 1979.

Lieberman, E. James, and Peck, Ellen. *Sex and Birth Control: A Guide for the Young,* revised ed. New York: Harper & Row, 1981.

Drugs and Alcohol — What You Don't Know Can Hurt You

Casewit, Curtis W. *The Stop Smoking Book for Teens.* New York: Julian Messner, 1980.

Gold, Mark S., M.D. *800-COCAINE.* New York: Bantam, 1984.

Kakis, Frederic J. *Drugs: Facts and Fictions*. Danbury, CT: Franklin Watts, Inc., 1982.

Levy, Stephen J. *Managing the "Drugs" in Your Life: A Personal and Family Guide to the Responsible Use of Drugs, Alcohol, and Medicine*. New York: McGraw-Hill, 1983.

Marshall, Shelly. *Young, Sober, and Free*. Center City, MN: Hazelden Press, 1978.

Strack, Jay. *Drugs and Drinking*, revised ed. Nashville: Nelson, 1985.

Way, Walter L. *Drug Scene: Help or Hang-up*, 2nd ed. Englewood Cliffs, NJ: Prentice-Hall, 1984.

Eating Problems and Self-Image — The Broken Mirror

Bennett, William, M.D., and Gurin, Joel. *The Dieter's Dilemma: Eating Less and Weighing More*. New York: Basic Books, 1982.

Chernin, Kim. *The Obsession: Reflections on the Tyranny of Slenderness*. New York: Harper & Row, 1981.

Landau, Elaine. *Why Are They Starving Themselves? Understanding Anorexia Nervosa and Bulimia*. New York: Julian Messner, 1983.

Levenkron, Steven. *The Best Little Girl in the World*. New York: Warner, 1978.

O'Neill, Cherry Boone. *Starving for Attention*. New York: Continuum, 1983.

Crisis Time

A Ten-Point Plan for Recognizing and Resolving Major Crises

Englebart, Lenald S. *You Have a Right — A Guide for Minors*. New York: Lothrop, Lee & Shepard, 1979.

Greenberg, Harvey R., M.D. *Hanging In: What You Should Know about Psychotherapy*. New York: Four Winds Press, 1982.

Gilbert, Sara. *What Happens in Therapy*. New York: Lothrop, Lee & Shepard, 1982.

Quinnett, Paul G. *The Troubled People Book: A Comprehensive Guide to Getting Help*. New York: Continuum, 1982.

How to Keep Your Cool if Your Parents Are Getting Divorced

Atlas, Stephen L. *The Official Parents Without Partners Sourcebook*. Philadelphia: Running Press, 1984.

Francke, Linda B. *Growing Up Divorced*. New York: Fawcett, 1984.

Gardner, Richard. *Boy's and Girl's Book about Divorce*. Highmount, NY: Aronson, 1983.

Getzoff, Ann, and McClenahan, Carolyn. *Step Kids: A Survival Guide for Teenagers in Stepfamilies*. New York: Walker, 1984.

Paylor, Neil, and Head, Barry. *Scenes from a Divorce: A Book for Friends and Relatives of a Divorcing Family.* Minneapolis: Winston Press, 1983.

Robson, Bonnie. *My Parents Are Divorced Too: Teenagers Talk about Their Experiences and How They Cope.* New York: Dodd, Mead, 1980.

"I Think I'm Pregnant"

Ewy, Donna, and Ewy, Roger. *Teen Pregnancy: The Challenges We Faced, the Choices We Made.* New York: New American Library, 1985.

Foster, Sallie. *The One Girl in Ten: A Self-Portrait of the Teen-Age Mother.* Claremont, CA: The Arbor Press, 1981.

McGuire, Paula. *It Won't Happen to Me: Teenagers Talk about Pregnancy.* New York: Dell, 1983.

Richards, Arlene K., and Willis, Irene. *Under 18 and Pregnant.* New York: Lothrop, Lee, & Shepard, 1983.

Rossow, Linda, and Owens, Carolyn. *Handbook for Pregnant Teenagers.* Grand Rapids: Zondervan, 1985.

Loneliness, Depression, and Suicide

Cohen, Daniel, and Cohen, Susan. *Teenage Stress: Understanding the Tensions You Feel at Home, at School, and among Your Friends.* New York: M. Evans, 1984.

Eagan, Andrea Boroff. *Why Am I So Miserable if These Are the Best Years of My Life?* Philadelphia: Lippincott, 1976.

Gardner, Sandra, and Rosenberg, Gary. *Teenage Suicide.* New York: Julian Messner, 1985.

Kalgsbrun, Francine. *Too Young to Die: Youth and Suicide,* revised ed. New York: Pocket Books, 1984.

Madison, Arnold. *Suicide and Young People.* Boston: Houghton Mifflin, 1981.

Mack, John E., and Hicker, Holly. *Vivienne: The Life and Suicide of an Adolescent Girl.* New York: New American Library, 1981.

Oslshan, Neal H. *Depression.* Danbury, CT: Franklin Watts, 1982.

Myers, Irma, and Myers, Arthur. *Why You Feel Down and What You Can Do about It.* New York: Charles Scribner's Sons, 1982.

When a Parent or Friend Dies, Sexual Victimization, Breaking the Law

Booher, Dianna D. *Rape: What Would You Do If. . ?* New York: Julian Messner, 1981.

Burnham, Betsy. *When Your Friend Is Dying.* Grand Rapids: Zondervan, 1983.

Dobelis, Inge N., ed. *Reader's Digest Family Legal Guide: A Complete Encyclopedia of Law for the Layman.* New York: The Reader's Digest Association, Inc., 1981.

Daugherty, Lynn B. *Why Me? Help for Victims of Child Sexual Abuse (Even if They Are Adults Now)*. Racine, WI: Mother Courage Press, 1985.

Dolan, Edward F., Jr. *You Legal Rights: An Handbook for Teenagers*. New York: Julian Messner, 1983.

Grossman, Rochel, and Sutherland, Joan, eds. *Surviving Sexual Assault*. New York: Congdon & Weed, 1982.

Krementz, Jill. *How It Feels When a Parent Dies*. New York: Knoph, 1981.

Kübler-Ross, Elisabeth. *Questions and Answers on Death and Dying*. New York: Macmillan, 1974.

Landau, Elaine. *Child Abuse: An American Epidemic*. New York: Julian Messner, 1985.

Pall, Michael L., and Streit, Lois B. *Let's Talk about It: The Book for Children about Child Abuse*. Saratoga, CA: R and E Publishers, 1983.

Richter, Elizabeth. *Losing Someone You Love: When a Brother or Sister Dies*. New York: The Putnam Publishing Group, 1986.

Reaching for Independence

College Admissions

Barron's Educational Service Guides

(All published by Barron's Educational Series, Inc., Woodbury, N.Y.)

> *Barron's Compact Guide to College.*
>
> *Barron's How to Prepare for College Entrance Exams.*
>
> *Barron's How to Prepare for the American College Testing Program (ACT).*
>
> *Barron's Profiles of American Colleges.*
>
> *Barron's Guide to the Two-Year Colleges.*
>
> *Barron's Computer SAT Study Program.*

de Olivera, P., and Cohen, S. *Getting In! The First Comprehensive Step-by-Step Strategy Guide to Acceptance at the College of Your Choice*. New York: Workman, 1983.

Fiske, Edward B., and Michalak, Joseph M. *The Best Buys in College Education*. New York: Times Books, 1985.

Hegener, Karen C., ed. *Peterson's Competitive Colleges*, 4th ed. Princeton: Peterson's Guides, Inc., 1985.

———. *The College Money Handbook, 1986*, 3rd ed. Princeton: Peterson's Guides, Inc., 1985.

Moll, Richard. *The Public Ivys: A Guide to America's Best Public Colleges and Universities*. New York: Viking-Penguin, 1985.

———. *Playing the Private College Admissions Game*. New York: Viking-Penguin, 1980.

Shanahan, William F. *College: Yes or No? The High School Student's Career Decision-Making Handbook*, 2nd ed. New York: Arco, 1983.

On Your Own

Angel, Juvenal L. *The Complete Résumé Book and Job-Getter's Guide*. New York: Pocket Books, 1980.

Beatty, Richard H. *The Résumé Kit*. New York: Wiley, 1984.

Cole, Sheila. *Working Kids on Working*. New York: Lothrop, Lee & Shepard, 1980.

de Long, C. Frederick. *Laughing All the Way to the Bank: The Earning Money Formula*. New York: Richards Rosen Press, 1982.

Lee, Rose P. *A Real Job for You: An Employment Guide for Teens*. White Hall, VA: Betterway, 1985.

Mitchell, Joyce Slayton. *The Men's Career Book: Working and Life Planning for a New Age*. New York: Bantam, 1979.

————. *See Me More Clearly: Career and Life Planning for Teens with Physical Disabilities*. New York: Harcourt Brace Jovanovich, 1980.

Seed, Suzanne. *Fine Trades*. Chicago: Follett, 1979.

Index